THE BATTLE OF FRANCE AND FLANDERS 1940

◆

SIXTY YEARS ON

THE BATTLE OF FRANCE AND FLANDERS 1940

◆

SIXTY YEARS ON

Edited by

BRIAN BOND

and

MICHAEL D. TAYLOR

LEO COOPER

First published in Great Britain 2001 by
LEO COOPER
an imprint of Pen & Sword Books Ltd
47 Church Street, Barnsley, S. Yorkshire S70 2AS

Copyright © 2001 by Brian Bond and Michael D. Taylor
and individual contributors

ISBN 0 85052 811 9

A catalogue record for this book is
available from the British Library

Typeset in 11/13 Sabon by
Phoenix Typesetting, Ilkley, West Yorkshire

Printed and Bound in England by
CPI UK Ltd

CONTENTS

NOTES ON CONTRIBUTORS

Brian Bond   is Professor of Military History at King's College, London and President of BCMH. His Lees Knowles Lectures, *Britain and the First World War: the Challenge to Historians*, delivered in November 2000, will be published by Cambridge University Press in 2002.

Michael Taylor   is a member of the BCMH Committee with a special interest in the 1940 campaign. He is currently researching a book on the performance of the Field Force.

Peter Caddick-Adams   is a Lecturer in the Department of Defence Management and Security Analysis at Cranfield University. As a Territorial Army Officer he served in Bosnia with UNPROFOR. His publications include *By God They Can Fight! A History of 143 Brigade* (Shrewsbury, 1995).

Michael Piercy   is a retired head teacher who took an MA in War Studies at King's College, London in 1993. He is a member of the BCMH team which is preparing a data base on British divisions in the First World War.

Jeremy Crang   is a Lecturer in the History Department and Assistant Director of the Centre for Second World War Studies at Edinburgh University. His publications include *The British Army and the People's War, 1939–1945* (Manchester University Press, 2000).

John Cairns   was formerly Professor of History at the University of Toronto. He has published numerous scholarly articles on France and Britain at war in 1939–1940 including 'Some Recent Historians and the "Strange Defeat"

	of 1940' in *The Journal of Modern History* (March, 1974).
John Buckley	is a Senior Lecturer in the Department of War Studies at the University of Wolverhampton. His most recent book is *Air Power in the Age of Total War* (U.C.L. Press, 1999).
Robin Brodhurst	is a former Greenjacket officer who is now Head of History at Pangbourne College. He has recently published *Churchill's Anchor. The Biography of Admiral of the Fleet Sir Dudley Pound* (Pen & Sword, 2000).
Stephen Badsey	is a Senior Lecturer in the Department of War Studies at RMA Sandhurst. He has published on a great variety of subjects ranging from the South African War to the Falklands and Gulf Wars. His strong interest in the First World War is exemplified by his contribution to Brian Bond and Nigel Cave (eds) *Haig: a Reappraisal Seventy Years On* (Leo Cooper, 1999).
John Drewienkiewicz	is a Major-General whose most recent appointment was Senior Army Member, Royal College of Defence Studies. He has a wide and varied experience of service in the Balkans.
Martin Alexander	has recently moved from a chair at Salford University to become Professor of International Relations at the University of Wales, Aberystwyth. His numerous publications include *The Republic in Danger. General Maurice Gamelin and the Politics of French Defence, 1933–1940* (Cambridge University Press, 1993).
Mungo Melvin	was formerly Colonel, Defence Studies at the Staff College Camberley and is currently, as a Brigadier, Chief Engineer of the Rapid Reaction Corps in Germany. He has published numerous articles in the Strategic and Combat Studies Institute *Occasional Papers*, and in other military journals.

FOREWORD

In July 2000 the British Commission for Military History (BCMH) devoted its weekend conference at Bedford to a reappraisal of the Battle of France and Flanders sixty years after the dramatic events which left Germany in command of Western Europe, France defeated and in political turmoil and Britain with its Army in disarray and in expectation of imminent German invasion.

Most of the papers collected here in a revised form were delivered and discussed at the conference, and all but two of the contributors are BCMH members. We have consequently drawn on the special interests and expertise of our members and have not attempted either a complete narrative history or systematic coverage of all the controversies or of all national viewpoints: there is, for example, no essay focusing on the Belgian role in the operations or on the confused second phase of the German offensive in June which culminated in a second British evacuation from Cherbourg and other western ports. We have, however, aimed to produce a volume which has coherence and is much more than a miscellany. We re-examine the key phases of the campaign, including the astonishing German breakthrough at Sedan; the failure of the Anglo-French forces to organize and execute a significant counter-offensive; the brilliant manoeuvre which saved the Field Force when the Belgians suddenly accepted a ceasefire; the inspired improvisation of a defensible bridgehead at Dunkirk; and the air and naval aspects of the campaign. There is also an original and provocative account of British reporting of operations, and a brilliant analysis of French attitudes during the final days of the evacuation, based on a wide range of archival sources and interviews, which has been edited from a much longer essay. Finally, these profoundly influential operations have been placed in their historical context by surveys of the post mortems and controversies generated amongst participants and scholars in France, Germany and Britain and, in the British case, with an additional essay on the impact of the campaign on military doctrine which has hitherto been virtually unexplored.

Even after sixty years, the repercussions of the 'sixty days that shook the West' are far from over and the vast historiography steadily increases. We offer no apology for adding another stone to the edifice and hope that these essays will stimulate further research and writing, both on the topics covered and on others which we have had to leave aside.

Brian Bond, President BCMH.

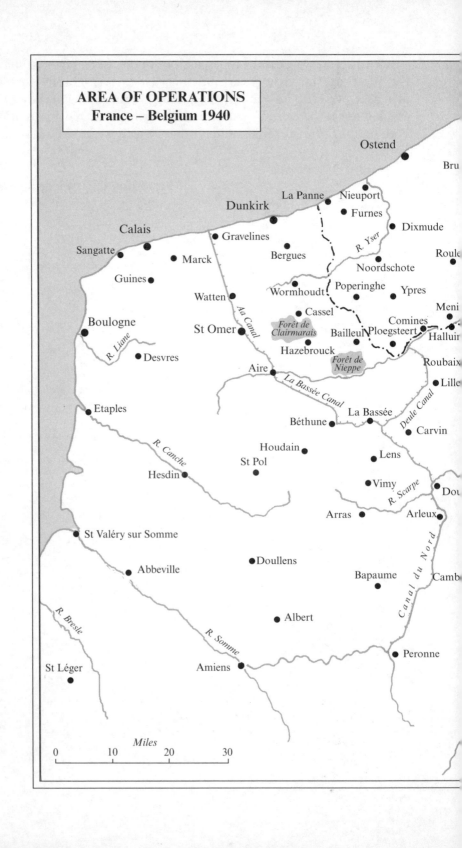

AREA OF OPERATIONS
France – Belgium 1940

Ostend

Bru

La Panne   Nieuport
Dunkirk   Furnes
Calais   Gravelines   Dixmude
Sangatte   Bergues   R. Yser   Roule
Marck   Noordschote
Guines   Wormhoudt   Poperinghe   Ypres
Watten   Cassel   Comines   Meni
Boulogne   St Omer   Forêt de   Bailleul   Ploegsteert   Hallui
                        Clairmarais   Hazebrouck   Forêt de   Roubaix
Desvres   Aire   La Bassée Canal   Nieppe   Lille
                                    La Bassée   Deule Canal
Etaples   Béthune   Carvin
R. Liane   R. Canche   Houdain   Lens
St Pol   Vimy   R. Scarpe   Dou
Hesdin   Arras   Arleux
St Valéry sur Somme   Doullens   Canal du Nord
Abbeville   Bapaume   Camb
R. Bresle   Albert
St Léger   R. Somme   Peronne
Amiens

Miles

0   10   20   30

INTRODUCTION:
PREPARING THE FIELD FORCE,
FEBRUARY 1939 – MAY 1940

BRIAN BOND

In retrospect it is hard to believe that the British Government did not commit even the small, regular contingent of its Army (the Field Force) to the Continent, in event of German aggression in the West, until February 1939. True, the Field Force was by now entirely dependent on motorized and mechanized transport, but it was smaller than the British Expeditionary Force of 1914, less well-trained and badly deficient in vital stores and equipment. "Better late than never," noted Major-General Henry Pownall in his diary in April, "but late it is, for it will take at least eighteen months more . . . before this paper Army is an Army in the flesh."[1]

In February 1939 this political decision fell far short of French expectations. Only the first four regular Divisions were definitely committed, with the first two due to reach their assembly area in France 30 days after mobilization. The French would have to carry a heavy burden alone in the first phase while the Field Force slowly assembled. Allied strategy would initially have to be defensive, irrespective of the reasons for going to war.

By the end of April the British government had further complicated the enormous problems of rapid rearmament by doubling the Territorial Army (to a paper target of 340,000); each existing T.A. unit was duplicated, thus creating twelve new infantry divisions, which stretched resources to the limit. A limited form of conscription was also introduced. As Pownall noted in his diary "it is a proper Granny's knitting that has been handed out to us to unravel. . . . What an unholy mess our politicians have made of the rebirth of the Army through shortsightedness, unwillingness to face facts and prejudice against the Army."[2] But at least, he reflected, it would be better to get the worst

1

of the inevitable muddles over before the outbreak of war. Pownall of course was *parti pris* but he *was* in a position to say "I told you so", having foreseen the necessity for a Continental commitment ever since Hitler's advent to power.

Until the political commitment was made, practical staff arrangements with the French were studiously avoided. Consequently, during the Munich crisis it would have been extremely difficult for the Army to mobilize and impossible to despatch it to France. It was therefore a remarkable achievement that in the autumn of 1939 the Field Force was mobilized efficiently, transported to allotted French ports and moved to its assembly area according to plan. This was due to months of painstaking work, in liaison with the French, by Brigadier L.A. Hawes and a small team of officers at the War Office. When Hawes began his work he found there was no accurate information about conditions in France, particularly about ports and railways. Worse still, there were no up-to-date maps of France.[3]

Because of the risk of air attack it was agreed that the main ports of disembarkation were to be in Normandy and the Bay of Biscay.[4] Different ports were to be used for the landing of troops, equipment, supplies and stores, the main ones being Havre, Cherbourg, Nantes and St Nazaire which would entail long and complex lines of communication and a huge administrative 'tail'.

By the summer of 1939 maps had arrived, the naval escort arranged and a deception plan set up to persuade the enemy to concentrate his expected submarine attacks further east against the Channel ports. As late as mid-August detailed arrangements had been made for the dispatch of only two divisions, but these were expanded to cover four just before the outbreak of war.

Meanwhile strenuous efforts were made on both sides to foster closer Anglo-French relations at various levels. Good will was encouraged by frequent visits and exchanges. In June, for example, the French Commander-in-Chief, General Gamelin, came to London to see the Tattoo, but also to settle important military matters, including the nature and scale of British military missions at French headquarters, the air defence of the Field Force, and its concentration area. Pownall proudly informed the French that the first two divisions of the Field Force could now arrive 19 days after mobilization and the whole regular contingent in 34 days.[5]

Some vital matters were amicably settled a month later when Hore-

Belisha, Churchill, Gort and others visited Paris for the 14 July celebrations. The assembly area for the British forces would be Le Mans, and their concentration area around Picquigny on the Somme north-west of Amiens. The Field Force would eventually take over a sector of the frontier on the French left between Maulde and Halluin. To First World War veterans like Gort and Pownall the scenario being anticipated seemed eerily similar to 1914. This view was underlined by agreement that the British Commander-in-Chief would be subordinate to General Georges (Commander of the North-Eastern Front), but with the right to appeal to his own government. In these, and later, discussions after the outbreak of war the British representatives, from Gort downwards, felt acutely conscious of their weak bargaining position because of their small contribution to the land forces of the alliance. Thus in attending the ceremonial march past down the Champs Elysées on 14 July, Churchill was heard to remark, "Thank God we've got conscription or we couldn't look these people in the face".[6]

At the highest political level Chamberlain proposed, and Daladier agreed, that a Supreme War Council should be set up to meet whenever necessary in Britain or France. The Council would have no executive authority, leaving final decisions to the two governments and any additional allies such as Belgium. This was a marked improvement, in timing and definition of military responsibilities, on the Supreme War Council belatedly set up in November 1917, but it could not resolve divergent national approaches to the war, or strategic issues such as long-range bombing. Gamelin also opposed the creation of a permanent inter-allied staff in London. Furthermore, both sides had acute internal problems such as civil-military mistrust and bitter rivalry between Gamelin and Georges in France; whereas in England Gort (and later Ironside too) were scarcely on speaking terms with the War Minister, Hore-Belisha.[7]

Apart from its lack of a single armoured division organized for war in Europe (as distinct from North Africa) in 1939, the Field Force's greatest weakness lay in the paucity of air support under its own control. This weakness was the inevitable result of extremely poor Army–RAF relations throughout the inter-war period, for which both Services bore some responsibility. The Air Ministry's pre-occupation with its independent bombing policy, and later with home defence (Air Defence of Great Britain), and the War Office's uncertainty over the

Field Force's role, meant that the employment of air power in close support of ground forces remained unresolved at the beginning of 1939.

The huge projected expansion of the Army to at least 32 divisions from Spring 1939 appeared to give the War Office leverage for a large increase in air support under the control of the Field Force. In June a War Office memorandum called for an allocation to the Army of 1,440 first-line aircraft with special emphasis on the roles of close-support and short-range, tactical bombing. The Air Ministry objected strongly to the notion that any aircraft, other than the small Air Component, should be placed under military control. The Chief of Air Staff, Sir Cyril Newall, warned that the dissipation of bomber squadrons into 'small packets' over a wide front would prevent the concentration of maximum effort at the decisive point.[8]

Consequently the Field Force sailed to France with the very modest air support of the Air Component, consisting of two bomber recon-naissance squadrons, six Army co-operation squadrons, four fighter squadrons and two flights of a headquarters communication squadron. The commander of the Advanced Air Striking Force of medium bombers was completely independent of the Field Force, receiving his orders direct from Bomber Command. The role of the AASF on the Continent was not to collaborate with land forces, but simply to bring British bombers nearer to targets in Germany. This peculiar arrangement provoked the wry comment from General Ismay that "It almost seemed as though the Air Staff would prefer to have their forces under Beelzebub rather than anyone connected with the Army."[9] British lack of close air support would prove to be an enor-mous handicap in the operations in May 1940, and it would take more defeats and more bitter controversy before really effective battlefield co-operation was achieved between the RAF and the Army.[10]

In the summer of 1939 the military forces in Britain were in a profound state of disarray due to the sudden changes which had been imposed on their priorities, size and organization. Conditions of near-chaos could not be remedied in the few months available. The most disturbing aspect was that, despite years of pundits invoking the lessons of the First World War, Britain seemed bent on creating a mass infantry army that would be suitable only for a static war of attrition. Although the Field Force contained eleven mechanized cavalry regi-ments and five Royal Tank Regiment battalions, its mixture of light, cruiser and heavy infantry support tanks was in most respects no match for the Panzers. In July a review of the difficulties of the regular divisions of the Field Force revealed that there were available only seventy-two out of 240 heavy anti-aircraft guns with only 30 per cent of the approved scale of ammunition and only 144 out of 240 anti-tank guns. The field-artillery regiments had not yet received any of the new 25-pounder guns. In the final pre-war progress report from the War Office small arms, cordite, gauges and fuses were among the items in short supply. Only sixty infantry tanks were available against a total requirement of 1,646. As for training, financial restrictions had prevented any large-scale Army manoeuvres being held for several years: exercises in September 1939 had been planned to get even I Corps into good order. Consequently, the first four divisions of the Field Force went to France inadequately trained and short of every type of equipment, especially guns, ammunition and tanks. The remainder of the Territorial units at home were little more than a token force of semi-trained troops, lacking equipment for realistic training.[11]

As for transport, the Field Force could now claim to be fully motorized and not at all dependent on horses. In reality the situation was little short of desperate. Major-General Montgomery, recently appointed to command the 3rd Division, recalled in his *Memoirs* that on mobilization transport had to be supplemented by requisitioning from civilians firms:

> "Much of the transport of my division consisted of civilian vans and lorries from the towns of England; they were in bad repair and, when my division moved from the ports up to its concentration area near the French frontier, the countryside of France was strewn with broken-down vehicles." He also noted that the Field Force had an inadequate signals system, no administrative backing, and no organization for high command; all had to be improvized on mobilization. He was dissatisfied with his division's anti-tank weapons, and remarked that he never saw any tanks of the single Army Tank Brigade either during the winter or the operations in May 1940.[12]

Montgomery's damning conclusion was that the Field Force had been dispatched to a modern war against a most formidable enemy with weapons, equipment and transport which were completely inadequate.

Fortunately for the Field Force, and in contrast to the experience of the BEF in 1914, it was not plunged into an early encounter with the *Wehrmacht*. Despite widespread fears of a massacre from the air or from submarines, the first four divisions were transferred to France without a single life being lost. The main troop landings began at Cherbourg on 10 September and at Nantes and St Nazaire two days later. By the end of the month more than 160,000 service personnel with over 23,000 vehicles and a vast tonnage of equipment and supplies had arrived in western France. On 3 October I Corps (1st and 2nd Divisions) commanded by Lieutenant-General Sir John Dill began taking over part of the front line allocated to the Field Force, followed nine days later by II Corps (3rd and 4th Divisions) commanded by Sir Alan Brooke. The 5th (Regular) Division arrived in December.[13] Though only a token force in comparison with the French Army, this was still a considerable achievement for 'the Cinderella Service' which only a year previously had been earmarked for an extra-European role against inferior opposition.

When the expected German autumn offensive in the West did not occur, there began a period of 'Phoney War' or 'sitzkrieg' marked by minimal military activity along the whole Anglo-French-held frontier and accompanied by complacent popular assumptions about 'hanging out our washing on the Siegfried Line'. In reality these were dreary, dull and potentially demoralizing months, particularly when a ferociously cold spell set in at the end of the year.

The main activities were marching, digging trenches and constructing pill-boxes. Slow progress on these frontier defences provided the occasion for the dismissal from the War Office of Hore-Belisha, whose well-meant but badly-presented criticisms gave Gort and Pownall at GHQ their opportunity to remove a detested politician who, they felt, was not giving them proper support in the War Cabinet.[14] This whole affair was suffused with irony because, at the very time the 'pill-box' issue erupted, Britain's military leaders were (however reluctantly) endorsing Gamelin's strategy for an advance into Belgium in event of a German attack, or earlier if invited by the neutral Belgian government.

The well-worn phrase 'all quiet on the Western Front' was certainly appropriate for the Field Force right through the severe winter of 1939–1940. Press coverage was very restricted and in any case there were few newsworthy incidents. Regimental histories describe this as a dreary period of digging and wiring (in a depressing industrial area all too familiar from the First World War), inter-spersed with weapon-training and route marches. Diarists among the other ranks noted that there was very little range-firing and no inter-arms training outside their battalions. A company commander summed up his unit's experience as 'Equipment poor and late in delivery. Training all right but orthodox, eg., movement at night neglected. Our commanders were too rigid in their attitude. They did not learn enough about enemy tactics'. Senior officers seem to have largely ignored the 'blitzkrieg' tactics demonstrated in Poland. Even members of tank crews did very little training in tanks, partly due to shortage of fuel, but also because it was feared that tank tracks would be observed by enemy spotter aircraft. Diaries and letters mention many days of idleness, often in grim accommodation, and of whiling away the time in cafés.[15] Apart from a few units which were given a chance to experience carefully controlled forays in the French Saar sector (including 51st Highland Division, which happened to be detached from the British sector on 10 May 1940), there was very little activity on the ground. Not surprisingly, many soldiers expressed feelings of impatience or boredom, and even eagerness for 'the balloon to go up'.

We now know that from October 1939 onwards Hitler repeatedly issued directives to the *Wehrmacht* to launch Plan Yellow (the Western offensive), but that these orders were again and again postponed, initially because the German generals urged caution in the light of lessons being assimilated from the Polish operations, and latterly because of the severe weather. From the Anglo-French viewpoint these frequent false alarms, conveyed to them on good authority from sources in Berlin, necessitated high states of alert and movements to the frontier in dreadful conditions invariably ending in anti-climax and the sapping of morale.[16] More seriously, these false alarms served to exacerbate anti-Belgian prejudices in the sense that the latter appeared to be clinging unrealistically to their neutral status, even to the extent of handicapping would-be allies who were being frustrated in their attempts to save Belgium from German occupation. Pownall's diaries provide a running commentary on the folly and iniquity of Belgian policy and behaviour.[17] This was just one of the ominous signs than an improvised alliance between France, Britain and Belgium would not function smoothly under the pressures of battle.

Following the dispatch of the five regular divisions to France in the Autumn of 1939, a further eight Territorial Army divisions were sent

7

out between January and the end of April 1940. These divisions were in general hastily put together, with imported drafts from other units to complete establishments, short of regular officers and senior NCOs and in varying states of equipment and training. With the exception of 50th (Northumbrian Division), all the Territorial brigades had a stiffening of one regular battalion. Three unofficially designated Labour Divisions (12th, 23rd, and 46th) were not equipped or trained to fight, but they too were swept up in the maelstrom of the retreat and virtually annihilated. Major-General John Drewienkiewicz reaches a sombre verdict in his study of the battle performance of the Territorial Army divisions: heroic though some of their actions were, as for example at Cassel and Hazebrouck, none managed to impose any significant delay on the German advance.[18] Indeed the Field Force as a whole was neither equipped nor trained for a fast-moving war against a first class opponent. It was essentially dependent on the French High Command's strategy and direction, and on fighting a static, or slow-moving, defensive campaign not so very different from that of 1914–1918.

In the early months of 1940 some politicians, including the Prime Minister, Neville Chamberlain, were inclined to believe that Hitler had 'missed the bus' and that there would be no great German offensive in the West. Others, including Churchill (First Lord of the Admiralty) and Ironside (Chief of the Imperial General Staff), thought that the Allies could seize the initiative by embroiling Germany in a campaign in Scandinavia. Consequently, in March and early April 1940, there was a tendency to neglect the needs of the Field Force in France in favour of possible operations in Finland and Norway. Not merely was there a delay in the build-up of personnel and supplies to the Field Force, but a brigade (15th Brigade from 5th Division) was actually recalled to fight in Norway.[19]

This diversion had important consequences for the organization and command structure of the Field Force. Had III Corps (commanded by Sir Ronald Adam) been fully formed before 10 May, Gort would almost certainly have appointed an Army Commander to run the battle while he was left free to deal with onerous issues of policy, strategy and liaison with two other allies. Since Gort had anyway been promoted 'above his ceiling', it was asking too much of him to fight the battle at the front (which he would have much preferred), while simultaneously having to cope with increasingly difficult command problems involving not only allies but also his own government, which was to show itself to be hopelessly out of touch with fast-moving events.

When the German onslaught began early on 10 May:

> The Field Force's leading formations advanced quite efficiently to the line of the River Dyle in Belgium as agreed with their allies, and for a few days the line was held with deceptively little enemy action. Once the retreat began, however, due to the German breakthrough further south, confusion and even worse soon occurred. Only a static or slow-moving campaign had been planned and communications (in all senses) soon collapsed under the unexpected strain. There had been sufficient motor transport for a planned advance but not for an improvised retreat on roads congested with refugees. There was soon an acute shortage of fuel. The British had relied almost entirely on the Belgian public telephone system, which now collapsed. Radio communications had been restricted for security reasons and now proved useless, as did field telephones. Thus orders could not be transmitted with any confidence and, in effect, confusion reigned.[20]

Thus was the scene set for the largely disorganized retreat to the coast, redeemed in part by gallant defensive actions, the brilliant manoeuvre described by Michael Piercy, and the skilful organization of the eastern sector of the Dunkirk perimeter described by Jeremy Crang.

As I wrote in *Time to Kill*:

> From the military historian's viewpoint the main conclusion must be that the other ranks and junior officers paid the price for the government's belated acceptance of a continental role with inadequate equipment and tanks, an almost total lack of close air support, unimaginative training still based essentially of First World War attitudes, and mediocre leadership. The speed and decisiveness of the Allied rout came as a terrible shock to those who understood the situation, resulting in some bitter criticisms of the politicians and generals held responsible. Understandably too, though it now seems rather shameful, much of the blame was transferred to Britain's recent allies, France and more especially Belgium for the latter's sudden announcement of a ceasefire on 28 May. But there was also a sentiment of profound respect for the Wehrmacht, and particularly for the Panzer divisions and the Luftwaffe.[21]

From a later perspective it is clear that this humiliating retreat and evacuation was 'a blessing in disguise' in that it signified an escape from the Continental commitment until 1944 and hence obviated the terrible prospect of repeating the experience of 1914–1918.

Notes

1   Brian Bond, (ed) *Chief of Staff: the Diaries of Lt. Gen. Sir Henry Pownall* (Leo Cooper, 1972) Vol I, p. 178. See also Brian Bond, *British Military Policy between the Two World Wars* (O.U.P., 1980) passim.
2   *Pownall Diaries*, pp. 201–2. See also Peter Dennis, *The Territorial Army 1907–1940* (Royal Historical Society, 1987).
3   Bond, *British Military Policy*, pp. 334–5. See also Major-General L.A. Hawes, 'The Story of the "W" Plan: the move of our forces to France in 1939' in *The Army Quarterly* (July 1971), pp. 445–6.
4   For a map with full details see L.F. Ellis, *The War in France and Flanders, 1939–1940* (H.M.S.O., 1953), p. 18.
5   Bond, *British Military Policy*, pp. 319–20.
6   Ibid., p. 320. I am indebted to Peter Caddick-Adams for permission to use details from his unpublished paper 'The British Army in France in 1940'.
7   Ibid., p. 321.
8   Ibid., p. 324–5.
9   Ibid., p. 326.
10 See for example, Charles Carrington, *Soldier at Bomber Command* (Leo Cooper, 1987).
11 Bond, *British Military Policy*, pp. 328–9.
12 Ibid., p. 329. Field Marshal Viscount Montgomery, *Memoirs* (Fontana pbk edn, 1961), pp. 49–50.
13 Bond, *British Military Policy*, p. 336.
14 *Pownall Diaries*, pp. 256–75. A.J. Trythall, 'The Downfall of Leslie Hore-Belisha' in *Journal of Contemporary History* (Vol 16, 1981), pp. 391–411.
15 Brian Bond, 'The British Field Force in France and Belgium, 1939–1940' in P. Addison and A. Calder (eds), *Time to Kill: the Soldier's Experience in the West, 1939–1945.* (Pimlico, 1997), pp. 42–3.
16 Brian Bond, *France and Belgium, 1939–1940* (Davis-Poynter, 1975), pp. 63–92.
17 See for example, *Pownall Diaries*, pp. 310–11.
18 Bond in *Time to Kill*, op. cit., pp. 40–1. K.J. Drewienkiewicz's study of the performance of the Territorial Divisions in 1940 is an unpublished

thesis written at the Royal College of Defence Studies in 1992. For a more positive view see Peter Caddick-Adams, *By God They Can Fight! A History of 143 Brigade* (Shrewsbury, 1995).

19   *Pownall Diaries*, pp. 284–90.
20   Bond in *Time To Kill*, p. 44.
21   Ibid., p. 48.

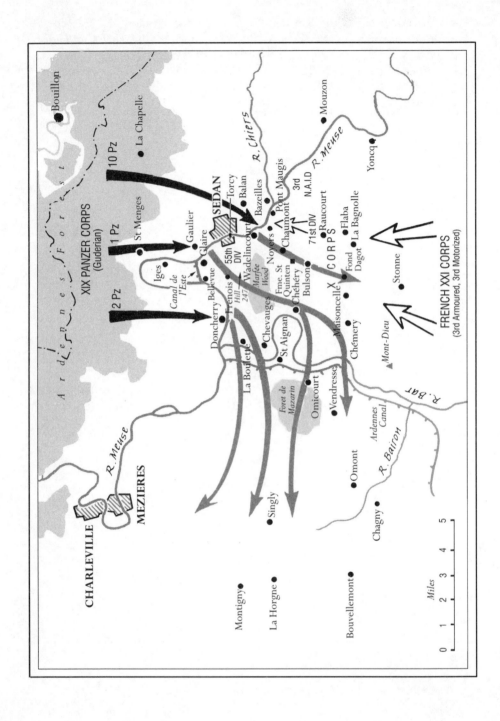

THE GERMAN BREAKTHROUGH AT SEDAN, 12–15 MAY 1940

PETER CADDICK-ADAMS

The Ardennes region of Luxembourg, southern Belgium and north-east France is renowned for its hills, valleys and, above all, forests. Beautiful country for walking or shooting, but to be avoided by an army in a hurry. Only a few relatively minor roads wind their way through the trees and thus the region was considered by the French to be unsuitable for motorized columns as a viable attack route: French war games of the 1930s calculated that an attacking force might take 9–10 days to work its way from the German border through the Ardennes to the River Meuse, a distance of about 70 miles. German war games during the autumn and winter of 1939–40 suggested that it might take as little as sixty *hours* to penetrate the forests and reach the Meuse, the gateway to France. In the event, Guderian's *panzers* managed it in fifty-seven hours.

The original German strategy for the invasion of the West, named *Aufmarschanweisung Gelb* (Deployment Directive Yellow), envisaged a Schlieffen-like thrust into northern Belgium and Holland, rather as the Germans had done in 1914. This is what the allies – the British and French – expected, and the capture of German war plans from a crashed plane in January 1940 reinforced this perception. Directive Yellow originated from OKH, but the brilliant tactician, 53-year-old Generalleutnant Erich von Manstein, proposed an alternative. A northern army would still thrust into Belgium as it was expected to do, thus distracting the allies' attention, but a southern army would attack through the poorly-defended Ardennes, then turn north and cut off the French and British forces. The Germans expected the cream of the allied armies to be sent into Belgium – France's best armoured divisions and the whole of the BEF – where they would be encircled and destroyed. The British military historian Basil Liddell Hart later

13

called the German advance into Belgium 'the matador's cloak', at once enticing the allies into Belgium and distracting them from the real attack further south.

The main component of France's defence was a series of underground fortresses, inter-connected reinforced concrete bunkers mounting heavy artillery, anti-tank and machine guns, protected by acres of anti-tank obstacles, ditches and barbed wire and which stretched from the Swiss frontier to the Belgian border. This was the Maginot Line, named after the French defence minister who survived fortress warfare at Verdun in 1916 and initiated the project in the 1920s. Unfortunately, the Maginot Line did not extend further north than the Ardennes. At the time of building, Belgium was an ally and a Maginot Line along the Franco–Belgian border was considered diplomatically impossible. In addition there was the issue of prohibitive cost and the technical difficulties of construction arising from the fact that much of France's border with Belgium lay in areas with a high water table. Shortly after the Line's completion in 1936, however, Belgium opted for strict neutrality and France had to consider the option of entering her neighbour's territory the moment she was invaded by Germany. This was felt to be a 'when', not an 'if', and France had learned from the First World War that if she was to preserve her northern industrial regions the invader must be stopped short of the French frontier.

French military doctrine of the 1930s centred on the concept of 'the methodical battle'. This in turn required a rigid centralization and strict obedience to top–down orders, thus stifling initiative in low-level commanders. Field commanders were thus neither trained nor intellectually equipped to respond to the unexpected. Unit commanders were also encouraged to remain in their command posts, the theory being that there they could exert the most influence, their hands being 'on the handle of a fan', the fan being their subordinate units. While not leading by personal example, they could thus ensure the smooth integration of all operations.

The first phase of any new war was to be defensive, the enemy halted by concentrated artillery fire and stubborn defence in depth rather than by dynamic counter-attack. Local reserves would be placed in front of any enemy who penetrated a position, a process known as *colmater*, or filling, with the idea of gradually slowing any advance to a standstill. Only when superiority in men and material had been accumulated would the battle change to the offensive, both locally in terms of operational counter-attacks and strategically. Within this framework, the role of French armour was as infantry support, a sort of slow-moving mobile artillery, deployed in small groups along the front.

The whole process lacked a sense of urgency and was further hampered by inadequate communications. Few radios were available and communication relied on the telephone or messengers. The first was open to disruption by enemy action in the forward areas and the second was so slow that senior and middle ranking commanders remote from the action were quickly out of touch. The flaws in such a system seeking to counter swift-moving armoured warfare are obvious in hindsight.

In contrast, German doctrine stressed decentralization and personal initiative at all levels. In general, German officers commanded units at one rank lower than their British contemporaries, with majors commanding battalions, captains companies and colonels regiments (the equivalent of a brigade). At the same time officers and NCOs were routinely trained to be able to command at one level up, so that sub-unit commanders had more responsibility than their British and French adversaries and were able to take more senior commands in moments of crisis.

Tactically, German methods evolved from those of the *Sturmtruppen* of the First World War, where small bands of stormtroopers probed the front looking for a weak spot, then attacked. This doctrine was considered less wasteful of manpower than the formal set-piece attack supported by massed artillery, so beloved of the French, and could be applied to armour as well. The mission-orientated system of command that many armies use today evolved from this tradition of identifying a commander's intent, and acting to achieve that intent even if beyond the strict remit of formal orders.

Momentum was a key principle in German doctrine and applied to every arm – assault pioneers as well as tanks or infantry. Reserves were used to reinforce success, not react to enemy initiatives, and the resulting maintenance of momentum was demonstrated often in the 1940 campaign, and again in 1941 in Russia. Also, the concept of the all arms battle was fully imbued into the Wehrmacht by 1940, uniquely among the armies of the time German field commanders being able to call quickly for Luftwaffe dive-bomber support in neutralizing centres of opposition. Full use was made of radios between the various arms, ground-to-air and tank-to-tank, making an enormous contribution to control of the battle.

Allied strategists reasoned that the Wehrmacht would attack through northern Belgium because the terrain would give their panzers room to manoeuvre in open country. Thus the Allies, under the supreme command of 68-year-old General Maurice Gamelin, adopted a defensive plan for Belgium in November 1939, plan 'D'. It was based on the concept of rushing into northern Belgium and creating stop lines to slow down or halt the German advance, allowing time to build up overwhelming reserves with which to make a decisive counter-attack, in accordance with established French military doctrine. These stop lines ran along rivers, particularly the Escaut (Scheldt) and the Dyle – hence Plans 'E' and 'D'.

Gamelin commanded primarily by messenger from his HQ, the gloomy Château de Vincennes, outside Paris, and had no direct radio links with his field forces. Using an unwieldy chain-of-command, Gamelin – also responsible for troops in the Alps, Syria and North Africa – issued orders via his deputy, General Georges, commander of the North-East Front. Georges had three Army Groups under him, of which General Billotte's No. 1 Group was earmarked to move into Belgium. Billotte commanded four French armies and the British Expeditionary Force (BEF). It was the 54-year-old Grenadier Guardsman, General Lord Gort, 6th Viscount, four times wounded, nine times mentioned in despatches, MC, DSO and two bars, and a VC won in 1918, who commanded the ten divisions of the BEF. Though under French command, he had the right of appeal to the British government before executing any order 'which appears to you to imperil the British Field Force'. Whilst the First, Seventh and Ninth French Armies and the BEF of Billotte's Group were to advance into Belgium, General Charles Huntziger's Second Army was to remain in France covering the Ardennes sector, as far south as the Maginot Line.[1]

The winter of 1939–1940 was the coldest of the century and the English Channel froze at Boulogne. The harsh weather severely restricted the training of the British and French armies, but such activity as was possible was directed mainly to creating defensive lines. Some have argued that this in itself sapped the aggressive spirit. More importantly, although the German all-arms tactics, soon to become known as 'blitzkrieg', had already been demonstrated in Poland, the Allies made little attempt to learn from them, or alter their doctrine. As Colonel Robert Doughty observed: "Tragically for France, a corps in a position that turned out to be crucial in the fight against the Germans, with troops that desperately needed additional training, focused most of its energies and resources on improving and building fortifications, rather than improving the fighting skills of its units and men."[2] The observation was being made about French units at Sedan, but it could equally well apply to the whole French Army and BEF at this time.

Although the Maginot Line itself petered out at Longuyon (near Luxembourg), a series of concrete bunkers had been built to cover the Meuse in the Sedan sector. Some were still incomplete by May 1940, but all were well sited on high ground on the south bank, overlooking the river. Whilst such field fortifications gave the French some confidence, what of the troops manning them?

The right flank of Huntziger's Second Army was the hinge between Army Group No. 1 and the beginning of the Maginot Line, defended by Army Group No. 2. A German penetration at this point would circumvent the Maginot Line altogether, and both threaten Paris and the rear of Billotte's forces. But, of course, this front was protected by the natural obstacles of the Ardennes hills and forests, the Semois and Meuse Rivers, before even considering military forces. General Grandsard's X Corps was responsible for the defence of this area and he deployed to his front a light screening force of cavalry, some of it still horsed, manning a few roadblocks and strong points north-east of Sedan. Once these units had withdrawn across the remaining bridges in his sector, all crossing points would be blown in a series of reserve demolitions. His main defensive line was established on the south bank of the Meuse and, on 10 May, comprised the 55th and 3rd North African Infantry Divisions.

The 55th Division, on which the main German assault at Sedan would fall, had three Regiments (brigade equivalents) plus attachments. One regiment was in Corps reserve, but the Division had under command the three battalions of 147th Fortress Infantry Regiment and 11th Machine Gun Battalion. With one battalion in divisional reserve and one committed to the forward screen, the Division therefore had seven battalions in position for the battle, four of its organic battalions plus all three battalions of the Fortress Regiment, augmented by the machine-gun companies of the 11th Battalion.

With regard to anti-tank capability, 55th Division was not well served. Two of its regiments were missing the anti-tank guns from their regimental support companies and this lack was only partially made up by the allocation of nine 1916 vintage 37mm light infantry guns, of dubious value in the anti-tank role. On the positive side, the divisional anti-tank battery was complete with its eight modern 47mm guns and another battery of the same composition had been allocated from the General Reserve. Two 47mm naval guns also appear to have been assigned. In taking command of 147th Fortress Regiment the Division had access to this unit's twenty-two 25mm guns and it also appears to have appropriated three such guns from 11th Machine-gun Battalion. This made a total of fifty-six anti-tank guns against an establishment of fifty-eight, but this was still woefully inadequate to cover the Division's 17km front. The theoretical density of anti-tank guns in the defence was ten weapons per kilometre but the Division could manage only 3.3.[3] A further problem was the siting of the weapons. As its name suggests, 147th Fortress Regiment had been raised and trained to defend fixed defences and most of their guns were therefore, quite properly, placed inside the blockhouses. This gave them protection from the enemy but also restricted their fields of fire and the ease with which they could be moved.

Anti-tank mines, an inexpensive and relatively simply made device that might be thought ideally suited to a defensive position, were at a premium in the French Army as a whole and were particularly scarce in the relatively 'safe' sector of the Ardennes. In the event, less than 500 were issued to the Division.[4] Thus whole sectors of the line were without armour-killing or stopping capability. However, this was not considered a problem as no German tanks were expected to come clattering out of the Ardennes, and certainly not in a time-scale that would preclude the bringing up of the reserves of infantry, artillery, armour and air reserves that the doctrine of deliberate battle decreed.

Artillery provision was good, the Division being supported by its own and a large proportion of X Corps artillery, by the time the battle opened totalling 174 guns of 75mm and 155mm calibre, nearly three times the amount of artillery normally assigned to such a division. Such a concentration not only favoured a strong defence but also the local 'counter-attack by fire', another aspect of the French concept of deliberate battle. However, significantly for the outcome of the coming struggle, the Division possessed no integral air defence capability and the inability to hit back at the Luftwaffe proved to be an important drain on morale. The only AA battery in the area, a 2 Army asset, shot down one aircraft before moving prematurely out of the battle.[5]

Given the circumstances of terrain, defensive works and artillery support, it was not considered a problem that both the 55th Division and 147th Fortress Regiment were from the 'B' series. As such, both contained only a tiny component of regular personnel, the rest being older conscripts with minimal if any modern training. Research by Robert Doughty has shown that the average age of 55th Division's soldiers was 31, subalterns 33, captains 42 and senior officers 51.[6] In the event, these older reservists proved less than resilient, particularly in the face of the novel form of attack from dive-bombers. Whilst the damage done to the bunkers and casualties sustained from air attack were generally minimal, the defenders, with no previous experience of the high-pitched screaming of a Stuka assault, often panicked and ran away. No aircraft were available in immediate support; indeed X Corps HQ had only three spotter aircraft at its permanent disposal. Morale and unit cohesion had also been sapped by the policy of exchange postings between the 147th Fortress Regiment and units of 55th Division. Men trained for fortress defence could not quickly be converted to the skills required of field infantry, a difficulty exacerbated by the fact that units brought out of the line for training seldom went back to positions with which they were familiar. 71st Infantry Division was 2nd Army's reserve and was probably in a worse state of training than 55th Division. Also a B Division, 71st had initially been in the line to the right of 55th but was withdrawn for additional training at the beginning of April. On 12 May it was ordered forward to take up positions between 55th and 3rd North African Infantry Divisions but it never fully deployed and achieved little.

It was entirely appropriate that the German attack at Sedan was commanded by 52-year-old Generalleutnant Heinz Guderian, father of the panzer arm. He had studied at Sedan in 1918 when it was the Imperial German Army's staff college and in the year the Maginot Line was completed, 1936, he had published a textbook on armoured warfare, advocating fully mechanized divisions capable of punching a hole in the front line, *Achtung Panzer!* He advocated large formations of tanks, fighting *en masse* that would break through their opponents' defences, followed by motorized infantry who would mop up the enemy defenders. Up with the tanks would be armoured engineer units, whilst mobile artillery and anti-tank units would support the advance and protect the flanks. Guderian saw a tactical air force interdicting the deployment of the enemy's reserves and providing close support to the armoured thrusts. *Achtung Panzer!* is now famous, but at the time of its publication it was ignored by the British and French, though after the war Guderian himself acknowledged the influence of the British advocates of armoured warfare.[7] Yet within its pages is a blueprint of Guderian's part in the invasion and defeat of France.

Whilst Generaloberst Fedor von Bock's Army Group 'B' advanced into Belgium and Holland on 10 May 1940 with twenty-six infantry and three panzer divisions, the main German thrust through the Ardennes was undertaken by Generaloberst Gerd von Rundstedt's Army Group 'A', with forty-five divisions under his command. The cutting edge comprised three panzer corps: Hoth's XV (5th and 7th Panzer Divisions), Reinhardt's XLI (6th & 8th Panzer), and Guderian's XIX Panzer Corps, consisting of the 2nd, 1st and 10th Panzer Divisions, with the elite GrossDeutschland Infantry Regiment in support. Clearly, Guderian possessed the largest corps, including over 800 tanks of the Wehrmacht's senior panzer divisions: he had himself commanded 2nd Panzer between 1935–1938. Both XLI and XIX corps were grouped together into a Panzer Group under the conservative cavalry general, Ewald von Kleist, the appointment being a precautionary measure by Army High Command in Berlin, still unsure, suspicious, and probably jealous of the new arm and its potential. Ritter von Leeb's Army Group 'C' continued to watch the Maginot Line from the safety of the Siegfried Line opposite.

Included in General Hermann Hoth's XV Panzer Corps was the 7th Panzer Division, commanded by a relatively obscure 48-year-old infantryman, much decorated in the First World War, Erwin Rommel. He, too, had written a textbook in the inter-war years, *Infanterie Greift An (Infantry Attacks)*, which caught Hitler's eye. After commanding Hitler's personal guard battalion, he was given 7th Panzer only on 15 February 1940, with no previous experience of armoured warfare. Considering his dazzling performance in May, it is astonishing that three months earlier he had never handled an armoured formation. Rommel's division was first across the Meuse at Houx, on the evening of 12 May, almost 24 hours ahead of Guderian to his south at Sedan.

Guderian crossed the Luxembourg border at 0435 hours on 10 May and within 24 hours had scatted the Belgian Chasseurs Ardennais and elements of the French 5th Light Cavalry Division tasked with creating blocks on the roads through the dense terrain. French time-and-space studies anticipated a German arrival on the Meuse not before about 20 May, but, despite horrendous traffic control problems requiring often drastic action by senior commanders[8], 1st Panzer reached the

Meuse at 1400 hours on 12 May. Crucially, although the French detected panzers in the Ardennes on 10–11 May, the German attacks by Army Group 'B' to the north, including the spectacular assault by glider-borne troops on the Belgian fort of Eben Emael (the first such assault in military history) and the presence of tanks and large numbers of paratroops in Holland, persuaded the Allies that the Ardennes was not to be the focus of a major attack. Even reports from aerial reconnaissance over the Ardennes of long, motorized columns on 12 May did not alter this view. X Corps was reinforced from local 2 Army resources but there was no strategic realignment. At this stage the Germans, aware of Allied expectations, were still showing the Allies what they expected to see – much activity to the north and far less in the centre. There was little artillery bombardment accompanying Army Group 'A's advance, traditional before launching an attack, and Luftwaffe activity in the Ardennes was kept to a minimum.

The French were bundled back so roughly that they were unable to hold Sedan itself and by nightfall of 12 May the Germans had occupied the town and the north bank of the Meuse. Both French and German conventional military wisdom demanded that they then pause and concentrate for the crossing of this major water obstacle, faced with strong and determined defenders. But on 13 May, assisted by overwhelming air support, Guderian's three divisions – 10th Panzer at Balan – Wadelincourt – Pont Maugis to the east, 1st Panzer and GrossDeutschland at Gaulier – Glaire, and 2nd Panzer at Donchery to the west – eventually crossed the river.

Guderian's immediate objective was for his three divisions, crossing the Meuse simultaneously in line abreast, to seize the high ground to the south, overlooking the river. He then planned to pivot west and punch a hole through whatever remained of the French defences. Once across the river, to protect his left flank he planned to use Graf von Schwerin's GrossDeutschland Regiment and/or 10th Panzer to occupy the southern heights at Stonne and Mont Dieu against a counter-attack.

The Luftwaffe deployed 310 bombers, 200 stukas and 200 fighters to support the Meuse crossing on 13 May, operating in continuous waves. This was the heaviest air assault so far in military history. Only seven French aircraft appeared over Sedan that day and were chased away by the Luftwaffe. One French colonel wrote: "Around 0930 hours German aviation began to bombard the position. . . . After 1100 the aerial bombardment became more intense and was mixed with lulls until 1700. . . . The attacks were executed by successive waves, each including around forty bombers, fighters participating in the action by firing their machine guns."[9] At the key crossing site in the centre 1st Panzer did not have time to draw up detailed crossing orders so, with masterly improvisation, produced the plan prepared for a map exercise in March, merely changing the timings. Both 2nd and 10th Panzer each loaned an artillery battalion to support 1st Panzer's assault, which was XIX Corps' main effort.

1st Panzer Division's assault was led by Oberstleutnant Hermann Balck's 1st Infantry Regiment (brigade equivalent) of three battalions. The 47-year-old Balck became one of Germany's most successful soldiers, being promoted over his divisional commander; he later commanded in succession 11th Panzer Division in Russia in 1941, XLVIII Panzer Corps in Sicily in 1943, IV Panzer Army in the Ukraine in 1944, and Army Group G in Lorraine in 1944–1945. Of a curious military pedigree, his grandfather had been an officer in the Argyll and Sutherland Highlanders, whilst his great-grandfather had served on Wellington's staff in the Peninsula![10] Balck personally led elements of two battalions across at 1500 hours, using tanks and assault guns in a direct fire rôle against bunkers on the south bank. Using about 100 rubber dinghies, each battalion crossed near the now-abandoned cloth factory at Gaulier, where the river is about seventy metres wide. French artillery was largely silent during this crossing, the artillerymen cowering beneath the stukas. The Germans moved rapidly westwards, pushing towards Bellevue and Frenois, whilst Balck's third battalion crossed. The division's Motorcyle Battalion crossed in the north, via a small island at St Menges and, moving south, was across the Canal de l'Est by 1800 hours.

The principal opposition to 1st Infantry Regiment came from Hill 247 just east of Frenois and a series of bunkers between Frenois and Wadelincourt. The most obvious of these today is just north of the crossroads and west of the Glaire–Frenois road, in the grounds of the Château de Bellevue. This bunker, No. 103 on French military plans, was commanded by Lieutenant Verron, who remembered seeing a mass of French infantry fleeing to the rear during a lull in the aerial bombardment on the morning of 13 May. As his bunker had blind spots these fleeing infantrymen were supposed to defend, and with his communication lines cut, Verron realized his vulnerable position, but stayed put. A bomb hit Verron's bunker during the afternoon, without causing much damage, and he continued to hold up 2nd

Panzer's crossing at Donchery with enfilade fire. At about 1745 hours Verron's bunker was attacked with hand grenades, eventually forcing his surrender. Shortly after his capture, Verron was escorted to the presence of a German general, "who was peering over a map and talking into a radio to a small aircraft that circled above Frenois. The general looked him over from head to foot, and after having apparently satisfied his curiosity . . . Verron was returned to his men."[11]

If indeed a general, and not a regimental commander, (such as Balck, or GrossDeutschland's Count von Schwerin), this may have been Generalmajor Kirchner, commanding 1st Panzer Division, or conceivably Guderian himself. The latter records being "anxious to take part in the assault across the Meuse by riflemen," crossing by assault boat after Balck's Regiment, and being greeted on the opposite bank by Balck, who cheerfully exclaimed, "Joyriding in canoes on the Meuse is forbidden," echoing Guderian's own words, made during training months earlier.[12] The US military historian Colonel Robert Doughty makes the point that the German commander, whoever he was, was only a few hundred metres away from the battle at Frenois. By contrast, Doughty observes that at the same moment General Lafontaine, commanding 55th Division, was located in his command post at Fond Dagot, eight kilometres due south, and that the French X Corps commander, General Grandsard, was at La Berlière, twenty kilometres away.[13]: both presumably had their hands still firmly on the handle of the French fan! Guderian spent the day in his command post above La Capelle, overlooking Sedan, or on the banks of the Meuse itself.

Working in the cover of the clothing factory, 1st Panzer's engineers had constructed two rafts by 1940 hours and a sixteen-ton bridge by 2300. Deciding to leave his tanks concentrated on the north bank, it was artillery, AA guns and half-tracks that Guderian moved across the Meuse initially. It was towards midday on 14 May that Guderian met von Rundstedt, his Army Group commander, on 1st Panzer's bridge over the Meuse, whilst an air raid was actually in progress. Apparently, von Rundstedt asked "Is it always like this here?", to which Guderian could reply with a clear conscience that it was!

Balck's leadership is a perfect role model for maintaining *momentum*. He pushed his Infantry Regiment on at a cracking pace and they covered the two and a half kilometres from the Meuse to Bellevue in three hours, fighting all the way and rushing the bunkers under fire. During the next four hours his Regiment reached Cheveuges-St Aignan, a further three kilometres south, *en route* attacking and capturing the French bunkers holding up 2nd Panzer at Donchery. The latter stages of the move on Cheveuges were led by Balck personally, as the advance slowed whilst attacking up the high ground of La Boulette. Leaving his 1st Battalion to secure the heights, Balck pressed on and by 0300 hours his 2nd Battalion had reached Chéhéry, a further two and a half kilometres south, whilst his 3rd Battalion occupied St Quentin Farm. Balck's determination pushed the French defenders south and east, opening up a salient approximately 3 kilometres wide by 7 kilometres deep. His men had been in continuous action for twelve hours.

Oberstleutnant Graf von Schwerin's GrossDeutschland had more difficulty crossing at Torcy. Its 2nd Battalion was held up by fire from French bunkers astride a demolished bridge. Only sustained fire from 88mm flak guns eventually subdued the defenders, allowing two companies to cross by assault boat, but by nightfall only one and a half of GrossDeutschland's four battalions had managed to cross. Working closely with Balck's Infantry Regiment in the fight for the French bunkers, they, too, were delayed by fire from Hill 247 and house-to-house fighting in Torcy. 2nd Battalion finally took Hill 247 at around 1900 hours. The remainder of GrossDeutschland then crossed the Meuse overnight.

As with 1st Panzer, 10th Panzer relied on using orders issued for an earlier map exercise. This saved valuable time and also illustrates the flexibility fostered by German doctrine. The Division's main effort was to cross at Wadelincourt using 86th Infantry Regiment, followed by 69th Regiment. French artillery concentrations disrupted the approach of 10th Panzer through the night, and damaged the assault boats in Balan and Bazeilles. In consequence, 86th's crossing started late and came under heavy fire as the shock of the initial air attacks wore off. Only one of the initial rubber dinghies managed to cross, under command of Leutnant Hanbauer, others being caught in the crossfire. Hanbauer's small group managed to penetrate the barbed wire and attacked trenches and bunkers under covering fire from the far bank. Eventually Hanbauer captured the heights overlooking the crossing, enabling other units to cross.

Here Fedlwebel Rubarth of the 49th Engineer Battalion similarly led a platoon across the Meuse, covered by machine guns on the east bank. He suffered casualties before reaching the river line, but crossed safely, and rolled up a line of small bunkers. French artillery fire initially prevented reinforcements from joining him, and destroyed his boats.

At one stage he had to return to the river bank and request more ammunition:

> The enemy reassembled and attacked us from the right flank. After a hard fight, our men silenced the enemy fire. Gefreiter Brautigam, who was a close friend of all of us, sacrificed his young life in this fight. . . . Then we stop before a bunker with two firing ports. We attack it from two sides. One Frenchman, who had left the bunker and aimed his weapon directly at me, was rendered harmless by a hand grenade. We press forward towards the bunker. . . . Gefreiter Hose has meanwhile blasted open the entrance. . . . The crew, which recognizes the uselessness of further resistance, surrenders. A French machine gun from this bunker becomes a valuable weapon for us in another fight. . . . The enemy fire ceases, and we launch an attack forward in unison with an infantry platoon against the heights before us.[14]

Like Lieutenant Hanbauer, Sergeant Rubarth led his men up the hills directly overlooking his crossing point and broke the back of the local defences. For his exploits, Rubarth was commissioned in the field to Leutnant and awarded the Knight's Cross of the Iron Cross.

By 1730 hours 10th Panzer reported the west bank of the Meuse secure and by 1800 hours had captured Hill 246, south of Wadelincourt, linking up with GrossDeutschland. The French had withdrawn from the river banks and moved back to high ground, where they conducted a defence initially from Hill 246, then the French military cemetery. The capture of Hill 246 may also have put pressure on the French defending Hill 247 against Balck's Infantry Regiment of 1st Panzer, one and a half kilometres north-west. By 0545 hours on 14 May 10th Panzer had constructed a tank-carrying bridge at Wadelincourt.

Guderian's old division, 2nd Panzer, had manoeuvred slowly through the Ardennes, being tangled with other units, and consequently arrived late at its crossing point of Donchery on 13 May. By 1700 hours elements of 2nd Infantry Regiment, supported by tanks, had only reached the railway line, 500 metres short of the river, and were under heavy fire. All attempts to cross by assault boats failed due to the defensive fire brought down by bunkers on the south bank of the Meuse, and by French artillery support, which was apparently strongest in this sector. Hampered to an extent by the loan of one of its artillery battalions to support the main effort by 1st Panzer, 2nd Panzer used tanks, 88mm and 37mm guns to fire directly into the bunkers. However, it was not until Balck's Infantry Regiment from 1st Panzer Division had outflanked the bunkers to the rear and darkness had fallen that 2nd Panzer started to cross by rubber dinghies, from 2200 hours onwards. Oberfeldwebel Keddig of 2nd Panzer observed: "We fired off shell after shell, always at the recognized bunkers, to try and silence them. It became unbearably hot inside the tank's turret, which was filled with powder smoke. A beautiful summer evening lay across the countryside. But the firing of the French artillery continued with undiminished violence. We couldn't dream of opening any of the tank's hatches."[15] A bridge was completed at Donchery only by 0400 hours on 15 May.

The area around Sedan remains littered with concrete bunkers of varying shapes and sizes from which it is clear that they are not interconnected with underground passages, as with the Maginot Line. Access to the Sedan bunkers was by a series of short trenches and local defence was by barbed wire. Defence should have been provided by the 55th Divisional and X Corps artillery, but failed for three reasons. First, the air attacks not only destroyed some guns but so terrified the artillerymen that they began to panic, some running away. Second, telephone lines between the bunkers, their commanders and the gunners had not been dug in and were very soon cut by German artillery fire. Finally, French artillery support was strictly rationed, out of a short-sighted fear of running out of ammunition in what was anticipated as being a long-drawn-out battle for the bridgehead. Thus the bunkers were vulnerable to infantry assault and fell one by one. It has been observed by Colonel Robert Doughty that another reason for the speed of the rupture of the French defences was the Germans' ability to exploit unit boundaries, as an inability for neighbouring French units to work together soon became evident.[16]

Thus by late evening Guderian had not only achieved his aim of crossing the Meuse, breaching the main defences and securing the heights of La Boulette and the Bois de la Marfee, four kilometres south of Sedan, but Balck had led his tired men as far as Chehery, three kilometres beyond. Bundeswehr historian Major Winifred Heinemann makes the observation that to the casual observer the most striking aspect of the invasion was the Germans' mass use of tanks. But the events of 13 May, he argues, demonstrate that the panzers could not have crossed the Meuse without the support of their integral assault engineers, panzer infantry, motorized artillery, as well as close air support from the Luftwaffe. In fact no tanks crossed on 13 May – their achievement this day was in silencing the French bunkers across the river and demoralizing their opponents.[17] The first tanks to clatter into the bridgehead were from 2nd Panzer Brigade of 1st Panzer Division, whom Guderian personally directed over the bridge at Gaulier from 0200 hours on 14 May, in response to reports of French armour moving north towards the bridgehead. It is interesting to note that the successes of 13 May were due to the personal actions and leadership of a few sub-unit infantry commanders – Balck, Hanbauer and Rubarth we know of, but there were unnamed others whose actions inspired the Germans and demoralized the French, challenging the blitzkrieg myth of the triumph of the machinery of modern war over the individual.

Daylight on 14 May saw Guderian push GrossDeutschland south to join Balck on his left flank. Initially they were unsupported by panzers, but elements of an assault engineer battalion and a battalion of artillery had crossed the Meuse to their aid. His aim was to swing 1st Panzer Division west and prepare to break out from the bridge-head. GrossDeutschland's recce screen thereupon began probing towards Bulson via Chaumont, and to Chemery-sur-Bar via Connage. French tanks and infantry started the first of a series of disjointed local counter-attacks at Chaumont, Connage and Maisoncelle. At Connage, in a blaze of costly Napoleonic glory, French horsed cavalry were involved in the action. According to one observer, "The German 37mm anti-tank guns could penetrate the French tanks' armour plate only after several hits at the same point, and a few of the French tanks came within 200 metres . . . before they were halted by highly accurate fire. . . . Other French tanks attempted to go round the flanks, but they were halted when the six [anti-tank] guns formed a circular hedgehog position."[18]

This tells us not only that the French tanks were well armoured, and therefore a match for German infantry, but also that the morale and discipline of the Germans was very high. To stay in the same firing position, repeatedly firing at the same tank until it is only 200 metres away, takes guts. Whilst they initially pushed the German recce screen back, the timely arrival of 1st Panzer Division's armour after 0930 hours at all three sites was crucial to destroying the French tank attacks.

These counter-attacks were hurried affairs and the tanks and infantry, never having worked together before, had no chance for familiarization or co-ordination beforehand. The French 213th Infantry Regiment (the X Corps reserve regiment from 55th Division) and 7th Tank Battalion attacked north towards Bulson and Connage, via Maisoncelle, whilst 205th Regiment (from 71st Division, 2 Army's reserve) and 4th Tank Battalion attacked west towards Maisoncelle, from Raucourt-et-Flaba. Although the French advance went well initially, the arriving panzers routed the French. The tank battalions lost 70% of their armour and the infantry sustained high casualties, having little to counter German armour: the whole of the 213th Regiment, for example, possessed only four 25mm anti-tank guns. They lacked artillery support, too. Fleeing gunners and aerial attack had reduced the number of 55th Division and X Corps guns supporting the French from 174 to just twelve.

GrossDeutschland pushed on to Chemery-sur-Bar, which fell after a sharp fight at 1100 hours; this is an excellent early illustration of German kampfgruppe (battlegroup) improvisation. The 37mm anti-tank guns which attacked Connage and Chemery came from GrossDeutschland, only under command of 1st Panzer Division for the crossing; armour support came from 2nd Panzer Regiment of the Division, whilst the 43rd Assault Engineer Battalion (of 1st Panzer Division) acted as infantry. These three units had not worked together before, yet operated in perfect cohesion, breaking French resistance, beating off counter-attacks and destroying many French tanks. Although it can be argued that it was a waste of a valuable asset to commit the assault engineers as infantry, the principle of momentum overcame all, and there was simply no time to wait for enough infantry to come up to attack the village. The moment of victory was bitter-sweet, however, for a short time later a misdirected stuka attack killed the CO of 43rd Assault Engineers and several tank officers from 2nd Panzer Regiment, seriously wounding the Regimental commander.

As 1st Panzer Division continued to front XIX Corps' main effort, the armour of Generalmajor Rudolf Veiel's 2nd Panzer Division crossed at Gaulier at 1000 hours on 14 May. It cleared as far west as the Canal des Ardennes, and south to St Aignan, protecting the right flank of 1st Panzer. The immediate objective of Generalmajor Ferdinand Schaal's 10th Panzer Division in the east was to capture the high ground, still in French hands, which overlooked his bridge at Wadelincourt, and then to occupy the heights north-east of Bulson.

28

The French positions, which continued to hold up German traffic over their pontoon bridge, were centred around Noyers and the military cemetery and only surrendered at 1300 hours, having also been outflanked by elements of GrossDeutschland moving south to their rear. By the evening of 14 May 10th Panzer had entered Bulson and had received orders to attack Stonne, with GrossDeutschland in support, now detached from 1st Panzer.

During the afternoon of 14 May Guderian was faced with a major tactical dilemma. His aim was to punch right through the French defences and head west, but his bridgehead was far from secure, with French tanks now counter-attacking to his south. Nevertheless, his own armoured doctrine suggested that he should concentrate his panzers, rather than dissipate them around the bridgehead, and continue to attack the French. The events of 13 May had suggested that the speed, determination and overwhelming force with which his XIX Panzer Corps had attacked had thrown the defenders completely off balance. If he could exploit the momentum of his attack, then Guderian reasoned he could break out of the Sedan pocket. That afternoon, therefore, GrossDeutschland Regiment and 10th Panzer Division were ordered to secure the German left flank, in the area of Stonne, and the high ground of Mont Dieu, to the west of Stonne; they were to stay there until relieved by 16th and 24th Infantry Divisions, following on, but yet to cross the Meuse. 1st and 2nd Panzers were ordered to make for Rethel on 15 May, some 30 kilometres south-west of Sedan.

In retrospect, this was a brave decision by an optimistic commander who had faith in his own forces and read the French will to resist accurately. At the time the move was a gamble. At this stage neither 1st nor 2nd Panzer had all their forces across the Meuse, yet on the afternoon of the 14th both were ordered to move west as the XIX Corps main effort. 1st Panzer in particular had lost many officers in the battle and reported only a quarter of their tanks battle-ready on 14 May. Guderian's immediate commander, von Kleist, would have preferred Guderian to halt and secure his bridgehead, as his own superiors were urging, in the face of reports of French armour massing at Stonne and Vendresse. Guderian, ever the optimist, persuaded von Kleist that his armour should be allowed to continue to roll west, as he believed the French were close to total collapse.

To begin the move west, 1st Panzer sub-divided into two kampfgruppen or battlegroups: to the south the bulk of the armour was to move along the road from Chémery-sur-Bar to Vendresse whilst an infantry-heavy northern battlegroup was to use logging trails to move due west through the Forêt de Mazarin. Elements of the French 1st cavalry brigade, including horsed cavalry, and the 5th Light Cavalry Division held up the panzers at Vendresse for the whole day, withdrawing at 1700 hours, whilst the northern group moved easily through the forest, making their objective of Singly at 2300 hours, completely outflanking Vendresse.

On this day, 14 May, the Allies flew twenty-seven separate bombing raids against the Meuse bridges, involving 152 bombers and 250 fighters, but failed to inflict any damage. The Luftwaffe and 200 anti-aircraft guns along the Meuse inflicted heavy losses, including forty out of seventy-two RAF bombers shot down. In the words of its official history, "no higher rate of loss has ever been experienced by the RAF."[19]

15 May saw perhaps the bitterest fighting of the whole battle for Sedan. To the south-east, in a combined infantry, panzer and stuka attack, GrossDeutschland assaulted the heights around Stonne at 0700 hours, but were thrown back by tanks and infantry of the French 3rd Armoured and 3rd Motorized Divisions at 1100. These two divisions were part of the French XXI Corps under General Flavigny and included around 150 tanks. The now-exhausted Gross-Deutschland were reinforced with 69th Infantry Regiment of 10th Panzer and the French were in turn pushed out of Stonne at 1700 hours. French armour also counter-attacked at Yoncq, but was held by 10th Panzer, and at Maisoncelle and Chemery-sur-Bar, where they were halted by German anti-tank guns. It took six German infantry battalions, four tank battalions, three anti-tank companies, the armoured engineer and the armoured reconnaissance battalion of 10th Panzer just to hold this south-eastern flank against French counter-attacks during 15 May, belying the legend of an easy victory in France.

In view of the ferocious battles around Stonne, the French remained convinced that the German main effort was to be a move *south-east*, outflanking the Maginot Line. Thus, reinforcements from the French 55th and 71st Infantry Divisions were rushed to that sector of the battlefield and away from the real German main effort. The morale of the units marching north to the battle was eroded by the sight of other troops moving to the rear, including headquarters staff, officers and whole artillery units. Some were obviously fleeing in blind panic; weaponless and leaderless, whilst others retreated with more dignity as formed units, following their officers. This rout also severely slowed the movement of reinforcements, French tanks particularly finding that roads swamped with soldiers trebled their march times.

In the south-west the armoured battlegroup of 1st Panzer, having eventually cracked the tough nut of Vendresse, drew up against strong French defences at Chagny. Its northern battlegroup attacked La Horgne, 3 kilometres west of Singly, at first light. For the first time in the campaign Balck's now-depleted and tired Infantry Regiment was halted by the ferocity of the French defence, but Balck's personal appearance and direction of the battle thereafter ensured its capture in the late afternoon. Over half the French defenders, from two Moroccan and two Algerian battalions of the 3rd Spahis Brigade (cavalry), were killed at La Horgne, but they halted Balck's Regiment between 0700–1700 hours on 15 May. The fall of La Horgne persuaded the French defenders of Chagny to withdraw, rather than risk being outflanked. Gradually the French were being pushed back and, significantly, it was the exhausted German infantry of 1st Panzer who were clearing the way, with the tanks clattering along to their rear in support. Time and time again it was the infantry, not the panzers, who made the breakout from Sedan possible. Balck was later awarded the Ritterkreuz (the German equivalent of the VC) for his leadership on this day.

Despite the continued defence of Stonne, the French high command seemed to sense they could not contain Guderian's Corps. On the previous evening the BEF and French First Army in Belgium were ordered to pull back from the River Dyle, to begin moving on 16 May. At this time the French premier, Paul Reynaud, telephoned his British counterpart, Winston Churchill (who had replaced Neville Chamberlain on 10 May) and declared, "We are beaten: we have lost the battle."

The French 3rd Armoured and 3rd Motorized Divisions counter-attacked at Stonne again on 16 May, pushing GrossDeutschland and 69th Regiments off the heights overlooking the town, and held them for most of the day. The French 3rd Armoured Division, which was almost annihilated at Stonne, comprised two armoured brigades, each of H-39 and Char-B tanks. Both tanks were well armoured and the H-39 mounted a high velocity 37mm gun, capable of penetrating most German armour. Unfortunately, the division had only been formed in

31

March 1940 and was under strength and poorly trained. Equipment shortages were so extensive that there were no internal tank radios and heavy fuel consumption of the Char-B meant a limited operating radius. With piecemeal use of the French armour at Stonne and the fact that German artillery was used to destroy French anti-tank guns, whilst the panzers remained out of range, the French eventually retreated in the face of renewed German pressure, supported by the Luftwaffe, at 1500 hours. That evening GrossDeutschland and 69th Regiments conducted a relief-in-place with units of 24th and 16th Infantry Divisions, who had meanwhile crossed the Meuse and moved up in support. On 17 May 10th Panzer headed west to catch up with the rest of XIX Corps. During the counter-attacks at Stonne, the French 3rd Armoured Division lost 60% of its tanks. The French 2nd Armoured Division was also deployed to the area in a mixed road/rail move, but never reformed on arrival. Thus it, too, was deployed piecemeal and over a protracted period, due to frequent changes of orders. Throughout this period General Lafontaine of 55th Division and General Grandsard of X Corps appeared indecisive and had trouble asserting their authority, as events rapidly overtook them.

To the west 1st Panzer broke through into open country and Guderian's almost reckless advance was amply justified when, during 16 May, XIX Corps linked up with XLI Panzer Corps to the north, creating a two-corps front across the Meuse of five panzer divisions. Apparently Guderian amazed his troops by *overtaking* the advance elements of his own 1st Panzer, on the way to meet the commander of 6th Panzer at Montcornet, advancing from the north! Guderian had already had to talk von Kleist into continuing the advance, and now the problem arose again. General von Kleist was still under pressure to halt Guderian and expand and consolidate the Sedan bridgehead, as conventional military wisdom dictated. He ordered a halt on the 17th. Keen to exploit the success of his now nearly exhausted divisions, Guderian actually ignored this order and, when reprimanded by von Kleist, he submitted his resignation in disgust at not being able to continue the advance. Though initially accepted, this resignation was later refused, and indeed with von Kleist's connivance, Guderian was allowed to continue with a 'reconnaissance in force' during the 17–18 May. Thus, Guderian had achieved between 13–16 May something the whole German Imperial Army had failed to do in 1914–1918 – break through the main French defensive line.

1 Alistair Horne, *To Lose A Battle: France 1940*, (Macmillan 1969), Chapter 6, pp. 100–18.
2 Robert Allan Doughty, *The Breaking Point – Sedan & the Fall of France 1940*, (Archon, Connecticut 1990), p. 112.
3 Ibid., p. 118. For the order of battle of 55th Division see: *Guerre 1939–1945, Les Grandes Unités Françaises, Etat. Major de L'Armée de Terre – Service Historique*, Paris, 1967, pp. 635–42.
4 Ibid., Chapter 4, pp. 119–20.
5 Ibid., pp. 118–19.
6 Ibid., p. 121.
7 Horne, op. cit., pp. 43–7; B.H. Liddell Hart, *The Other Side of the Hill: Conversations with Germany's Generals*, (Pan paperback 1978), pp. 61–75. For a more sceptical view of Liddell Hart's alleged influence, see John J. Meersheimer, *Liddell Hart and the Weight of History*, Brassey's 1988, pp. 164–7.
8 For an account of XIX Panzer Corps' passage through the Ardennes, see *Guderian's XIX Panzer Corps and the Battle of France*, Florian K. Rothbrust, Praeger, 1990.
9 Lt.-Col. Pinaud, commanding 147 Fortress Regiment, quoted in Doughty, op. cit., p. 136.
10 Michael Glover, *A New Guide To the Battlefields of Northern France & the Low Countries*, (Michael Joseph 1987), p. 129.
11 Doughty, op. cit., pp. 172–5.
12 General Heinz Guderian, *Panzer Leader*, (Futura paperback 1974), p. 102.
13 Doughty, op. cit., p. 174.
14 Quoted in Doughty, op. cit., pp. 155–7.
15 Horne, op. cit., p. 260.
16 Doughty, op. cit., p. 185.
17 Chapter 3, in Harris & Toase (editors), *Armoured Warfare*, (Batsford, 1990), p. 68.
18 Doughty, op. cit., p. 211.
19 Denis Richards, *The Royal Air Force 1939–45*, Volume 1, HMSO 1953, p. 120.

ANGLO-FRENCH CO-OPERATION DURING THE BATTLE OF FRANCE

PETER CADDICK-ADAMS

This chapter will attempt to examine the reasons for the overall failure of the Anglo-French alliance to co-operate adequately in their struggle against the Germans in May–June 1940. It is not a military analysis of the French or British campaigns, but an evaluation of how the allied armies operated together, or might and should have operated together. I will argue that had there been more effective liaison, or a dedicated multi-national staff, it would have made a vast difference to the outcome of the campaign.

Following the First World War, France had conceived a strategic defence in conjunction with Belgium against the common enemy, Germany. The Maginot Line, built at great expense, defended the French frontier south and east of the Belgian Ardennes while the open and industrialized north was to be defended by field armies under the terms of the Franco-Belgian military alliance. However, as early as 1931 the Belgians were showing a strong preference for defence through neutrality rather than military alliance and in that year the Belgian Ambassador in Paris warned that French troops could not expect to enter Belgium without an explicit invitation. Belgium's paranoia at provoking Germany at such an early stage is interesting, two years before Hitler came to power. France's western defence strategy was finally wrecked by Belgium's decision to end the Franco-Belgian military alliance on 6 March 1936, followed by the announcement of strict neutrality seven months later. This meant that there was no opportunity for joint training, planning, or even of significant ground reconnaissance.

It was rather like removing the keystone from an arch. Defensive alliances with Czechoslovakia, Poland, the Soviet Union, Rumania and Italy, aimed at hemming Germany in to south and east, all proved ultimately of little value, while the only consistent strand of British defence policy in the 1930s was at all costs to avoid a continental commitment to fight another war in Europe.

The sophisticated apparatus of alliance and multi-national military command that had evolved by the end of the First World War had not survived the years of peace, even in theoretical form. Thus it was that when Britain at last recognized in 1939 the inevitability of a continental military involvement, no peacetime preparations had been made to staff a multi-national headquarters: it was assumed that each army would fight its own war, communicating via a network of liaison officers at individual headquarters. These took the form of Military 'Missions', in the British case typically led by a Major General or Lieutenant General, which were assigned, for example, to French and Belgian GHQs and to HQs of Army Groups and Armies. At a lower level, French officers, often from the reserve or called from retirement, were attached to the headquarters of most British units, although in this case their role appears primarily to have been to provide language and cultural bridges between the resolutely Anglophone British and the local population.

However, such *ad hoc* arrangements were no substitute for joint command and staffs. Edward Spears, who had made his name as principal French liaison officer in 1914, wrote on 23 May 1940, "liaison with the French was extremely unsatisfactory. Général Georges' liaison was functioning to some extent, thanks to the activity and competence of the officers concerned, but the main liaison organization at Vincennes with GQG, although there were some good men there too, had broken down as far as rendering any useful service was concerned. The French were giving them no news, and they were not organized to collect it."[1] Clearly, such poor liaison between allied headquarters was hardly a prelude to successful coalition warfare. Spears, an MP, had been appointed Major General on 22 May with the task of creating his own liaison network, reporting to Churchill via 'Pug' Ismay.

The British offer in July 1939 to establish a permanent inter-allied joint staff was politely declined by the French, perhaps understandably as the proposal was that it should be based in London. At the same time, at the strategic level Daladier did accept Chamberlain's suggestion that an Anglo-French Supreme War Council like that of the

First World War should come into being on the outbreak of hostilities, but not before. Fatally, it would have no executive control, leaving final decisions to governments.[2] One of its members, Ismay, recalled: "[it] served a useful purpose, but the lack of a permanent Anglo-French secretariat to maintain records, preserve continuity and ensure systematic procedure was a grave defect."[3] It will also be remembered that both Prime Ministers changed, as did many senior military figures, during September 1939–June 1940. Of multi-national staffing in general, the CGS of the BEF, Lieutenant General H.R. Pownall, recorded on 17 May: "The staff work about our joint withdrawal [from Belgium], First French Army, ourselves [BEF] and the Belgians is appalling."[4]

Consideration of the failure of the allied effort needs to be addressed in the context of the distressingly rapid collapse of the allied forces in May 1940, a collapse that was as much moral as physical. It should be remembered that within five days of the German invasion of 10 May the Dutch had thrown in the towel, the French defences on the Meuse had been thrust aside and members of the French government were openly talking of surrender, whilst Belgium was beginning to wobble. As early as 13 May General Pownall wrote in his diary: "All the Belgians seem to be in a panic, from the higher command downwards. What an ally!"[5] And again on 15 May, "Holland surrendered today, after five days of 'Blitzkrieg'. There was no chance that she would hold for long, but five days is a bit short. The worst effect is likely to be on Belgian morale, already thoroughly bad from top to bottom."[6] The same day General Ironside [CIGS] noted his diary: "This morning at 8 am, just as I was talking to Gort, the PM rang up and told me that he had been talking to Reynaud [on the telephone], who was thoroughly demoralized. He said that the battle was lost. The road to Paris was open. Couldn't we send more troops? Winston told him to keep calm, that these incidents happened in a war."[7]

Part of the distress over the 1940 collapse emanates from the force ratios. It was a defeat that was never anticipated and should not have happened. Both sides were pretty evenly matched on paper. Against the Germans' 136 divisions (of which seventy-five attacked in two Army Groups), the French fielded 100 divisions and the British ten, to which one could add twenty-two Belgian and ten Dutch divisions, for a total of 142.[8] Moreover, against ten German panzer divisions the

Allies could field seven armoured or mechanized divisions, comprising three French and one British armoured divisions and three French light mechanized divisions each with a strong tank element. (A further French armoured division (4th DCR) was hastily assembled on 15 May and although involved in much fighting was arguably never a fully integrated fighting force.) Another shock comes in a comparison of overall tank numbers, for the French could muster about 3,680 tanks, the British 300 and the Belgians around 270 against 3,465 German panzers, a position of Allied numerical superiority.[9] In the air, the Germans were more numerous but did not have a crushing superiority. The French *Armée de l'Air* had perhaps 1,120 modern aircraft, to which must be added around 125 Dutch and 180 Belgian aircraft and some 300 British from the approximately thirteen Hurricane and fourteen bomber squadrons which operated with the BEF's Air Component and the Advanced Air Striking Force, giving a total of around 1,700. The Luftwaffe fielded around 3,200 planes in the West, including 1,000 fighters, 1,360 bombers and 340 Stuka dive-bombers.[10] Thus the Germans were outnumbered by about 2:1 in the number of divisions deployed, faced near-parity in terms of armour but enjoyed around a 2:1 superiority in aircraft if one excludes the RAF resources remaining within the UK.

Against this must be put the quality and deployment of the allied forces. The German Army had been blooded in Poland and had the added advantage of being able to concentrate their forces where they chose. The allies had no recent operational experience and were strung along four hundred miles of frontier. In terms of armour the Germans concentrated their resources in ten operationally ready panzer divisions. Of the seven Allied armoured formations, the British 1st Armoured Division was simply not ready for war and arrived too late to join the main body of the BEF, as it reached France south of the Somme just as the Germans reached the Channel coast. Around half the Allied armour was deployed across the front in individual regimental-sized units dedicated to reconnaissance or infantry support. R.H.S. Stolfi has done much to re-assess the French tank strength in 1940 and concludes that the French High Command dissipated its armour in ill-co-ordinated and hasty attacks, which they should have concentrated to slow and contain the German advance.[11]

Bundeswehr historian Karl-Heinz Frieser argues that the German war machine in 1940 was both revolutionary and reactionary: revolutionary because of the existence of sixteen armoured and motorized divisions in the attacking force, and the way they were used, reactionary because, following in the panzers' wake, were infantry divisions who relied on horses for movement.[12] It is fair to argue that the Germans won in France *not* because of superior numbers or equipment, but rather because of better doctrine, their speed of manoeuvre and an ability to exploit French errors to the full. In fact, Colonel Robert Doughty and other modern scholars argue that the Germans did not so much win as the French collapsed, enabling the Germans to pick up the pieces, rather like a boxer caving in to his opponent at the start of Round One.[13] Certainly, Alistair Horne and others argue, the events of May–June 1940 came as much as a surprise to the Germans as they did to the French. Karl-Heinz Frieser goes so far as to suggest that in May 1940 Hitler lost control of the invasion, which developed a momentum of its own. The successful outcome enhanced the Führer's belief in his own genius (after all, he had backed Manstein's original plan against the inclinations of some of his most senior generals) and the resulting over-confidence propelled him into the fight with Russia a year later.

In examining evidence of inter-Allied co-operation in 1940, reference must be made to the British so-called 'counter-attack' at Arras of 21 May south-west of Arras. The SS Totenkopf and Rommel's 7 Panzer Division were bruised (Rommel was so surprised that he reported being attacked by five divisions![15]) by a scratch formation of two tank and two infantry battalions of the BEF and detachments of the French 3rd DLM. The origins and scope of this operation were largely misunderstood at the time and have been a source of confusion ever since, despite the attempt of the British official historian to put the matter into context.[16]

John Colville (Churchill's Private Secretary) recorded the British War Cabinet's reaction on Sunday 19 May 1940 to the news of the rapid German advance westwards from Sedan.

> After lunch came the astounding and, if true, nerve-racking news that the French army south of the BEF has melted away and left a vast gap on the British right. . . . At the moment Lord Gort's choice seems to be to retire to the sea, forming a bridgehead round Dunkirk or to fight his way south-eastwards [sic], leaving the Belgians to their fate, in order to rejoin the French. Lord Gort has asked for a Cabinet decision on the action he is to take. . . .

The Cabinet met at 4.30 and decided that the BEF must fight its way southwards towards Amiens to make contact with the French.[17]

On 20 May Ironside took this decision to Lord Gort's headquarters where the latter explained that it was impossible to carry out such an order. His forces were fully committed and he had placed his only reserves, 5th and 50th Divisions with 1st Army Tank Brigade, under General Franklyn of 5th Division with orders to mount a blocking or 'mopping up' operation on the roads south of Arras the following day. This purely local initiative was to relieve pressure on the town's garrison, by now all but surrounded on three sides. If a major effort such as that envisaged by the War Cabinet was to be undertaken it must be primarily with French resources.

Ironside and Pownall then visited Billotte at his HQ, the former writing,

I then found Billotte and Blanchard at Lens, all in a state of complete depression. No plan, no thought of a plan. Ready to be slaughtered. Defeated at the head without casualties. *Très fatigués* and nothing doing. I lost my temper and shook Billotte by the button of his tunic. The man is completely beaten. I got him to agree [to a plan]. . . . Gort told me when I got back to his HQ that they would never attack.[18]

Pownall recorded the same meeting:

They were in a proper dither, even Blanchard who is not *nerveux*. But the two of them and [Colonel] Alembert were all three shouting at one moment – Billotte shouted loudest, trembling, that he had no means to deal with tanks and that if his infantry were put into line they would not withstand attack. Tiny [Ironside] was quite good in speaking to them firmly and getting them to take a pull. . . . C-in-C [Gort] telephoned them (at Lens) to say he was putting in 50th and 5th Divisions to counter-attack southwards from the Scarpe tomorrow morning. We got the French to agree they would co-operate also with two divisions [attacking south towards Cambrai with elements of Prioux's Cavalry Corps co-operating on Franklyn's immediate right] (not so great an effort as they have at least eight in the neighbourhood). This is our last reserve. . . . We cannot do much more in the common cause.[19]

What comes across from these accounts is a clear sense that two very senior British Army officers saw it as necessary to force support from a reluctant French ally that they perceived as ineffective. Given the obvious panic at Billotte's headquarters, there is some justification for this view. However, Gort's reactions to events can be criticized for suffering from the opposite vice of inertia. Ironside recorded in his diary for 20 May that he had "asked Lord Gort under whose orders he was now acting. The answer was Général Billotte, who had a head-quarters under the Vimy Ridge near Lens. Billotte had given the BEF no orders for some eight days, nor had Gort complained to the Cabinet or to me." The lack of communication between Billotte's No. 1 Army Group and the BEF for the preceding *eight days* [i.e. 12–20 May] underlines just how little Anglo-French military unity there was at the operational/strategic level. It also says much about Gort's conception of the pace of operations. Despite his undoubted bravery (thrice wounded, VC, DSO and two bars, MC), one cannot help wondering if he was really equipped to deal with the kind of campaign unfolding around him, or whether he lacked personal drive and initiative: one cannot imagine the Montgomery of 1942–1944 content with receiving no orders for eight days!

As carried out, the Arras operation was a reinforced brigade action, a very small-scale affair. Although Gort had told Billotte on 20 May that he was putting two divisions into the field in fact only three tired Territorial infantry battalions and two weakened tank battalions took part. The balance of the infantry was used to bolster the Arras garrison, to take over part of the line on the Scarpe from either French or un-battleworthy British troops and to provide a back-stop on the Béthune Canal. British artillery was largely unable to deploy in support, although an anti-tank battery on the right accounted for several panzers in the closing stages. The two French divisions did not, as Gort had predicted, take part, but elements of the much-battered 3rd DLM provided considerable support to Franklyn's right flank. Despite friendly fire incidents causing casualties, arising from in-adequate local liaison and planning, there appear to have been no recriminations and relations between the French Cavalry and the British remained cordial.

Tactically, the counter-attack achieved little, but operationally it caused OKW and Hitler great nervousness and probably contributed to the 'halt order' of 24–27 May, which allowed the Dunkirk escape. But in failing to prevent the BEF leaving Dunkirk, as Dr Frieser has pointed out, the German achievement in Northern France was reduced from a strategic knockout blow to an operational victory. Controversially, Frieser believes that Hitler's ratification of the halt order, originally issued by his senior generals, was as much an attempt to re-impose, in a bizarre way, his authority over his generals (almost out of spite) and to regain control over the campaign which had run away on its own, as it was to respond to the perceived threat to his exposed flanks, a danger underlined by the Arras counter-attack.[20]

The need for a strategic response to dislocation of the Allied rear by striking at the lengthening panzer corridor from Sedan to the Channel coast had of course been recognized. As early as the Supreme War Council meeting in Paris on 16 May Churchill had demanded of Gamelin, "Now, my General, when and where are you going to counter-attack – from the north or from the south?"[21] Apparently unbeknown to Lord Gort[22], on 19 May Gamelin did indeed issue orders for such a counter-attack, stressing the urgency of the situation by saying outright that "It is all a question of hours".[23] Nevertheless, General Weygand, the newly appointed 73-year-old French Commander in Chief, cancelled this order the following day. Following a change of government, the new French Prime Minister, Reynaud, had sacked Gamelin and replaced him with Weygand, who arrived from Syria to take command on 20 May and wished to make his own appreciation before confirming any orders for major operations. Whatever Weygand's strengths, he – like Gort – clearly had no idea of the speed with which it was necessary to act. In today's terminology, the Germans had already overhauled the French decision-making cycle. Martin Alexander argues convincingly that part of the weakness of the French High Command was that throughout the March–May 1940 period Prime Minister Daladier and his C-in-C, Gamelin, were locked into a power struggle with their successors, Reynaud and Weygand, which hampered the military efficiency of all four. As further evidence of the pernicious effects of a failure to provide a unified command structure, Brian Bond notes that the British were unaware of the deep personal rift between Générals Gamelin and Georges (who commanded the North-East Front, which included the BEF).[24]

Weygand's own plan for retrieving the situation was discussed at a conference of senior field commanders held at Ypres on 21 May, at which, most unfortunately, Gort arrived too late to speak to Weygand. On 22 May, in the gloomy Château de Vincennes, Weygand explained his plan to Ismay (Churchill's staff officer). In essence, the Belgians would be asked to hold a shortened allied line in the north, freeing British forces to join with a number of French divisions in a south-wards attack on the German corridor, aiming to meet a French force attacking northwards from the line of the Somme. The preparations required to make this proposal practicable were complex and the earliest possible date for the attack would be 26 May.

Whatever may have been the shortcomings of the plan and its timing, Weygand made a good impression on at least some of the British higher command. Ismay recalled:

> Weygand's appearance was a pleasant surprise. He gave the appearance of being a fighter – resolute decisive and amazingly active. . . . One dared to hope that the Allied armies would now have the leadership that had hitherto seemed lacking. The meeting was short and businesslike. Weygand . . . proceeded to unfold his plan. This, in summary, was that the French First Army and BEF should attack south-west, while a new French Army Group that was now being formed from here, there and everywhere, under command of Général Frère, was to attack northwards from south of the Somme and join hands with them. The plan met with general agreement and the meeting ended on a note of strained optimism.[25]

Alas, Weygand had left the Ypres conference before Gort could arrive, and Général Billotte, commanding Army Group One, died when his staff car skidded into the back of a lorry whilst returning from the meeting. Rumours circulated that he had committed suicide. The resulting confusion meant that no senior Frenchman was able to impose his will and get the French northern armies moving. As Ironside recorded of the doomed Weygand manoeuvre and the time taken to plan it:

> this would have been an ideal plan if it had been issued and acted on earlier . . . it would certainly be too late by the time subordi-nate commanders had given their orders and positioned their troops. The gap between the German armour and its supporting

formations was gradually closing. Bombing delayed the arrival of the French Army Group in the south. Nearly the whole of the BEF was in contact with the enemy and would be difficult to disengage, while Billotte . . . the only Frenchman who knew of Weygand's plan, was dead. No successor was appointed for some days, and orders arrived late.[26]

Of Allied unity, Ironside observed that "the only chance is that Weygand's manoeuvre will be carried out. We have lost faith in the French power of attack. Whether it will come again is impossible for a foreigner to say. Only a Frenchman can incite them to advance."[27]

Although Gort had little faith in the plan he loyally withdrew his 5th and 50th Divisions from the Arras salient on 23 May in preparation for the proposed attack. His actions were misinterpreted by some Frenchmen as a withdrawal to the coast, an impression reinforced less than two days later when he decided on the evening of 25 May that the only hope for the BEF was evacuation for which he required both divisions to cover his line of retreat. This further poisoned already poor Anglo-French relations. Some French commentators of 1940 (Benoist-Méchin for example) believe that Gort deliberately absented himself from the Ypres meeting and that he was determined as early as 22 May to evacuate rather than fight. There is little evidence for such conspiracy theories and the explanation for his absence from the Ypres conference is the simple one of a combination of bad communications, the fact that he had just moved his HQ and roads crowded with refugees.

The successful evacuation from Dunkirk obscures the fact that the fighting in France was by no means over by the end of May 1940. With the evacuation of the BEF the allied armies north and east of the Arras-Boulogne panzer corridor had been crushed but to the south and west there were still formed bodies of British and French troops capable of offering resistance to a further German advance. These included British Lines of Communication troops, many of which were formed into *ad hoc* units, later an improvised Division, under Brigadier (later Major General) A.B. Beauman, Commander Northern District Lines of Communication based at Rouen. Some of these units were later to be used to reinforce the two British field formations also in the area, 1st Armoured and 51st (Highland) Divisions.[28]

51st Division had been in the Maginot Line on the Saar when the

Germans invaded on 10 May, from where they were withdrawn to form a British 'Group' with 1st Armoured Division south of the Somme. They arrived in the Bresle area on 28 May and came under command French IX Corps, part of French Seventh Army. Seventh Army was in effect a new command, tasked with defending the line of the River Somme from the coast to Amiens. The fighting elements of 1st Armoured Division had begun to disembark at Havre, later Cherbourg, only on 19 May, the day before the Germans cut off the BEF from its base by reaching the Channel coast at Abbeville.

To examine the state of Anglo-French liaison under what were crisis conditions it will be instructive to look at 1st Armoured and 51st Highland Divisions' involvement in the attempts by the French to reduce the German bridgehead at Abbeville.

On arrival in France 1st Armoured Division was grossly under strength and not battleworthy. Its two infantry battalions and one tank regiment had been sent to Calais; it was deficient in wireless equipment, had no artillery, bridging equipment or reserve tanks, and, because of the disruption to all forms of communication, generally travelled on its own tracks rather than by rail. (There were at this time no tank transporters except a handful in workshop recovery sections.) The Division's war establishment was 372 tanks, but due to production shortages it was able to field only 257. Of these some had not had their guns fitted, a task that had to be undertaken by units on arrival in their first concentration areas.

Immediately on arrival in France on 21 May Major General Roger Evans, OC 1st Armoured Division, received orders direct from GHQ BEF at once to secure crossings over the Somme. In the event this was wholly impractical, the Germans having a firm grip on the line of the Somme and secure bridgeheads across at several points. Nevertheless, the order was confirmed on 23 May. At the same time General Georges, commanding the North-Eastern Group of Armies which included those forces now seeking to defend the line of the Somme, also issued instructions to the Division via the Swayne Mission, the Liaison team at his Headquarters, to 'mop up' enemy elements in the Abbeville area. Yet a third set of instructions came simultaneously from General Robert Altmayer commanding the left wing of French Seventh Army, comprising 2nd and 5th French Cavalry Divisions. Altmayer believed Evans was under his command and he accordingly ordered that 1st Armoured Division should cover his left flank during a proposed attack on Amiens. Having confirmed his subordination to

GHQ BEF, Evans attempted to carry out their orders at the cost of a number of tank and personnel casualties.

The command situation was clarified on 25 May when Evans was ordered first to co-operate with the French and later the same day to place himself under command of French Seventh Army, General Frere.[29] Frere in turn subordinated the Division to Altmayer. When Altmayer's command became the new French Tenth Army at the end of May, the British divisions remained subordinated to him, 51 Division being under command of Ihler's IX Corps, 1st Armoured Division being Tenth Army troops. By this time, British Military Mission No. 17, led by Lieutenant General J.H. Marshall-Cornwall, had been sent by the War Office to co-ordinate the actions of the British Divisions with the Tenth Army Headquarters.[30]

In the first operation under Altmayer's command the problems that could arise through lack of prior Anglo-French staff co-operation were highlighted. The two armoured brigades of Britain's 1st (and only available) Armoured Division were equipped with lightly armoured but fast light tanks and cruisers, designed for exploitation in conditions of open warfare. French tanks were generally slower, but better armoured and more suited to the infantry support role. Nonetheless, Altmayer's first order was that 1st Armoured Division's 2nd and 3rd Armoured Brigades should support 2nd and 5th French Cavalry Divisions respectively in an attack on the Abbeville bridgehead scheduled for 27 May. Evans explained the limitations of his tanks but the attack went ahead as ordered.

2nd Armoured Brigade in particular found it difficult to advance in the face of a stubborn German resistance, including well-concealed and dug-in anti-tank guns, and in the absence of the amount of French artillery and infantry support promised. 3rd Brigade had an easier time but in both cases the British tanks were unable to exploit the advantages of their speed and manoeuvrability. In the words of the British Official History, "Nothing had been achieved. The German hold on the Somme and on their bridgeheads had not been disturbed". The overall result for the Division was some sixty-five tank casualties to enemy action. A further fifty-five tanks suffered mechanical breakdown, no doubt in the main brought on by the need to make all moves in the operational area on their own tracks. In both cases, a lack of spares made timely repair and maintenance of recovered tanks difficult.[31]

Following representations about the misuse of British armour from

General Evans and General Swayne, General Georges the following day, 28 May, issued a general instruction saying that the British division should not be employed except in circumstances suitable for its equipment, "unless battle conditions make other arrangements vitally necessary".[32] No doubt Altmayer, under an imperative instruction to reduce the Abbeville bridgehead, would have argued that battlefield conditions *had* made the use of British armour vitally necessary. To that extent at least it is doubtful whether prior staff-work making the French aware of the limitations of British armour would have materially affected the issue. In any event, the harm was done. The Queen's Bays and 10th Hussars of 2nd Armoured Brigade were so reduced in numbers that they had to be formed into a composite regiment, the third regiment of the brigade, 9th Lancers, having suffered rather fewer casualties. 3rd Brigade was sent back to Rouen to refit. British armour took no further active part in the Abbeville attacks on 28–30 May, although 9th Lancers remained in reserve.

What might have been achieved by a proper balance of forces, each tasked to an appropriate form of action, is indicated by the partial success of the French 4th DCR under De Gaulle when it attacked the Abbeville bridgehead on 29 and 30 May. The 37mm anti-tank guns of 57 (Bavarian) Infantry Division are recorded in their divisional history as plastering the French heavy tanks, without penetration. Only the aerials and pennants were shot away, the steel-cored warheads "bouncing off the front of the tanks like rubber balls". The French effort actually retook half the Abbeville bridgehead, the Germans losing half their officers and one third of their NCOs killed or wounded and about 200 prisoners. At one point two or more German battalions actually panicked and withdrew across the Somme, leaving their heavy guns. The GOC German XXXVIII Corps, von Manstein, cites in *Lost Victories* going into Abbeville to grip the situation. Three hours later the Germans regained their positions without contest:[33] the French had insufficient infantry to hold the ground won by their armour. At the end of four days' fighting the German position remained essentially unaltered, but in their two days' action 4DCR's fighting capacity was severely reduced by the loss of 105 tanks.

51st Highland Division relieved 4th DCR and parts of 2nd and 5th Cavalry Divisions between 30 May and 1 June, the division's three brigades eventually holding an impossible line of 24 miles. Altmayer was still under pressure to reduce the Abbeville bridgehead and he gave Major General Victor Fortune commanding 51st Highland Division the task, placing the French 31st Infantry and 2nd Armoured Divisions under command for the purpose.

At dawn on 4 June the attack went in between Abbeville and the coast, the French 2nd Armoured and 31st Infantry Divisions attempting to take high ground overlooking Abbeville with the British 152nd and 153rd Brigades having flank objectives. The attack bogged down, partly through a lack of time for proper reconnaissance – some of the French infantry arrived only a couple of hours before the attack – and partly through a failure of armour-infantry co-operation amongst the French forces. When some French infantry started to withdraw against orders, their commander ordered the accompanying tanks to fire at every Frenchman who sought an appointment elsewhere. This drastic action stopped the rot, but French armour also ran into a German minefield on ground supposedly held by 51st Highland Division. The Scotsmen had been ordered back the previous evening, but had not informed the flanking French units, and German troops had immediately advanced, laying mines along a natural bottleneck between two woods.

The cost of the day's confused fighting was about 1,000 allied troops and fifty armoured vehicles, and underlined the lack of Anglo-French liaison at a tactical level. Often this was due to the inadequate numbers of wireless sets in the allied armies. Tanks, infantry and armour could not communicate with each other or their own divisional HQs, so the inter-allied confusion was not, perhaps, surprising.[34]

Phase Two of the German offensive – *Fall Rot* (Operation Red) – began the following day, 5 June, and Tenth Army, 51st (Highland) Division included, was forced back 15 miles to the River Bresle, retreating again on 8 June. Arguably, at the strategic level the French had already surrendered, if only mentally. Earlier in May Reynaud's Cabinet had started to explore the idea of an armistice, with or without British acquiescence. Once started, this defeatism spread and Reynaud soon found it impossible to silence Pétain who wanted an immediate cease-fire to save France from further loss. Once Reynaud resigned on 16 June (to be replaced by Pétain), the die was cast for the unconditional surrender at Compiègne on 22 June. The downward spiral was reflected in the military sphere, French Tenth Army HQ, for example, completely ceasing to function for 48 hours between 8–10 June.

The way defeatism penetrated the French military was again illustrated on 12 June. Harried by Rommel's 7th Panzer Division, General Fortune's 51st Highlanders were bottled up on the coast at St Valéry-en-Caux, with the rest of Général Ihler's French IX Corps. Despite Fortune's desire to carry on fighting, and hope of evacuation Dunkirk-style by the Royal Navy, Ihler gave the order to surrender at 10 am. The bag of 46,000 prisoners of war included 8,000 Scotsmen. The taste of Anglo-French co-operation was turning sour.

There is one interesting statistic that hints at a riddle still to be unravelled. German casualties for the whole campaign were incredibly low – 27,074 killed, 111,034 wounded and 18,384 missing. During *Fall Gelb*, between 10 May to 3 June when they were attacking the allied armies when they were still fresh and operating according to plan, the *Wehrmacht* suffered an average of 2,500 casualties per day. But after the collapse of the main allied armies in the north, when then fighting was with the rump of what was an increasingly demoralised French Army, during *Fall Rot* from 4 June until the last effective fighting on 18 June, this figure more than doubled to over 5,000 men per day.[35] The post-Dunkirk fighting was clearly the toughest for the Germans, perhaps an indication of battle experience on the part of the French, or simply a measure of their desperation.

In conclusion, there were in fact many examples of allied co-operation in May–June 1940, but they were more in evidence in the lower echelons of command. Here, often at unit level, informal local agreements could often produce helpful results. But that was no more than could be expected of any situation where professional soldiers are required by circumstances to act in their mutual best interests. At the top, the Supreme War Council met infrequently before 10 May, and only five times thereafter; it added little to the Allied direction of the campaign, partly because of the frequent changes of personalities. The only formal attempt at integrating the operations of the forces was the network of Military Missions, and these were found wanting. It is difficult to escape the conclusion that one of the most serious failings of the allied armies was the lack of a unified command and staff structure. The hard-won lesson of the First World War in this respect had been forgotten. Perhaps King George VI spoke for his generals when he wrote to his mother after Dunkirk: "Personally, I feel happier now that we have no allies to be polite to and to pamper". If he did, then it indicated how difficult a road had to be followed in the years ahead before the successful establishment of the multi-national Supreme Headquarters that oversaw the liberation of Europe in 1944.

1   Maj-Gen Sir Edward Spears, *Assignment to Catastrophe*, Reprint Society Edition 1956, p. 162.

2   Brian Bond, *British Military Policy Between the Two World Wars*, Clarendon Press 1980, p. 320.

3   Lord Ismay, *The Memoirs of Lord Ismay*, Heinemann 1960, p. 103.

4   Brian Bond (ed.), *Chief of Staff, The Diaries of Lt-Gen Sir Henry Pownall, Vol. One 1933–40*, Leo Cooper 1972, p. 319.

5   Ibid., p. 314.

6   Ibid., p. 315. The editor of these diaries, Professor Brian Bond, notes that Pownall's references to the Belgians are consistently prejudiced and unjust as the Belgian Army bore the brunt of the invasion in their own country, without air cover, and enabled the BEF to escape from Dunkirk.

7   Col R Macleod & Denis Kelly (eds.), *The Ironside Diaries 1937–40*, Constable 1962, pp. 308–9.

8   There seems great confusion over the numbers of divisions actually employed by the Allies. This is because orders of battle were reshuffled after the invasion, and some historians have included fortress and garrison formations as field divisions. These numbers are taken from Richard Natkiel, *Atlas of Twentieth Century Warfare*, Bison Books 1982, pp. 104–5.

9   Every commentator seems to have different sets of Allied and German tank figures. These are from the well-researched Jean-Paul Pallud, *Blitzkrieg in the West, Then and Now*, Battle of Britain Prints 1991, pp. 63–4.

10 *Blitzkrieg in the West*, op. cit., pp. 65–9.

11 RHS Stolfi, 'Equipment for Victory in France in 1940', article in *History*, Vol. 55 (1970), pp. 1–20.

12 Lt-Col Dr Karl-Heinz Frieser, lecture to JHQ Centre, Heidelberg, 27 September 2000, and Frieser, *Ardennen Sedan, Militärhistorischer Führer durch eine europäische Schicksalslandschaft*, Report Verlag 2000. (German language). For an analysis of the German Army's reliance on horse transport, see R. L. DiNardo, *Mechanized Juggernaut or Military Anachronism? Horses and the German Army of World War II*, Greenwood Press, 1991.

13 Col Robert A Doughty, *The Breaking Point; Sedan and the Fall of France, 1940*, Archon Books, 1990.

14 Frieser, ibid.

15 Alistair Horne, *To Lose A Battle: France 1940*, Macmillan 1969, p. 444.

16 Major L.F. Ellis, *The War in France and Flanders*, HMSO 1953, pp. 87–8.

17 Sir John Colville, *The Fringes of Power, Downing Street Diaries 1939–55*, Hodder and Stoughton 1985, pp. 135–6.

18 *Ironside Diaries*, op. cit., p. 321.

19 Pownall Diaries, op. cit., pp. 323–4.

20 Frieser, op.cit.

21 *The Memoirs of Lord Ismay*, op. cit., p. 127.

22 Ellis op. cit., p. 113.

23 Ellis op. cit., p. 114.

24 Martin S Alexander, Chapter 1 in John Gooch (ed.) *Decisive Campaigns of the Second World War*, Frank Cass 1990, pp. 10–44; Brian Bond, *British Military Policy*, op. cit., p. 321.

25 *The Memoirs of Lord Ismay*, op. cit., p. 130.

26 *Ironside Diaries*, op. cit., p. 329.

27 Ibid., p. 331.

28 Ellis, op. cit., pp. 252–3 and 265.

29 Ellis, op. cit., pp. 255–8.

30 Basil Karslake, *1940 – The Final Act*, Leo Cooper 1979, pp. 132–3, also Ellis, op. cit., pp. 257–8, 262 and 275.

31 Ellis, op. cit., pp 259–61; B.H. Liddell Hart, *The Tanks: Vol. Two*, pp. 24–7.

32 Quoted in Ellis, op. cit., p. 261.

33 FM Erich von Manstein, *Lost Victories*, Arms and Armour Press 1982, p. 133.

34 Pallud, *Blitzkrieg in the West*, op. cit., pp. 408–13; Karslake, *The Last Act*, op. cit., pp. 121–51.

35 Pallud, *Blitzkrieg in the West*, op. cit., pp. 607–9.

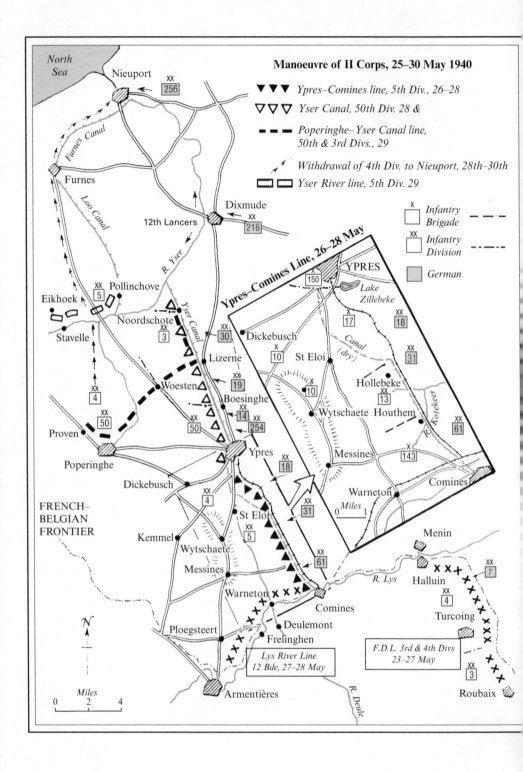

Manoeuvre of II Corps, 25–30 May 1940

▼ ▼ ▼ *Ypres–Comines line, 5th Div., 26–28*

▽ ▽ ▽ *Yser Canal, 50th Div. 28 &*

■ ■ ■ *Poperinghe–Yser Canal line,
50th & 3rd Divs., 29*

↗ *Withdrawal of 4th Div. to Nieuport, 28th–30th*

▭ ▭ *Yser River line, 5th Div. 29*

X	*Infantry Brigade*
XX	*Infantry Division*
▓	*German*

North Sea

Nieuport — XX 256

Furnes Canal

Furnes

Loo Canal

12th Lancers

Dixmude — XX 216

R. Yser

Eikhoek

Pollinchove — XX 5

Yser Canal

Noordschote — XX 3

Stavelle

XX 4

XX 50

Proven

Poperinghe

Lizerne — XX 30

Woesten — XX 19

Boesinghe — XX 14 XX 254

XX 50

Ypres — XX 18

Dickebusch — XX 4

Kemmel

St Eloi — XX 5

Wytschaete

Messines

Warneton — X X X

Ploegsteert

XX 31

XX 61

Deulemont

Frelinghen

*Lys River Line
12 Bde, 27–28 May*

Ypres–Comines Line, 26–28 May

YPRES — XX 150

Lake Zillebeke

X 17   XX 18

Dickebusch — X 10   St Eloi   *Canal (dry)*   XX 31

X 10   Hollebeke — X 13   *R. Kotekeer*

Wytschaete Houthem   XX 61

Messines — X 143

Warneton   *0 Miles 1*   Comines

R. Lys   Menin — XX 7

Halluin — XX 4

Turcoing

*F.D.L. 3rd & 4th Divs
23–27 May*   XX 3

Roubaix

**FRENCH–
BELGIAN
FRONTIER**

R. Deule

Armentières

N

Miles
0   2   4

THE MANOEUVRE THAT SAVED THE FIELD FORCE

M.R.H. PIERCY

By 6pm on 25 May 1940 General Lord Gort VC had decided to withdraw the British Expeditionary Force to Dunkirk for evacuation to England, a brave personal decision to which the force owed its eventual survival. Reluctantly, he had concluded that effective French support was now in doubt for the Anglo-French operation, planned for next day, to break out south-west to the Somme across the neck of the panzer corridor. The Field Force of the BEF, manning ninety-seven miles of the one hundred and twenty-eight-mile front of the Anglo-French enclave, was severely overstretched, despite adding to its five regular and four territorial divisions the three Territorial Labour Divisions, ill-prepared as they were. Cut off from its French bases and with enemy action preventing the use of Dunkirk as a port of re-supply, the BEF was on half-rations and too low on ammunition and fuel for more than one further major operation, be it breakout or withdrawal.[1]

Gort had become increasingly worried by reports he was receiving about the rapid decline of the Belgian Army, particularly intelligence from Lieutenant-General Alan Brooke commanding II Corps. That morning also the Belgian High Command had told Gort that its situation was critical.[2]

With the BEF's return to the Frontier Defence Line on the 23rd, II Corps was holding a line running south from Menin-Halluin on the River Lys. Flanking the Lys, with the Belgian Army on its left, was 4th Division, with 3rd Division, further right covering Roubaix. Right of II Corps was I Corps, with French 1st Army beyond. The Belgians held the line of the Lys, east from Menin, but, under attack from von Bock's Army group 'B', was withdrawing northwards. Its retirement had exposed an eight-mile gap beyond the Lys towards Ypres, screened only by the armoured cars of the 12th Lancers. By the 25th the enemy had begun probing westward from Menin along the north bank of the Lys, raising fears that von Bock was about to launch an attack westwards across the BEF's line of retreat to link-up with the panzers in the Allied rear. Brooke had ordered 4th Division to extend its left to cover II Corps' exposed flank and had sent the machine-gun battalions 1/7 Middlesex and 6th Black Watch, with a battery of 20th Anti-Tank Regiment, to hold the south bank of the Lys westwards to Comines. His concerns had led him to call on Gort at 02.00 that morning, the 25th. He persuaded the C-in-C to send the 143rd Brigade, the last of GHQ's reserves, to cover the gap between Ypres and Comines, to which meanwhile Brooke had despatched the 4th Gordon Highlanders, a machine-gun battalion.[3]

Highly classified German staff papers, dated 24th, were captured later that morning by a patrol of 1/7 Middlesex. They showed that von Bock had indeed just launched a westward offensive with three army corps. His XI Corps was to seize Ypres, covering the right of the main thrust by a reinforced IV Corps directed against the Wytschaete Ridge in the left rear of II Corps[4]: none of these included panzers. Returning to GHQ at 19.00 with these plans, Brooke found that Gort had already decided upon the withdrawal to Dunkirk. Summoning his corps commanders, Gort directed Lieutenant-General Sir Ronald Adam to relinquish III Corps and to prepare a defensive perimeter around Dunkirk. He instructed Brooke to develop and hold a defensive flank along the Ypres-Comines line, extending it northwards, behind which II Corps and the BEF could withdraw to Dunkirk.[5]

With the breakout abandoned, Gort had in reserve the four brigades of the 5th and 50th Division (5th Division had one brigade detached for operations in Norway and 50th Division, being a so-called 'motor division', had a two-brigade establishment). The 5th, with scarcely a break since its action at Arras, was ordered to the Ypres-Comines line that evening and its GOC, Major-General H.E. Franklyn, was appointed to command the defences there. Returning through Ploegsteert, Brooke was offered I Corps' Heavy Artillery to support 5th Division, a significant acquisition since II Corps had later to abandon its own south of the Lys when extricating 3rd and 4th Divisions from the Halluin-Roubaix salient on the 27th. The 50th Division, sent into reserve on the 25th, was ordered to Ypres next day. However, the 151st Brigade could not be relieved from its defence of

Carvin on the Canal Line until midnight and 150th Brigade was immobilized by traffic congestion. It was only with daybreak on the 27th, therefore, that the division embussed, arriving at Ypres later that day. Major-General G. le Q. Martel, its GOC, was placed in command at Ypres and ordered to establish a system of defence extending northwards along the Yser Canal as additional troops arrived. Beyond the 50th Division was the French 2nd Light Mechanized Division (D.L.M.) under II Corps' command.[6]

To reinforce the hard-pressed 5th Division Brooke elicited whatever extra units he could. On the 27th he persuaded Major-General H. Alexander, commanding 1st Division, to send him three battalions about to embus for Dunkirk. From GHQ he gained 13/18th Royal Hussars with its seven remaining light tanks. Some units did not arrive or did so only belatedly. The remaining twenty-eight tanks of the 1st Army Tank Brigade, ordered on the 26th to support a counter-attack by 5th Division next day, got lost; five of the tanks, including two Infantry Tanks Mk II, were later directed to the division by "a staff-officer" and fought with it "until complete mechanical failures". Also on the 26th Gort had ordered the remaining infantry of 23rd Division, estimated at the equivalent of three battalions, to 50th Division, but it was only on the perimeter on the 30th that the weary troops, bereft of all senior officers, finally made contact.[7]

The problems of command and control began at unit level with the shortage of maps, particularly of the coastal area. Often those available were of too small a scale to show roads and locations specified in orders. Communications also became increasingly difficult as the battle moved off the lines of buried cable; local telephones could not be used and military wireless proved unreliable. Congested roads, under frequent air attack, impeded all military traffic, even staff cars and despatch riders, a galling problem for the most thoroughly mechanized army in the campaign. Nevertheless, despite the concerns of his staff for their commander's safety, Brooke exercised command by personal contact, visiting his commanders to issue verbal instructions, often obliged to return to amend them as he endeavoured to improvise a co-ordinated response to the evolving battle. Often he had to issue orders without reference to Gort or to GHQ, because for much of the time he did not know where they were.[8] Nevertheless he remained seemingly imperturbable throughout.

Gort's orders faced Brooke with a complex task. He had firstly to establish a defensive flank facing east and hold it against two or more enemy army corps; in the course of II Corps' withdrawal the flank would have to side-step progressively northwards. Secondly, west of the defensive flank he had to establish in succession three south-facing 'lay-back' lines, through which the divisions could withdraw incrementally from the defensive flank as it edged northwards. The first of these layback lines was to be along the north bank of the Lys. The next would be provisionally along the axis Poperinghe–Ypres although the divisional commanders responsible would determine the precise line as circumstances dictated. The third was to be the Yser River Line, through which II Corps would withdraw into the Dunkirk defensive perimeter. Brooke's immediate task was to withdraw 3rd and 4th Divisions, which were in positions "well forward in the Halluin–Roubaix salient. Success would depend upon holding the Ypres–Comines line long enough for them to be extricated".[9]

The three brigades despatched to the Ypres–Comines line occupied it on the 26th, the 143rd arriving first, followed from noon by the 13th and 17th Brigades of 5th Division. Confronting the three British brigades were three enemy divisions, 61st, 31st and 18th of the enemy's IV Corps. The Ypres–Comines Canal was disused and dry, apart from a little mud, and in few places presented a serious defensible obstacle. East of it ran the Ypres–Comines railway line, serving to restrict the defenders' field of fire. West of the Canal was the Ypres–St. Eloi–Warneton road and west of that, some two or three miles from the canal, lay the key strategic feature, the ridge dominated by the villages of Messines and Wytschaete from which it took its name. Upon arrival the 143rd Brigade had spread itself along the eight-mile gap between Ypres and the Lys, but with the advent of 5th Division had concentrated right to cover the three miles south of Houthem. On its left was 13th Brigade, behind the canal over the next two miles north to Hollebeke. North from here the canal line diverged north-west from the railway line. The 17th Brigade, still de-bussing as the enemy made contact at Houthem, defended the railway line well forward of the canal over the next three miles. The front of 5th Division ended at Zillebeke Lake, just under a mile south-east of Ypres. The canal bridge between 13th and 17th Brigades had previously been blown, inhibiting mutual support. There was barbed wire enough for only a few key points. The 12th Lancers screened Ypres until the arrival of 50th Division; they had expected to find French or Belgian troops there but on arrival discovered only a British Pioneer battalion in the town and some Belgian engineers about to demolish a bridge west of it.[10]

The 'Battle of Wytschaete', fought over three days, 25–28 May, witnessed the most bitter fighting of II Corps' manoeuvre. As it intensified, Brooke progressively reinforced Franklyn's command. The 13th/18th Royal Hussars and the three battalions from 1st Division, namely 3rd Genadier Guards, 2nd North Staffordshire Regiment and 2nd Sherwood Foresters, arrived on the 27th. To 5th Division's machine-gun battalion, 9th Manchester Regiment, Brooke added the two previously holding the south bank of the Lys. Artillery dominated the battle. Although stripped of one infantry brigade 5th Division had kept its three artillery regiments and was also supported by the 18th Field Regiment RA of 48th Division and the 97th Army Field Regiment RA from I Corps. Especially effective was I Corps' four medium regiments, which fired five thousand rounds in thirty-six hours and destroyed enemy concentrations on several occasions. Only in October 1942, preceding El Alamein, was such weight of fire next used by British gunners.[11]

The battle became very confused. In the course of the 26th enemy patrol activity grew more intense and spread across the whole front. Supported by heavy mortar and shellfire, the enemy advanced in rushes through any weak spots and by nightfall had penetrated the thinly held front of 143rd Brigade, but 4th Division sappers expelled those Germans who had crossed the Lys at Comines. Fire continued throughout the night and the day and night following. At first light on the 27th the enemy attacked in force all along the line. The front was penetrated at both Hollebeke and Houthem, on either flank of 13th Brigade and between its two forward battalions. Another attack got past the left flank of 17th Brigade, which was still without firm contact with 150th Brigade as they continued improvising a defensive line behind some railway wagons south-east of Ypres. As 17th Brigade fell back from the railway to the canal, 13th Brigade withdrew to conform, but the movement caused confusion with troops pulling back too far, some back to the St Elio–Warneton road. Parties of stragglers even reached Warneton in the south and in the north to within a mile of Wytschaete, both key positions in Brooke's intended manoeuvre.[12]

Aware from the captured enemy staff papers that the attack south of the Lys by the German 7th Division was merely a holding operation,

Brooke ordered Major-General Bernard Montgomery to extend 3rd Division to its left, freeing first the 10th Brigade of 4th Division and then the 11th to move to the support of 5th Division. East of Wytschaete the enemy had almost reached the guns of the 91st Field Regiment when, at 23.00, they were halted by advanced elements of 10th Brigade; overnight the guns were withdrawn to Kemmel Hill. Both brigades had established a firm defensive line east of Wytschaete by 09.00 next morning, but had not covered the gap on the left of 17th Brigade. In the south the enemy had by the evening of the 27th advanced to within mortar range of Warneton bridge.[13]

The situation was largely restored later that evening. At 19.00 on the right front of 143rd Brigade sappers of 4th Division supported a local counter-attack led by the Colonel of the 6th Black Watch that regained the line of the Kortekeer River. Next, at 20.00, Franklyn counter-attacked south of Houthem with two battalions of 1st Division, the Genadiers and North Staffordshires. He had decided to knock the enemy off balance rather than simply to putty up some sort of defensive line. The operation was designed to gather up the scattered elements of the 13th and 143rd Brigades and bring them back into line along the canal. Supported by tanks, a dismounted Hussar squadron, with the surviving brigade carriers used as tanks and with parties of sappers and gunners as infantry, the counter-attack advanced under a creeping barrage and established a line on the Kortekeer River, only a mile short of the canal, linking up with the line established by 143rd Brigade. Some ground was later lost, but, under a supporting barrage from field, medium and heavy artillery, a satisfactory defensive line was eventually stabilized east of the St Eloi–Warneton road. Next morning, the 28th, under heavy bombardment from mortars, artillery and dive-bombers, the enemy attack resumed, intensifying in the afternoon. The medium artillery halted the enemy by evening and on 13th Brigade front a good tactical line was established.[14]

That night, 28–29th, the 5th Division, the 143rd Brigade and the 4th Division's 10th and 11th Brigades broke off contact with the enemy as best they could and, too intermingled to withdraw separately, retired together through the Poperinghe–Ypres line that had that evening been established by the 3rd and 50th Divisions. The Ypres–Comines line had been severely tested but Franklyn's command had held, "by its eyelids", and "had saved II Corps and the BEF".[15]

The War Diary for the German IV Corps[16] for the battle presents an interesting perspective of British defensive tactics. It considered that attacking British defences was unusually difficult. The positions were difficult to detect even after the defenders had opened fire, none was spotted from the air. British barrages were well directed, falling to within two hundred metres of the defenders. German troops were allowed very close before small arms fire began and were often allowed, seemingly deliberately, to penetrate between positions and then cut off, while an accurate barrage was directed against troops following up. British tanks were employed as mobile machine-gun nests, hull-down but moving when spotted. In counter-attacks tanks would take up forward positions, fire a few bursts and then switch to another point. Such tactics made it very difficult for German anti-tank guns to engage them. British troops were described as fit and tenacious, possessed of high morale, even if the territorials were judged to lack the training of regulars. Both sides, it noted, suffered relatively high casualties, of whom proportionately few were taken prisoner in battle.

The 7th Guards' Brigade in its War Diary characterized the Germans, in turn, as enterprising and aggressive, seemingly quick to spot and exploit defensive weakness. It also noted the demanding pace of operations against the Germans. Brooke judged them to be "wonderful soldiers". However, the German IV Corps had spent three precious days, with mounting casualties, probing for weak spots in the British positions. Although possessing the strength to have broken through in a single concentrated thrust, it was no doubt as much deceived as deterred by the weight of artillery in support of 5th Division. The German Army generally was also unpractised in night operations, a skill II Corps, and especially Montgomery's 3rd Division, had mastered and which enabled it repeatedly to baulk von Bock's attempts at outflanking.[17]

With the Ypres–Comines line held, the first and most difficult stage of II Corps' move was completed.[18] By the early morning of the 28th the defensive flank had completed a major step sideways, withdrawing from positions south of the River Lys and extending beyond Ypres northward along the Yser Canal. The 50th Division, left of the 5th, covered Ypres and the Yser Canal to Boesinghe and the 3rd, having withdrawn with 12th Brigade during the night from the Halluin–Roubaix salient, had come in on the left of the 50th Division along the canal to Noordschote. The 2nd DLM had gone into reserve in the left rear of 3rd Division, and the 12th Lancers, now under Montgomery's command, had been instructed to cover the eighteen-mile gap left of 3rd Division, from Noordschote to Nieuport, opened by the Belgian retreat.[19]

The Yser Canal north of Ypres was a busy commercial waterway and presented a significant defensible obstacle. On the 27th the 12th Lancers, then responsible for its defence, had been joined by a company of machine-gunners of 2nd Middlesex, part of 3rd Division's advance party. The western approaches to Ypres had already come under shellfire when at 10.15 on the 27th 50th Division HQ entered the town. That evening as 150th Brigade took up its position in and to the south of Ypres the enemy was already in contact. During the night 151st Brigade came up along the west bank of the Yser Canal to Boesinghe, where that afternoon French and Belgian sappers had demolished the road and rail bridges. The German attack on Ypres and the Yser Canal defences had been slower to develop than that against 5th Division. In the event the German IV Corps had not been supported by XI Corps, which had advanced northwards on the left of the Sixth Army's assault on the Belgian Army, so passing east of Ypres. It was therefore IV Corps, extending to its right, that initially engaged 50th Division.[20] Only later in the day, following the Belgian capitulation, did the four divisions of XI Corps appear further north along the Yser Canal.

Early on the 28th the main enemy attack at last began either side of Ypres. The tentative contact south of the town between 150th and 17th Brigades was lost as enemy infantry penetrated north of Zillebeke Lake. Newly arrived at Wytschaete, the 11th Brigade was not in a position to counter-attack but 150th Brigade delivered an attack with a mixed force of motorcycle infantry of 4th Royal Northumberland Fusiliers, and sappers, gunners and Lancers fighting as infantry. Although reinforced with the division's only reserve battalion, 8th Durham Light Infantry, contact with 17th Brigade was not restored. A new flank for 150th Brigade was contrived south-west of Ypres along the road to Dickebusch, joining 10th Brigade east of Wytschaete, but the left of the 17th Brigade, to the support of which Brooke had initially despatched 11th Brigade, remained in the air as, in the last hours of the 28th, it fought to avoid encirclement.[21]

As the enemy XI Corps wheeled left, the attack developed against the front of 151st Brigade and beyond, along the Yser Canal. Despite heavy bombing and shelling of 50th Division, the fighting north of

Ypres never developed the intensity of the battle along the Yser–Comines line, where the lack of a major water-line seemed to offer the enemy prospects of a swift success. The 151st Brigade destroyed several enemy attempts to cross the Yser Canal in rubber boats and the brigade's artillery dispersed two enemy troop concentrations and, about 20.00, destroyed an attempt to bridge the canal. Further north that morning, towards the canal's junction with the River Yser, the 12th Lancers had wiped out a German mounted patrol attempting to swim across; the horseflesh was greatly appreciated by the starving locals. About 15.00 the enemy made a small lodgement on the western bank that was eliminated by machine-guns of 2nd Middlesex and fifteen tanks of 2nd DLM.[22]

Around 07.00 on the 28th also, Montgomery's 3rd ('Iron') Division had come into line on the left of 151st Brigade. The successful completion during the night of its spectacular manoeuvre had been a great relief to Brooke. He had judged it necessary on the 26th to countermand his order for the division to move that night; elements of 5th and 50th Divisions would still have been moving into line then and Brooke had to delay the withdrawal of 3rd Division for twenty-four hours to avoid entangling the lines of march of the three divisions. Fortunately, against all British expectations, the Belgian Army had held out until 04.00 on the 28th, just hours before 3rd Division arrived along the Yser Canal.[23]

The manoeuvre had called for 3rd Division to break off contact with the enemy and to travel in darkness to just east of Armentières, where it was to cross the Deule and Lys Rivers. It then had to advance twenty miles northwards along minor roads in front of the British gun-line and within four thousand yards of the unstable battlefront of 5th Division, to occupy in daylight unreconnoitred positions along the Yser Canal in contact with the enemy.[24]

Montgomery, a superb trainer of men, had prepared 3rd Division for just such a night movement. Supremely confident, he had planned it as if it were one of his many divisional exercises. An advance party had been sent in daylight on the 27th to establish positions for 8th and 9th Brigades; 7th Guards Brigade, the divisional rearguard during the withdrawal, was on arrival to become divisional reserve. During the 27th 9th Brigade, reinforced with 1st Coldstream Guards, had covered the fronts of 4th Division's 10th and 11th Brigades, sent earlier to support 5th Division. As the positions were thinned out in darkness the Coldstreamers, one weak company allotted to each battalion front, moved about firing occasional shots, until withdrawing at midnight.

The Corps' heavy anti-aircraft guns had already been sent to Dunkirk but, to avoid the risk of traffic-jams, its other Heavy and Medium Artillery had to be abandoned, even at the risk of betraying British intentions to the enemy. Infantry had priority, carried in unit, artillery and commandeered civilian vehicles. Routes had been reconnoitred, marked out, guides posted and movement carefully controlled by wireless. Montgomery, leading with his command group, had forced his way through all congestion. The roads east of Armentières were few and poor, but at likely bottlenecks 4th Division sappers had built pontoon bridges alongside existing road bridges, preparing both for subsequent demolition; its other sappers had gone ahead to prepare south-facing defences along the northern bank of the Lys from Comines through Warneton, to just east of Armentières, the first 'lay-back' line. The 12th Brigade of 4th Division was II Corps' rearguard. Its carriers covered the withdrawal of 3rd Division to the bridges at Deulemont and Frelinghen, while its own marching columns crossed at Warneton. Once the two divisions had crossed, all the bridges were demolished. Bypassing Ploegsteert, 3rd Division had moved east of Kemmel Hill, from where massed British artillery exchanged fire with the enemy. It travelled through Messines and Wytschaete and, avoiding the badly bombed Poperinghe, had taken up positions from Boesinghe to Noordschote on the left flank of II Corps. Brooke had feared that 3rd Division would be delayed by traffic congestion as it passed through the maelstrom of military traffic, French and British, and the hordes of refugees, and that the Luftwaffe would catch it *en route* in daylight. In the event bad weather that morning had grounded enemy aircraft. The division had arrived barely in time; the 12th Lancers, sappers and DLM had been fending off enemy attacks for three hours when at 07.00 the first of the Division arrived.[25]

Visiting Montgomery, "who had as usual accomplished the impossible", Brooke confirmed arrangements for the next two stages of II Corps' manoeuvre during the night of 28/29th. The 3rd and 50th Divisions were to pivot westward from Lizerne on the Yser Canal to Poperinghe, to form the second 'lay-back' line through which, in the early hours of the 29th, the 4th and 5th Divisions were to withdraw, to establish in turn the third 'lay-back' line on the Yser River. Awaiting Brooke at Corps HQ were reports from GHQ and the

12th Lancers of an entirely new threat. Now, within hours of the Belgian surrender, a large German column was driving down the Belgian coast road into Nieuport, the key point to the eastern section of the Dunkirk perimeter. The town was held only by *ad hoc* forces and its bridges had still not been prepared for demolition. Brooke, who had believed that the moves he had planned for the next two nights would finally ensure the safety of II Corps, found the news "disconcerting". Worse was soon to follow. Shortly afterwards the 12th Lancers reported that the enemy was also appearing in strength at Dixmude on the River Yser, the place Brooke apparently intended as the eastern defensive point of the proposed Yser River Line. Once again the threat was to be countered by II Corps' operational dexterity.[26]

It had been fear of a Belgian collapse that had determined Gort upon Dunkirk; the capitulation of its army now, at 04.00 on the 28th, threatened those plans with disaster. Von Bock had reacted speedily to the Belgian surrender, directing his Sixth and Eighteenth Armies into the eighteen-mile gap north of Noordschote, uncovered by the capitulation and screened only by the 12th Lancers with its few remaining serviceable armoured cars. The Lancers had been ordered to move north, destroying all the bridges over the canal and water-line, still seen as the final stretch of II Corps' 'defensive flank'. On reaching Dixmude one Lancer patrol had sighted three German staff cars leaving an 'unauthorized parley' and had rightly assumed that they would immediately report the lack of British defences there. Scarcely had the sappers of the Royal Monmouth Engineers accompanying the patrol demolished the bridge than German motorcyclists appeared and an enemy column of some two hundred and fifty trucks of lorried infantry with artillery was seen entering the town. Montgomery, to whom it was reported, sent more sappers to bolster the defence of the crossing-point but declined to commit his reserve brigade. Instead he ordered 2nd DLM to cover 3rd Division's withdrawal that night by screening the Loo Canal, which accordingly became the replacement 'defensive flank' for II Corps.[27]

In the early hours of the 29th, the 50th and 3rd Divisions established the second 'lay-back' position on the line Poperinghe–Lizerne–Noordschote. Having destroyed its artillery and covered by its remaining carriers and the 4th/7th Dragoon guards of 2nd Division, the 150th Brigade withdrew from the Yser Canal and by 08.00 was digging in east of Poperinghe. The line on its right, north-west to

Proven, was found to be undefended, although it was supposed to form part of a general BEF line; I Corps had seemingly continued its withdrawal to the Yser River. Brooke therefore instructed Martel to cover the right flank of 50th Division with the machine-gunners of [4th] Royal Northumberland Fusiliers and a screen of 13th/18th Royal Hussars. On its left the 151st Brigade, which had retired from the canal under heavy shellfire at 04.00, came into line east to Woeston. The 3rd Division completed the line, its 9th Brigade falling back obliquely from its junction at Lizerne with 8th Brigade, which continued to hold the Yser Canal north to Noordschote.[28]

The 4th and 5th Divisions retired together that night from their positions on the Ypres–Comines Line, after destroying the heavy and medium artillery, withdrawing through the Poperinghe–Lizerne line. Under Brooke's original instructions they were together to hold the Yser River Line. North of Poperinghe 4th Division re-grouped, 12th Brigade having retired from the Lys 'lay-back' line and the 10th and 11th from their defensive positions east of Wytschaete Ridge. The 5th Division found disengaging from the battle much more hazardous. Having enveloped the exposed left of 17th Brigade, the enemy had cut off its individual battalions. By 11.00 the encircled remnants of 2nd Royal Scots surrendered; only part of one company of the 2nd Northamptonshire Regiment got away, although a counter-attack by 10th Brigade carriers enabled a party of 6th Seaforth Highlanders to get clear; the Brigade now totalled only four hundred and forty-one officers and men. The 13th Brigade had fared better; 10th Brigade's interventions had checked the enemy long enough for it to withdraw, with 143rd Brigade, both retiring through 50th Division with little further enemy interference other than bombing and shelling.[29]

With these movements II Corps' 'defensive flank' south of Lizerne had been removed, allowing Army group 'B' to link up at last with the panzers at Cassel, which was being defended by 44th Division. Although the panzers were unwilling to join his operation, von Bock now launched an attack against the Poperinghe–Noordschote line, intending to envelope the right of 50th Division at Poperinghe and to isolate 8th Brigade, still along the Yser Canal. His preliminary bombardment on the 29th was too late to catch 150th Brigade, falling on positions already vacated, but the 151st Brigade, the divisional rearguard, was overtaken mid-afternoon and was able to withdraw to the Yser River Line only after a punishing action. The 3rd Division had begun its withdrawal that afternoon, the 7th Guards Brigade route-marching to Furnes. Still in their defensive positions, the 8th and 9th Brigades had been heavily shelled from 18.00. Now free to cross the Yser Canal south of Lizerne, an enemy attack got behind 8th Brigade and it was only with serious loss that at 21.00 it was able to join 9th Brigade withdrawing into the Yser River Line.[30] Heavy as they were, von Bock's attacks had lacked co-ordination.

The situation at Nieuport meanwhile was grave. At 11.00 on the 28th an undemolished bridge had been seized by an enemy column of motorcycle troops, unseen until too late among the hordes of refugees. They had been engaged by a patrol of the 12th Lancers, supported by all and sundry able to hold a rifle. Although the defenders had been reinforced by two tanks of the 15th/19th Royal Hussars and about another hundred gunner-riflemen with four eighteen-pounders of 76th Field Regiment, they had been unable either to regain or destroy the bridge, while the enemy, part of the Eighteenth Army's IX Corps, had grown in strength. Now II Corps found a reserve to despatch to the defence of Nieuport, the 4th Division[31], just freed from the duty to hold the eastern section of the Yser River Line by the decision to establish the defensive flank along the Loo Canal.

The final 'lay-back' line along the River Yser was little more than a series of defensive positions covering likely crossing places, "impossible to hold against a determined attack". Brooke's original intention had been for one brigade from each of 4th and 5th Divisions to hold the line, the others continuing into the perimeter. The new shorter flank along the Loo Canal flank, although freeing the 4th Division, presented more bridges to be demolished, required those over the Furnes–Nieuport Canal to be destroyed sooner and surrendered a deep defensive zone. However, II Corps now lacked both the men and the means to hold the line originally intended along the lower Yser River. By 07.00, 29 May, the Yser River Line was occupied. The 143rd Brigade, supported by 1/9 Manchesters, now with only six machine guns remaining, and the personnel of an artillery regiment as infantry, manned positions about Eikhock, a mile north of Stavelle. On its left, strengthened with more gunner-infantry, 17th Brigade were astride the Furnes–Ypres road. The 13th Brigade continued the line to the Loo Canal and along it north to Pollinchove. Now without tanks and low in morale, the 2nd DLM held the ground west of the Loo Canal beyond Pollinchove, reinfored with the remnants of the French 60th Infantry Division from Belgium.[32]

In the course of the 29th and the morning of the 30th II Corps moved into the Dunkirk defences. As the roads funnelled towards the perimeter traffic congestion intensified, a situation aggravated both by the loss of roads east of the Loo Canal and by French motor and horse-drawn traffic crossing II Corps' line of march to reach the western sector of the Dunkirk defences that were to be held by the French Army. Military police rigorously excluded all non-essential traffic, allowing entry only to twenty-five-pounder gun-teams, anti-tank guns, machine-gun trucks, rifle battalion trucks, bren-gun carriers, ambulances, water trucks, bridging equipment, wireless trucks and a few staff cars. The 4th Division, denied its route through Dixmude, made slow progress, the 12th Brigade reaching Nieuport only that evening, the 10th Brigade at midnight and the 11th early next morning, the 30th.[33] The division took over the defence of the town and positions either side from the miscellany of defenders keeping the enemy at bay.

The 7th Guards Brigade was the first of 3rd Division to reach the perimeter, taking over the defence of Furnes and a short section of the Furnes–Nieuport Canal from 20.00 on the 29th, but suffering badly from sniping and mortaring from across the canal as they came into line. The divisional sappers defended the canal to the left as far as Wulpen, the junction with the 4th Division's 10th Brigade; the sappers remained to strengthen the badly depleted 8th Brigade which took over the front at 04.00 next day. Arriving with the 8th Brigade, the 9th took over the Bergues–Furnes Canal to Bulscamp, with the 7th guards Brigade on its left and the 151st on its right. On 50th Division's final move into the perimeter traffic congestion had separated its two brigades; the 150th had arrived at 02.00 on the 30th but it was 11.00 before 151st reached the perimeter, losing a company of the 8th Durham Light Infantry when the approach of the enemy caused the entry bridge to be blown. The 151st was strengthened with the addition of 3rd Grenadier Guards and some infantry of 23rd Division. The division dug in, as far as strength permitted, the 150th on the right, in contact with I Corps at the France–Belgian border.[34]

The enemy had not considered the Yser River Line worthy of an organized assault. The retiring columns were harassed all day with mortaring, sniping and minor skirmishes on their rearguards, the main columns being shelled and attacked by aerial bombing and machine-gunning. The 143rd Brigade retired from its positions at 23.59 on the 29th and 5th Division's rearguard, 17th Brigade, at 04.45 on the 30th;

with 5th Division were the remnants of the three battalions of 1st Division and of three machine-gun battalions. Once within the perimeter each brigade formed a composite battalion and went into reserve.[35]

By midday on the 30th II Corps was within the Dunkirk perimeter.

The manoeuvre of II Corps had been, of course, part of a wider military situation. Much of the enemy's military efforts had been expended upon Britain's allies. Brooke was clearly right in stating that allies "had given way on all flanks", but the Belgian Army and, at Lille, the French 1st Army had absorbed much of the energies of Army Group 'B' and of the Luftwaffe, capitulating only on the 28th and 31st May respectively. The enemy had also made mistakes, the inexplicable 'halt order' of the 24th, the poor co-ordination of the Army Groups, the growing pre-occupation with the looming 'Battle for France' and possibly a serious under-estimation of the number of troops it had trapped in the enclave. Elsewhere also, actions by other units of the BEF had bought time for the withdrawal to Dunkirk, the stand of 145th Brigade at Mont de Cats for example and 44th Division's grim defence of Cassel.[36]

Within this context the manoeuvre of II Corps, however, was a thing apart. It had been a continuous operation over five days, moving an active front in contact with superior forces over forty or more miles, responding swiftly to every evolution of the enemy but never seriously dislocated. The tactics of II Corps – dogged defence by day and a succession of extensive night movements – had kept it one pace ahead of von Bock.[37] It had been a notable feat of arms and it had saved the Field Force.

Before leaving Dunkirk on the 30th Brooke took farewell of his command. The original divisions of II Corps, the 3rd and 4th, were still effective fighting formations of some thirteen and twelve thousand men respectively. The two brigades of 50th Division each numbered about twelve hundred, but each of the two brigades of 5th Division he estimated as six hundred each at best; the 143rd probably had no more. On the 25th, however, Gort had thought only 25% of the BEF would be saved. The German Chief-of-Staff, Franz Halder, noted on the 30th that "the pocket was sealed later than it should have been and sealed on the coast", allowing "countless thousands to get away to England".[38]

Brooke had enabled the Field Force to reach Dunkirk; it had yet to get away.

The Unit War Diaries and Cabinet Papers cited are from the Public Record Office, Kew, to whom my thanks are due, as they are also to the Liddell Hart Centre for Military Archives, to the Imperial War Museum and to the British Library.

1   *London Gazette*, 17.10.41, Gort's Despatches, p. 5923–4; *Official History*, L.F. Ellis, "The War in France and Flanders, 1939–40", (London, 1954), (hereafter O.H.), pp. 141–3 and 148–9; the logistical constraints upon Gort are from a recent but restricted publication.

2   B. Bond (ed) *Chief of Staff: The Diary of Lieutenant-General Sir Henry Pownall*, Vol. 1, (London, 1972), pp. 330 and 339–40; Liddell Hart Centre for Military Archives, King's College, London (LHCMA), Alanbrooke Papers 5/1/2 Diary 12 April – 30 May 1940 (hereinafter Brooke 'Diary'), 25 May; LHCMA 5/1/2, Alanbrooke 'Notes on My Life' (Hereinafter Brooke 'Notes') p. 164; G. Blaxland *Destination Dunkirk: The Story of Gort's Army* (London, 1973) (Blaxland 'Dunkirk') p. 245 and map p 246; B. Bond *Britain, France and Belgium, 1939–40*, (Bond 'Belgium') pp 81–7 and 90.

3   O.H. map p. 122; Brooke 'Diary' for 25th; CAB/106/293 'A Short Account of the Operations of II Corps in the campaign of the B.E.F. in the Low Countries, 1940' by Mr Hare (Hare 'Low Countries') 25th; Entries for 24th–26th in W.Ds of 4th Division and of 11th and 12th Brigades, WO/167/230, 368 and 370.

4   O.H. pp. 148–50; Brooke 'Diary', 25th and 'Notes' pp. 166–7; WO/167/29(6) W.D. of G.H.Q., App. 13; Blaxland 'Dunkirk' pp. 250–1; the author identified and interviewed Sgt. Burford, whose capture of the documents earned him merely a "mention".

5   Blaxland, pp. 255–6.

6   O.H. pp. 90 'et seq'; Brooke 'Diary' for 25–27th and 'Notes' p. 169; WO/167/300, 402 and 404, W.Ds for 50th Division and 150th and 151st Brigades for 27th.

7   Brooke 'Diary' for 27th; WO/167/262, 414, 453, 459 and 460, W.Ds of 23rd Div, 1st Army Tank Brigade, 13th/18th Royal Hussars and 4th and 7th Royal Tank Regiment.

8   CAB/106/240 'There and Back' by X (Col. C.E. Ryan, formerly of I Corps Staff) p. 17, [a consignment of requisite maps was sent and mislaid]; see Ryan p. 15 also for comparative journey times; Brooke 'Diary' 25–29th and 'Notes' p. 181 on his style of command; CAB/106/252 "Operations of II Corps during the Retreat from Louvain to Dunkirk" by F.M. Lord Alanbrooke, (Brooke 'Retreat') p. 7; N.

Hamilton, *Monty: the Making of a General, 1887–1942* (London 1981), (Hamilton 'Monty') p. 358; references to congestion and difficulties of communication are too many to enumerate; the scale of the maps was often too small to establish company positions or permit accurate artillery fire.

9　Brooke 'Notes' p. 172; Hare 'Low Countries' p. 12.

10　WO/167/221, 372 and 378, WD's for CRE 3rd Division and 13th and 17th Brigades for 27th; Hamilton 'Monty' p. 380.

11　The title 'Battle of Wytschaete' is from W.D. 13th Brigade, WO/167/372; Brooke 'Diary' for 27th and 'Retreat' pp. 5–7; Hare 'Low Countries', 26th–27th; claim by former staff officer of 5th Division that appeared in a recent but restricted publication.

12　WO/167/372, 378 and 379, W.Ds of 13th, 17th and 143rd Brigades for 26–27th and WO/167/300, 402 and 404, W.Ds for 50th Division and 150th and 151st Brigades for 27th; Hare 'Low Countries', 27th; Blaxland 'Dunkirk' pp. 262–5.

13　WO/167/218, WD 3rd Division, entry at 13.50 on 27th; WO/167/230, W.D. 4th Division 27th–28th; WO/167/500, WD 91st Field Regiment RA, 27th–28th; Brooke 'Retreat' pp. 6–7; Hamilton 'Monty' pp. 378–9.

14　WO/167/372, 378 and 397, W.Ds of 13th, 17th and 143 Brigades for 27th; Brooke 'Diary', 27th, Hare 'Low Countries' 27th; Blaxland 'Dunkirk', pp 256–7; O.H., pp. 194–6.

15　Brooke 'Diary' 28th and 30th and 'Notes', p. 182.

16　CAB/106/281, Miscellaneous Paper No. 3, "Experiences gained in action against English troops: Extract from Reports by IV Corps, dated 30.7.40", (in translation).

17　WO/167/359 W.D. 7th Guards Brigade, May 1940 'Lessons'; Brooke 'Diary', 23rd.

18　Brooke 'Notes', p. 180.

19　Ibid., p. 818 'Diary', 28th; Hare 'Low Countries', 28th; WO/167/362 W.D. 8th Brigade 00/23, dated 27th; WO/167/453 W.D. of 13th/18th Royal Hussars for 27th; WO/167/364, 370, 404, 452, W.D.s for 9th, 12th and 15th Brigades and 12th Lancers for 28th.

20　WO/167/218, 402, 404, 452, 453 and 912 for W.Ds of 3rd Division, 150th and 151st Brigades, 12th Lancers, 13th/18th Royal Hussars and of 17th Field Company, R.E. for 27th; O.H. see maps for 27th and 28th, preceding pp. 201 and 225 to compare IV and XI Corps dispositions.

21　WO/167/378 WD of 17th Brigade for 27th–28th; WO/167/300, 402, 404, W.Ds for 50th Division and 150th and 151st Brigades for 28th; Brooke "diary", 28th; Blaxland 'Dunkirk', pp. 267 and 274–5.

22　WO/167/218, 362, 364, 404 and 452, W.Ds of 3rd Division, 8th, 9th and 151st Brigades and 12th Lancers.

23   Brooke 'Diary' 28th; Hamilton 'Monty', pp. 357 and 378–9; Blaxland 'Dunkirk', p. 312.

24   Ibid., p. 357; Brooke 'Notes', p. 178.

25   Imperial War Museum, Montgomery Papers, BLM/14, 15 and 17; Hamilton 'Monty', pp. 337, 343, 348 and 378–80; Blaxland 'Dunkirk', p. 269; WO/167/218, 359, 362, 370 and 912, W.Ds of 3rd Division, 7th, 8th and 12th Brigades and 17th Field Company R.E.; WO/167/364 W.D. 9th Brigade, "Tactical School Lecture by Brigadier W. Robb, D.S.O, M.C., on 'Operations in Belgium, May 1940'," dated August 1940 (Robb "Lecture") "Withdrawal from Tourcoing, 27th and 28th".

26   Brooke 'Diary' 28th and 'Notes', p. 182; Brooke 'Retreat', p. 89; Hare 'Low Countries', p. 13; WO/167/452, W.D. of 12th Lancers, 28th; WO/167/218, W.D. of 3rd Division, 28th; Blaxland 'Dunkirk', pp. 312–3; Montgomery had sent his 'Chief of Staff', Major 'Marino' Brown to Brooke with reports of the new threat to Nieuport, but the major was shot dead en route, seemingly attempting to clear a traffic jam among French troops.

27   WO/167/218, and 452, W.Ds of 3rd Division and 12th Lancers, 28th; WO/167/230, W.D. 4th Division 00/8 App 18; CAB/106/256; W.D. 101 Field Coy. RE, 'Royal Monmouth Engineers', Diary of Lt. DA Smith MC RE, for 28th; Blaxland 'Dunkirk', pp. 312–4; Hamilton 'Monty', p. 381; O.H., p. 202.

28   Brooke 'Diary' 28th–29th; Hare 'Low Countries', 28th; WO/167/218, 359, 362, 402, 404, W.Ds 3rd Division, 7th, 8th 150th and 15th Brigades for 28th–29th; WO/167/364, Robb 'Lecture', 28th–29th; OH, p. 202 and map facing.

29   Gort's Despatches, p. 5928; O.H., pp. 202 and 212; WO/167/366, 368, 370, 372, 378 and 397, W.Ds 10th, 11th, 12th, 13th, 17th and 143rd Brigades for 28–29th; WO/167/302 W.D. 8th Brigade 00/24 of 28th.

30   Brooke 'Diary' 29th; O.H., pp. 216–18; WO/167/362, 364, 402 and 494, W.Ds for 8th, 9th, 150th and 151st Brigades for 29th.

31   WO/167/220 and 364, W.D. C.R.A. 3rd Division for 27th and of 9th Brigade; Robb 'Lecture' for 28–29th; Hare 'Low Countries', p. 13; see also note 33 below.

32   WO/167/372 and 378, W.Ds for 13th and 17th Brigades for 29th; Brooke 'Diary' 28th.

33   Brooke 'Diary' 29th; WO/167/302, W.D. of CRA 50th Division App. H; WO/167/230, 366, 368 and 370, W.Ds 4th Division, 10th, 11th and 12th Brigades for 29th.

34   WO/167/218, 359, 362, 402 and 404, W.Ds 3rd Division, 7th Guards Brigade and 8th, 150th and 151st Brigades for 29th.

35   WO/167/378 and 397, W.Ds for 17th and 143rd Brigades for 29th and 30th.

36 Bond 'Belgium', pp. 100–5; Jacobsen H.A. and Rohwer J (eds) *Decisive Battles of World War II – the German View* (1965), pp. 65–6.
37 O.H., p. 321.
38 Brooke 'Diary' 26th; British Library, 'Franz Halder Diaries Vol. IV, Campaign in France, 10th May – 30th October 1940', (typewritten translation), entry for 30th May 1940.

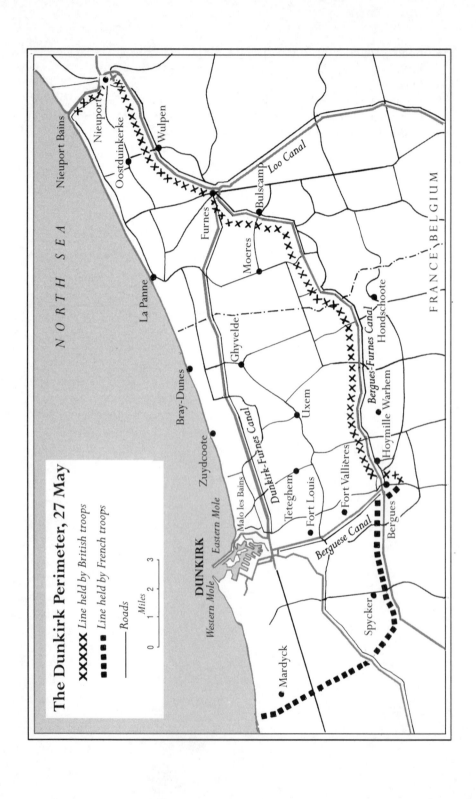

The Dunkirk Perimeter, 27 May

xxxxx *Line held by British troops*

▪▪▪▪▪ *Line held by French troops*

—— *Roads*

Miles
0 1 2 3

NORTH SEA

Nieuport Bains

Nieuport

Oostduinkerke

Wulpen

Bulscamp

Loo Canal

Furnes

Moeres

La Panne

Ghyvelde

Hondschoote

Warhem

Bergues-Furnes Canal

Uxem

Hoymille

Fort Vallières

Bergues

Bray-Dunes

Zuydcoote

Teteghem

Fort Louis

Dunkirk-Furnes Canal

Berguese Canal

Malo les Bains

Eastern Mole

DUNKIRK

Western Mole

Spycker

Mardyck

FRANCE

BELGIUM

THE DEFENCE OF THE DUNKIRK PERIMETER

JEREMY A. CRANG

The popular image of the British Expeditionary Force at Dunkirk in 1940 is of long lines of forlorn soldiers waiting patiently on the beaches to be rescued by the Royal Navy. Shocked by their rapid defeat, they snake helplessly down to the shoreline to meet the little ships.[1] But a short distance inland a gallant rearguard battle was fought for several days to defend the Dunkirk perimeter and enable the evacuation to take place. Without this determined final stand many more British troops would have been captured by the Germans: the 'miracle' of Dunkirk might not have appeared quite so wondrous.

On 26 May General the Viscount Gort, the Commander-in-Chief of the BEF, was authorized to withdraw his beleaguered force to the coast. That evening Lieutenant-General Sir Ronald Adam, the commander of III Corps, was summoned to Gort's HQ at Premesques. Adam, who had served under Gort before the war as Deputy Chief of the Imperial General Staff and shown great coolness under pressure during the campaign, was ordered to hand over his Corps and go back to Dunkirk to organize the defence of the perimeter and the evacuation of the BEF. He was to be assisted in this task by several staff officers from GHQ: Lieutenant-General Lindsell (Quartermaster-General), Major-General Pakenham-Walsh (Chief Engineer) and Lieutenant-Colonel the Viscount Bridgeman (GS01).[2]

Early on 27 May Adam left for a conference with the French at the Hotel du Sauvage in Cassel. Before the main meeting commenced Adam met General Fagalde, commander of the French troops at Dunkirk, and agreed a plan for the defence of the bridgehead. Under the scheme, which had been skilfully drawn up by Bridgeman, a perimeter would be established between Gravelines and Nieuport Bains. It was to be thirty miles wide and up to seven miles deep. The

73

French would man the line from Gravelines to Bergues, and the British from Bergues to Nieuport Bains. The position of the Belgian army was considered too 'obscure' for it to be included in the plans. The area afforded promising defences: the perimeter lay along a series of canals that ringed Dunkirk and the surrounding countryside was low-lying, beditched and criss-crossed by small waterways. The sea dykes had been opened and the land inside the canal line was beginning to flood. It was not good tank country.[3]

Adam and Fagalde then joined the main meeting. The French representatives present included Admiral Abrial, commander of the Dunkirk area, General Blanchard, commander of the First Group of Armies, and General Koeltz, representing General Weygand. The plans agreed for the defence of the bridgehead were not questioned, but it appeared that the main purpose of the conference was to stimulate the French into offensive action.[4] According to Adam, Koeltz made a rousing appeal on behalf of Weygand that the time had come to stop the retreat and attack the Germans everywhere: "No one said anything for a bit and then General Fagalde rose and said that he would return to his headquarters at once and order an attack on Calais, driving the Germans before him. We British looked at him in astonishment, but the French applauded him." Flabbergasted, Adam left the meeting as quickly as was decently possible.[5]

Adam and his staff officers proceeded to Bergues. On the way the party was machine-gunned by a flight of Belgian biplanes with German markings. While taking cover in the roadside ditch, Pakenham-Walsh was wounded in the shoulder.[6] On arrival in Bergues, Adam visited Major-General Thorne, the commander of 48th Division, whose HQ was in the town. He enquired about the possibility of co-opting some of the reserves to man the perimeter. Thorne was too deeply engaged in battle to spare any troops. He did, however, agree to lend his divisional artillery commander, Brigadier Frederick Lawson (later Lord Burnham), to establish the defence line.[7]

After reconnoitring the perimeter, Adam drove to La Panne where he set up his HQ in the town hall. This seaside resort had the advantage of a direct undersea telephone line to England. The line had been laid so that the Belgian King Albert could keep in close touch with the London Stock Exchange while at his holiday villa.[8] Adam then went to Dunkirk where he met Fagalde, along with Captain Tennant, then senior British naval officer, at the French HQ in the Bastion. The French commander explained that, under pressure from the Germans, he would have to pull in his troops to the west of Dunkirk. Adam could not resist reminding him of his *cri de guerre* earlier that day: "I told him that, after his morning's promise to General Koeltz, I expected to hear that he was on his way to Calais. 'Oh,' he said, 'after General Koeltz's moving words, someone had to say something, and no one else appeared to be ready'."[9] Later that day the French withdrew from Gravelines and retired to a new line running from Mardyck to Spycker to Bergues.[10]

In the meantime the British sector of the perimeter was taking shape. Under Bridgeman's plan, the bridgehead was divided into three corps areas. II Corps would defend the eastern end of the perimeter and be evacuated from the beaches at La Panne, I Corps would hold the centre and withdraw from Bray–Dunes and III Corps would man the western end and embark from Malo-les-Baines. Orders were issued that vehicles should be left outside the perimeter, and in each corps supply dumps were established by Lindsell.[11]

Lawson began the task of organizing the defence line from among the troops filtering into the perimeter. He established his HQ in Furnes and divided his front into several sections of equal length. Units that came in were despatched to these sections. Leaderless groups of soldiers, and individuals, were kept 'on ice' until suitable officers could be found to accompany them to the defences. Most of the troops, recalled Lawson, were well-disciplined and in surprisingly good heart. But a number were suffering from nervous strain: "These stragglers were roped in by my staff captain, who was sent on a shepherding mission into the highways and byways with orders to put on a soft hat, smoke a cigar (which I gave him) and restore public confidence."[12]

Back at La Panne, Adam was concerned about the small number of men being taken off the beaches. He spoke to the War Office on the telephone, pointing out that the number of naval personnel and small craft were inadequate and that unless more were provided it would prove impossible to re-embark the BEF: "I am afraid I was somewhat rude about the arrangements."[13] Adam decided to send Captain Moulton, a Royal Marines officer, to Admiral Ramsay at Dover with a map indicating where the troops were concentrating.[14]

There was more bad news. The 2nd Anti-Aircraft Brigade had been given the task of protecting the bridgehead from the Luftwaffe. Its orders were to keep the guns going to the last. Spare gunners were to join the infantry and the wounded were to proceed to the beach. Somewhere down the line the orders became garbled: *all* gunners were to go to the beach. The anti-aircraft commander, Major-General Martin, reasoning that if the gunners were to be evacuated then the guns were no longer required, ordered them to be destroyed in case they fell into enemy hands. Sometime after midnight he reported to Adam's HQ. He saluted smartly and proudly announced that all the anti-aircraft guns had been spiked. A near-incredulous Adam paused for a while before responding, "You . . . fool, go away."[15]

By 28 May Lawson had, by superhuman efforts, succeeded in manning the perimeter. Adam Force, as it was termed, was largely composed of gunners and engineers with a few infantry. It was hoped that, as the divisions of the BEF fell back upon the coast, these troops could be replaced by frontline units. For the time being improvisation was the order of the day.[16]

During the morning Adam learnt that the King of the Belgians had asked for an armistice. This posed a serious threat to the eastern end of the bridgehead. If the Belgians laid down their arms the Germans might reach the defence line before the rest of the BEF arrived. Captain Gordon-Lennox, one of Adam's staff officers, was despatched by car to Ostende and Dixmude to assess the situation. On his journey he came into contact with the 12th Lancers and asked them to protect the flank. They rushed their armoured cars into Nieuport just in time to thwart a German probe into the town.[17]

The Germans brought up more troops. The area around Nieuport was manned by Adam Force recruits under Brigadier Clifton of the 22nd Armoured Reconnaissance Brigade. These included men from the 53rd and 2nd Medium Regiments Royal Artillery, 1st Heavy Anti-Aircraft Regiment Royal Artillery, and 7th Field Company Royal Engineers, all fighting as infantry. Despite coming under heavy fire, this scratch force held off the enemy attacks.[18]

During the day Gort set up his HQ at King Albert's holiday villa in La Panne and the corps commanders moved into the perimeter. Adam met Lieutenant-General Brooke, commander of II Corps, to discuss the situation. They were old friends from their days together as sub-alterns in the Royal Horse Artillery. Brooke was asked to move troops back urgently to help defend the eastern end of the perimeter.[19]

In the meantime traffic congestion was becoming a problem in the bridgehead. En route to a further meeting with Fagalde Adam discovered that the La Panne to Dunkirk road was blocked with French army lorries. Drastic action was required: amid much cursing, the vehicles were bulldozed off the road. The evacuation was now proceeding more smoothly, but there were still bottlenecks at the beaches. Adam again contacted the War Office to urge that more naval forces be provided.[20]

On 29 May the BEF continued to withdraw into the bridgehead. Some units were sent directly to the beaches whilst others were integrated into the perimeter. The Germans continued to probe Clifton's troops in the Nieuport area. A number of subterfuges were used by the attackers to penetrate the line, including, it was reported, disguising themselves as nuns. But, with the assistance of naval gunfire, the defenders held on until relieved by Brooke's forces.[21]

Adam met with officers from Gort's HQ and agreed a plan for the final withdrawal and embarkation. III Corps would embark first, followed by II Corps, and then by I Corps, which would act as the rearguard. Accompanied by Tennant, Adam visited Abrial in Dunkirk to explain the British plans and re-assure him that efforts would be made to take off French troops. The French commander seemed satisfied, but it was a difficult meeting since he had been under the impression that British front-line units would man the perimeter to the last: "Abrial was pretty sour and as he had received no orders [thought] that it was to be a fight to the end."[22]

Corps had now assumed responsibility for the perimeter and during the evening control of the bridgehead passed from Adam to Gort's HQ.[23] In the meantime more naval forces had arrived and the rate of evacuation was speeding up. The beaches were crowded with French soldiers expecting to embark and some British shipping was made available for these troops.[24]

By 30 May most of the BEF had reached the perimeter. To the relief of Lawson, Major-General Montgomery's 3rd Division marched over the bridge into Furnes, with the 7th Guards Brigade leading. The guardsmen were in such good order that they looked as though they were on a day's exercise at Pirbright. "It is difficult to describe the heartening effect of the march-in," recalled Lawson. "To see those men, and Monty so superbly on top of his form, made me think that if we could only get out of the present embarrassment there might be a future somewhere." Lawson handed over and proceeded to the beach.[25]

The major German attack this day was aimed at the canal north of Furnes. The enemy were beaten off, but the 4th Royal Berkshires suffered heavily. The Germans renewed their assault and succeeded in crossing the canal. Major Campbell of the 1st Coldstream Guards organized a counter-attack. He and his runner went forward with grenades, supported by covering fire from one of the platoons, to dislodge the enemy. Although Campbell was fatally wounded, the guardsmen succeeded in driving the Germans back across the canal.[26]

Adam, meanwhile, had been ordered to embark and he headed for the beach. There he met Lawson who, by coincidence, ran into his son among the dunes. Lawson senior insisted that his son shave and, for good measure, requisitioned one of the bottles of whisky he was carrying: "Three were too many for a boy of 19." Adam and Lawson found a canvas boat and managed to reach a waiting destroyer. On board Adam shared a cabin with Brooke who had also been instructed to return home.[27]

Gort's problem was now to thin out the troops in the bridgehead while maintaining an adequate defence of the perimeter. His task was complicated by the government's decision that French and British troops would be embarked in equal proportions. It thus seemed likely that a defence line would have to be manned for longer than had been anticipated if all the troops were to get away. At the same time the pressure on the eastern end of the bridgehead was mounting and it was clear that the existing perimeter could not be held there for much longer. Gort visited Abrial in Dunkirk to discuss the situation. It was agreed that on the night of 31 May – 1 June the line would be re-located along the Franco–Belgian frontier. During the day the evacuation was nearing its peak and III Corps proceeded to the beaches.[28]

On 31 May there was fighting all along the perimeter, but the focus of German attention was again the eastern end of the line. Although the decision had been taken to withdraw at the end of the day, the line had to be held in the interim.[29] At Nieuport the Germans crossed the canal and attacked the 1st/6th East Surreys. They were soon in danger of being surrounded. The 1st East Surreys, their 'sister' battalion, came to the rescue. The enemy were halted, but every man was needed. At one point the two battalion commanders manned a bren gun together, one firing, the other feeding in ammunition.[30]

Near Furnes the depleted 4th Royal Berkshires, along with the 1st Suffolks, fell back in the face of further German attacks. Lieutenant Jones of the 2nd Grenadier Guards was despatched to report on the situation and, if necessary, organize a counter-attack. Arriving at the scene, Jones rallied the dispirited troops and, at the point of a bayonet, led them back to their former positions.[31]

Later that day the enemy switched their attention to Nieuport once more. The East Surreys were by now exhausted. It seemed doubtful that they could continue to hold out. But help was at hand. As the Germans massed for the attack, eighteen Blenheims of the RAF, supported by six Albacores of the Fleet Air Arm, bombed the enemy and broke up their concentrations. The British soldiers cheered at this unexpected assistance.[32]

Back at La Panne Gort had been ordered to leave the bridgehead. He went to see Abrial to make his farewells and then handed over to Major-General Alexander, commander of 1 Division, who had been selected to command the I Corps rearguard. Alexander had been chosen for this task, somewhat controversially, over Lieutenant-General Barker, the commander of I Corps. Barker was showing signs of strain and it is possible that Gort believed that Alexander had a better prospect of getting the remaining troops away. The Commander-in-Chief forlornly cut the medal ribbons off the spare uniform he was leaving behind, so as to avoid them becoming souvenirs and propaganda for the enemy, and was taken on board a waiting mine-sweeper.[33]

Alexander visited Abrial to confer about the position. The French commander, still hoping that the British would continue the fight, thought that it was possible to contract the bridgehead further and hold a perimeter running from Bergues to Uxem to Ghyvelde and then to the sea (the intermediate line). Alexander believed this impractical. Not only would the line be so close to the beaches that the enemy's artillery fire would make evacuation impossible, but the fighting condition of the troops was such that prolonged resistance was not possible. After consultation with the War Office, Alexander informed Abrial that the remaining British troops would withdraw on the night of 1–2 June.[34] The evacuation was now at its zenith. At the end of the day II Corps abandoned the eastern end of the perimeter and, apart from some troops who were assigned to help the French hold the Franco-Belgian border, proceeded to the beaches.[35]

On 1 June the Germans launched their most determined assault on the perimeter so far. This time they targeted the southern sector of the line. At Hoymille the enemy crossed the canal under cover of a heavy bombardment and penetrated the positions of the 2nd Warwickshires. The 1st Loyals were ordered to counter-attack. The ground was water-logged through flooding and movement was painfully slow. The German machine-gun fire was deadly and there were many casualties.

The advance came to a standstill and the troops were forced to return to their start line. The Commanding Officer of the Loyals, Lieutenant-Colonel Sandie, ordered a further attack "with more vigorous action". This time it succeeded and the enemy were halted.[36]

Opposite Warhem the 5th Borderers also came under attack. They warned the 2nd Coldstream Guards, who were to the left of them, that they were about to withdraw. Major McCorquodale – a resplendent Coldstreamer who shunned the new army battledress declaring that 'I don't mind dying for my country but I'm not going to die dressed like a third-rate chauffeur' – threatened to shoot any Borderers who retreated. This did not stop them falling back and the Guards' flank was exposed.

One of McCorquodale's subalterns, Lieutenant Langley, had occupied a cottage near the canal with a party of guardsmen. They set up two bren-gun nests in the attic and fired on the advancing Germans. Three lorries were set alight which blocked the canal road. At one point the firing pin of one of the brens melted. Eventually an enemy shell hit the roof and Langley was wounded. He was taken away in a wheelbarrow and somehow managed to get to a casualty clearing station. By the evening the battalion was still holding its front, but the guardsmen were much depleted. Among those who fell that day was McCorquodale.[37]

The 1st East Lancashires were defending the canal between Hoymille and Warhem. Captain Ervine-Andrews, a burly Stonyhurst-educated southern Irishman, was in command of 'B' Company. After an intense bombardment, the Germans attacked during the morning and, finding their way blocked to the front, crossed the canal on either side of the company. Ervine-Andrews' men, running perilously short of ammunition, were in danger of being cut off. At this moment Second-Lieutenant Griffin arrived with three bren carriers and a fresh supply of ammunition. This relieved the situation and the Germans were held back from the flanks.

At midday, following another intense bombardment, the enemy again attacked on the company front. Ervine-Andrews was informed that one of his forward positions was about to be overrun. The outpost was a barn, located at a point where a small tributary joined the canal. The roof was alight, the bren gun had jammed and the Germans were closing in. Under heavy fire, Ervine-Andrews ran to the barn. He climbed onto the roof and, from among the blazing rafters, shot seventeen of the attackers with a rifle. By now the bren was back in action and he accounted for more of the enemy with it. The German attack faltered.

By mid-afternoon the situation was becoming critical. It was only a matter of time before the Germans renewed their assault and the company's ammunition was again running low. Ervine-Andrews ordered Lieutenant Cetre back to Battalion HQ to report the position. Cetre returned to the front line with more ammunition and instructions to hold the position until the last round and then retire. Soon the last shot had been fired and Ervine-Andrews ordered his company to withdraw. The survivors had to wade across flooded fields, sometimes up to their necks. At a check point the company met the Lancashires' Commanding Officer. The order was given to 'march to attention' and the soldiers strode past as though on parade.

Two months later Ervine-Andrews, who had been evacuated from Dunkirk with his battalion, was having a meal in a West End restaurant. During the meal the wireless was switched on for the nine o'clock news. To his astonishment he heard it announced that the King had awarded him the Victoria Cross for his action at the canal line.[38]

In the meantime Alexander had realized that it would not be possible to embark all the remaining British troops during the night since the ships were now under heavy fire. He met with Abrial and agreed that those left in the bridgehead would form an inner defence line around Dunkirk. At the end of the day I Corps withdrew from the perimeter and, retiring through the French who were manning the intermediate line, proceeded towards the coast.[39]

On 2 June the British soldiers holding Dunkirk had an easier day. Apart from heavy shelling, they suffered little interference. Further forward, the French now bore the brunt of the fighting. All along the line the Germans pressed forward, but the French troops put up stern resistance. During the afternoon the Germans attacked Bergues and captured the town. They then advanced to Fort Vallières, just three miles from Dunkirk. Scraping together every man he could find, Fagalde organized a counter-attack which halted the enemy.[40]

At Dunkirk the last of the British troops were taken off during the night. Alexander and Tennant toured the beaches in a small naval craft to make sure no one had been left behind. Alexander shouted through a megaphone, "Is anyone there, is anyone there?" Having satisfied themselves that everyone had been embarked, they boarded a destroyer which, by this time, was under sporadic machine-gun fire.[41]

During 3 June the Germans continued their attack on the bridge-head. The French again put up stubborn resistance, but the line began to cave in. The defenders were squeezed into a small pocket around Dunkirk. Abrial and Fagalde decided that during the coming night the final French evacuations would take place. The ships returned and took off as many French troops as possible. The two French commanders also embarked and the following morning those soldiers remaining in the town surrendered to the Germans. The guns at last fell silent.[42]

Amazingly, the British army had escaped from Dunkirk. In accounting for this 'miracle', a vital role was played by the officers and men of the BEF who gallantly held the perimeter defences during the evacuation. In particular, credit should be given to Adam for his organization of the bridgehead. "The defence of the Dunkirk perimeter," notes David Divine, "was his achievement."[43] The insouciance of the Germans also played a part. Due to a combination of factors – Hitler's 'halt order', the difficulties of the terrain, the exhaustion of the troops, poor coordination between formations, over-estimation of the effectiveness of the Luftwaffe and the impending push southwards – they failed to press home their attacks on the perimeter until the evacuation was well under way.[44] The contribution of the French must be acknowledged too. Not only did they man the western end of the perimeter throughout the evacuation, but they also acted as the rearguard while the last of the British troops were embarked. As the ships slipped away from Dunkirk at dawn on 4 June many of the French troops who had bravely fought to hold back the Germans were left at the harbour.[45] From the French perspective, Jacques Mordal observes that "no episode in the epic of Dunkirk caused more heartbreak".[46]

Notes

I am grateful to the Trustees of the Liddell Hart Centre for Military Archives for permission to quote from the Adam papers.

1   See, for example, *The Times* online: <http://www.the-times.co.uk/onlinespecials/britain/dunkirk/index.html> (consulted 31 August 2000).
2   Lord Gort's Second Despatch, *The London Gazette*, 17 October 1941, pp. 5923–5; Major L.F. Ellis, *The War In France and Flanders 1939–1940* (London, 1953), pp. 174–5; Public Record Office, War

Office papers, WO 197/118, Account of Operations of Adam Force, by Lieut-Gen. Sir Ronald Adam, 17 June 1940; PRO, Cabinet papers, CAB 44/68, BEF in France and Flanders 26 May – 31 May 1940, by Lt-Col. H.F. Joslen, p. 14; Liddell Hart Centre for Military Archives, Pakenham-Walsh papers, diary entry, 26 May 1940.

3   LHC, Adam papers, Adam 3/10, biographical notes by Gen. Sir Ronald Adam, 1946, p. 27. I am grateful to Isobel Forbes Adam, Gen. Adam's daughter, for providing me with a copy of these notes; LHC, Bridgeman papers, 2/3, The Campaign of the BEF May 1940, p. 15; PRO WO 197/188, Account of Operations of Adam Force; Gort's Despatch, p. 5925; W. Lord, *The Miracle of Dunkirk* (Ware, 1988). pp. 20, 76–8; P. Wilson, *Dunkirk: From Disaster to Deliverance* (Barnsley, 1999), p 79; D. Divine, *The Nine Days of Dunkirk* (London 1964), pp. 95–6; G. Blaxland, *Destination Dunkirk: the Story of Gort's Army* (1973), pp. 309–10; Ellis, *France and Flanders*, pp. 178, 197; N. Harman, *Dunkirk: the Necessary Myth* (London, 1980), p. 140.

4   Ellis, *France and Flanders*, pp. 197–8; Gort's Despatch, pp. 5925–6; Lord, *The Miracle*, p. 78.

5   LHC Adam 3/10, biographical notes, pp. 27–8.

6   PRO WO 197/118, Account of Operations of Adam Force; LHC Adam 3/10, biographical notes, p. 28; LHC Pakenham-Walsh, diary entry, 27 May 1940.

7   PRO WO 197/118, Account of Operations of Adam Force; LHC Adam 3/10, biographical notes, pp. 28–9; Gort's Despatch, p. 5926.

8   PRO WO 197/118, Account of Operations of Adam Force; Lord, *The Miracle*, pp. 79–80; Harman, *Dunkirk*, p. 158.

9   LHC Adam 3/10, biographical notes, p. 29.

10 Lord, *The Miracle*, p. 78.

11 Gort's Despatch, p. 5926; Ellis, *France and Flanders*, p. 180; Lord, *The Miracle*, p. 79; Divine, *Nine Days*, p. 96; PRO WO 197/118, Further Notes on Administrative Points, by Lieut.-Gen. W.G. Lindsell, 20 June 1940.

12 Lord Burnham, 'One Man's Dunkirk', *Daily Telegraph*, 31 May 1965, pp. 14, 17. I am grateful to The Hon. Mrs Whitehead, Lord Burnham's daughter, for providing me with a copy of this article.

13 PRO WO 197/118, Account of Operations of Adam Force.

14 Lord, *The Miracle*, pp. 81–3.

15 Ibid., pp. 80–1.

16 PRO WO 197/118, Account of Operations of Adam Force; Lord, *The Miracle*, p. 79.

17 PRO WO 197/118, Account of Operations of Adam Force; R. Atkin, *Pillar of Fire: Dunkirk 1940* (London, 1990), pp. 182–3.

18 PRO 197/119. Report on Operation in Vicinity of Nieuport 28–30 May

1940, by Brig. A.J. Clifton, 28 June 1940; Ellis, *France and Flanders*, p. 211.

19 Lord, *The Miracle*, pp. 111–12; PRO WO 197/118, Account of Operations of Adam Force; LHC Adam 3/10, biographical notes, p. 30.

20 PRO WO 197/118, Account of Operations of Adam Force; LHC Adam 3/10, biographical notes, p. 30; Blaxland, *Destination Dunkirk*, pp. 311–12; Ellis, *France and Flanders*, p. 213; CAB 44/68, BEF in France and Flanders 26 May – 31 May 1940, p. 111.

21 Lord, *The Miracle*, p. 146; PRO 197/119, Report on Operation in Vicinity of Nieuport 28–30 May 1940; Divine, *Nine Days*, pp. 107–8.

22 PRO WO 197/118, Account of Operations of Adam Force; LHC, Lindsell papers, 1/5, Narrative of Events Covering the Period 21 May to Night of 2–3 June at Hazebrouck and Dunkirk, by Brig. R.G. Parminter; LHC Adam 3/10, biographical notes, p. 31; Gort's Despatch, p. 5929.

23 PRO WO 197/118, Account of Operations of Adam Force.

24 Gort's Despatch, p. 5929; Ellis, *France and Flanders*, pp. 219, 223.

25 Ibid., p. 225; Burnham, 'One Man's Dunkirk', *Daily Telegraph*, 1 June 1965, p. 16.

26 Ellis, *France and Flanders*, pp. 225–6; M. Howard and J. Sparrow, *The Coldstream Guards 1920–1946* (London, 1951), pp. 38–9.

27 PRO WO 197/118, Account of Operations of Adam Force; LHC Adam 3/10, biographical notes, pp. 31–2; Burnham, 'One Man's Dunkirk', 1 June, p. 16.

28 Gort's Despatch, p. 5930; Ellis, *France and Flanders*, pp. 225, 230–1; Divine, *Nine Days*, pp. 165–6; W.J.R. Gardner, *The Evacuation from Dunkirk: 'Operation Dynamo' 26 May – 4 June 1940* (London, 2000), pp. 56, 65.

29 Ellis, *France and Flanders*, p. 235.

30 Lord, *The Miracle*, pp. 198–9.

31 Ibid., p. 199; N. Nicolson and P. Forbes, *The Grenadier Guards in the War of 1939–1945* (London, 1949), p. 39; Wilson, *Dunkirk*, p. 105.

32 Lord, *The Miracle*, pp. 199–200; Ellis, *France and Flanders*, p. 235.

33 Gort's Despatch, p. 5930; Divine, *Nine Days*, p. 166; Atkin, *Pillar of Fire*, pp. 189–91.

34 Gort's Despatch, p. 5934; Ellis, *France and Flanders*, pp. 239–40; N. Nicolson, *Alex: the Life of Field Marshal Earl Alexander of Tunis* (London, 1973), pp. 105–8; W.G.F. Jackson, *Alexander of Tunis as Military Commander* (London, 1971), pp. 106–7; B. Bond, *France and Belgium 1939–1940* (London, 1975), pp. 177–8.

35 Gardner, *The Evacuation*, p. 84; Ellis, *France and Flanders*, p. 235.

36 Lord, *The Miracle*, pp. 208–11; Ellis, *France and Flanders*, p. 242; Capt. C.G.T. Dean, *The Loyal Regiment (North Lancashire) 1919–1953* (Preston, 1955), pp. 106–7.

37 Lord, *The Miracle*, pp. 201, 231–3; Howard and Sparrow, *The Coldstream Guards*, pp. 52–3; Wilson, *Dunkirk*, pp. 92–8; J.M. Langley, *Fight Another Day* (London, 1974), pp. 48–55.

38 H.L. Kirby and R.R. Walsh, *The Seven VCs of Stonyhurst College* (Blackburn, 1987), pp. 108–15; R.R. Walsh, *Lieutenant Colonel Harold Marcus Ervine-Andrews, Victoria Cross* (Blackburn, 2000), pp. 14–15. I am grateful to Raymond Walsh for providing me with copies of these sources.

39 Gort's Despatch, p. 5934; Ellis, *France and Flanders*, p. 243; Divine, *Nine Days*, pp. 199–200; Gardner, *The Evacuation*, p. 85.

40 Gort's Despatch, p. 5934; Lord, *The Miracle*, pp. 249–50; Blaxland, *Destination Dunkirk*, p. 342.

41 Gort's Despatch, p. 5934; Ellis, *France and Flanders*, p. 245; Field Marshal Earl Alexander of Tunis, *Memoirs 1940–1945* (London, 1962), p. 79; Nicolson, *Alex*, p. 113.

42 Lord, *The Miracle*, pp. 254–5; Ellis, *France and Flanders*, p. 245–6; Blaxland, *Destination Dunkirk*, p. 344; Divine *Nine Days*, pp. 226–7.

43 Divine, *Nine Days*, p. 275.

44 H.A. Jacobsen and J. Rohwer (eds), *Decisive Battles of World War Two: the German View* (London, 1965), pp. 64–7; K. Maier et al, *Germany and the Second World War*, vol 2, *Germany's Initial Conquests in Europe* (Oxford, 1991), pp. 291–5; Ellis, *France and Flanders*, pp. 214, 225–7; Lord, *The Miracle*, pp. 208–10.

45 Divine, *Nine Days*, pp. 234–5; L. Deighton, *Blitzkrieg: From the Rise of Hitler to the Fall of Dunkirk* (London, 1979), p. 263; Bond, *France and Belgium*, p. 181.

46 Quoted in Divine, *Nine Days*, p. 235.

THE FRENCH VIEW OF DUNKIRK

JOHN C. CAIRNS

Anglo-French disagreements and misunderstandings, leading to mutual recrimination and bitterness, reached a climax at Dunkirk. Gort had been contemplating the evacuation of his forces from the Channel ports since 18 May. On the evening of 25 May he had made the agonizing, unilateral decision to abandon any last hope of a southward drive to link up with French forces south of the Somme and ordered a general retreat to the coast. This decision was accepted and confirmed by the War Office the following day when rear echelons began to embark. In sharp contrast, neither Weygand nor the French government was prepared to permit French troops to be evacuated and regarded the British move as a betrayal of the allegiance. Moreover, since no preparatory instructions had been given, the French navy was ill-prepared to embark troops even when the necessity to do so became apparent.

John Cairns' deeply-informed account, based on an unrivalled knowledge of French sources and interviews with many of the leading participants, begins on the morning of 28 May when the Belgian forces had ceased fighting, thus intensifying German pressure on the ever-shrinking allied-held perimeter around Dunkirk. (Brian Bond).

The French had done little enough to prepare for evacuation. At 9:30 a.m. on 29 May Admiral Jean Abrial, since 19 May designated as in command of all French troops from Boulogne to Dunkirk, deemed the port unusable ("Sea withdrawal of substantial units seems impracticable") though strong air and naval support would permit further resistance and beach evacuation of 'useless people'. General Maxime Weygand, French C-in-C since Maurice Gamelin was sacked on the evening of 19 May, raged against "that King!" (Leopold III of Belgium): "What a swine! What a rotten swine!"), while 'gingering up'

General Alphonse Georges, French Commander North-East Theatre, and reiterating holding fast 'to save what can be saved'. He nevertheless endorsed the arrangements being made in Dover for evacuation. A Pas de Calais Flotilla of small ships was created to work under Abrial and Vice Admiral Bertram Ramsay.[1] But Weygand gave no order to embark French troops. General Louis Koeltz, the French Army's Assistant Chief of Staff, passing through London, talking "as if the withdrawal . . . was quite a normal military operation", seemed oblivious to it all.

Resistance to evacuation remained strong not merely because of the odds, but chiefly because the enemy seemed poised *not* to attack Britain but to drive south when the Dunkirk camp fell. Asked that day, "Is your only hope an error in German strategy?" Colonel R. Noiret, GQG's Chief of Operations, said, "it was better to keep the Armies in being and hope for an error than to undertake something that must fail and with losses unacceptable in a democratic country." Removal of recent British reinforcements, he emphasized, would have a "disastrous effect on French morale."[2] The northern redoubt was to buy time. But late on the 28th General Georges Blanchard, since 25 May Commander of the French First Group of Armies (GA1), pressed for preparations to embark units of 1 Army getting through to the coast. And before midnight Churchill finally rejected mediation and a "too hasty acceptance of defeat", which would neither be "honourable" nor save them from "the fate of Denmark or Poland". This was bad news for Weygand, Marshal Pétain, Georges, Édouard Daladier (since 19 May French Minister of Foreign Affairs), and many others, all convinced that negotiation must start before the armies collapsed. Evacuation and loss of the redoubt, followed by breach of the Somme–Aisne line, would be disastrous. That evening the Marshal put the case to Paul Reynaud, the French Premier.[3]

General Champon, head of the French Military Mission to the Belgian Army Headquarters, tried tempers in Dunkirk, Dover, Paris and London as he insisted on the immediate evacuation of his large organization. Dramatic scenes involving drawn revolvers, francophobe demonstrations and shrill messages ended with the Mission's embarkation that day, 29 May. But it had poisoned the atmosphere.[4] Possibly more damaging was Blanchard's accusation that Lord Gort, C-in-C of the BEF, had exposed 1 Army's flank by withdrawing "on the [British] government's order, despite my representations". Captain William G. Tennant, British Senior Naval Officer and Admiral

Ramsay's representative at Dunkirk, reminded the Admiralty that the French "at Dunkirk feel strongly that they are defending Dunkirk for us which is largely true." Brigadier J. G. Swayne, head of the Military Mission to Georges' headquarters, pressed for high-level denial of any intention to abandon France.[5] As yet there were only indications of an emerging French policy: General Joseph Doumenc, French Chief of Staff, signalled Blanchard to hold the bridgehead "in order to permit progressive sea evacuation". Weygand asked Admiral François Darlan, the French naval chief, to hasten preparations.

Meantime Gort's instructions remained contradictory. Critical of Blanchard's apparent inactivity, he and Lieutenant General Sir Henry Pownall, Gort's Chief of Staff, told Colonel Jacques Humbert, Chief of Staff to GA1, that they had no authority to embark French troops; all beaches east of Dunkirk were for British forces. When Humbert observed that he had been told otherwise the day before, Pownall said he would give them beaches when they produced French ships. Gort's "spontaneous" offer of two British ships each night "never worked," Brigadier Otto Lund noted, "the French were all over the beaches and mole and got in where they could. . . . They were not in good order!" Gort himself, as he informed the CIGS, Sir John Dill, believed that "every Frenchman embarked is at cost of one Englishman" and his instructions were "that safety of BEF is primary consideration. . . . Remains of 1st French Army on arrival will deserve embarkation but by no means all those now in this area." Major General Sir Richard Howard-Vyse, leading the British Military Mission to GHQ, though warning that "a limit to the possibilities of resistance . . . might well be close at hand", assured Weygand of British solidarity. But when Churchill insisted on places for French troops on British ships, and perhaps lifting two 1 Army divisions and replacing them by British units pro tem, the War Office rode him off, saying the matter was best left to Gort. Churchill telegraphed Reynaud before midnight, May 29, to say: "We wish French troops to share in evacuation to fullest possible extent",[6] but fair words buttered no parsnips. And neither he nor Dill had yet demanded that the French produce a clear evacuation policy.

So heavy were the RN's losses that day that the Admiralty concluded the harbour was too hazardous to use and withdrew its most modern destroyers. As more French troops entered the crowded perimeter incidents increased. Officers of each nationality observed violent encounters involving fixed bayonets, rifle fire and oars.[7] Abrial asked Blanchard to give Gort strict orders to abandon materiel outside the camp. But Blanchard was finished: "I don't command anything here," he told General Léon Fornel de la Laurencie, commanding French III Corps. Nevertheless he instructed one of his Generals, "No matter what the state of your men, you've got to assure defence of the bridgehead. This defence comes before any other consideration, no matter what it may be."[8]

Gort feared Abrial might even stop all embarkation unless he received firm orders from GQG: "He was already beginning to ride rather rough over the whole evacuation business." He had in fact declared he would not evacuate anyone (later admitting to have not embarked units that could have got away). Believing the war to be lost, he thought the sole honourable solution was "a resolute stand without thought of retreat". Equally firm, General Robert Fagalde (Commander French XVI Corps and, since 24 May, of all troops in the ports of Calais, Boulogne and Dunkirk) sent Lt. General Sir Ronald Adam (commander British III Corps and, since late on 25 May, charged by Gort with forming a bridgehead around Dunkirk) a letter saying that if British forces did not "radically" alter their attitude, "I shall not hesitate to order French troops to take action against British activities and embarkations by every means and particularly *by using their weapons*." To stop such threats and recriminations, Dill thought that the Foreign Secretary, Lord Halifax, should speak to Reynaud while he himself talked to Weygand. The "quite straightforward" line he proposed, however, might well have made matters worse: "We should say . . . that through the failure of their Army we have lost the BEF."[9]

Weygand was harshly critical. "Every people has its virtues and defects," he remarked to Colonel P. A. Bourget. "Apart from his distinguished qualities, the Englishman is motivated by almost instinctive selfishness." Skeptical of assurances that Gort had not exposed GA1's flank, he doubted that Blanchard had "had opportunity to withdraw [all] his troops if he wished". But apart from the fact that his conception of the bridgehead scarcely admitted the idea of evacuation, he was poorly and tardily informed by deferential subordinates. Slow to act, he was less than imperative with Darlan (in no way a subordinate), who, having long discounted the feasibility of maritime evacuation, delivered an imperious rebuke at the hint of criticism from Abrial or anyone else. "You are aware," he telegraphed General Doumenc on May 30 "that the Marine, alerted only three days ago to an evacuation contingency always thought to be very difficult, is making maximum effort.[10]

Thus Weygand was much on his own when, trying again to force the pace at a meeting he had asked Reynaud to call on the morning of May 30, he handed him a memorandum saying he had no weapons to prevent a sudden collapse and no hope of raising fresh armies, for which in any event there was neither clothing nor equipment. He could only try to hold the Somme–Aisne line. The British must be informed and asked for maximum and immediate help – two or three divisions, tank units, anti-tank and anti-aircraft weapons, and the full assistance of their air force. Should the front be breached, the Government would have to take "decisions of the first importance". Though they also discussed Reynaud's notion of a possible redoubt in the Breton peninsula (Weygand told him next day it was not feasible), the focus was on the northern bridgehead as part of a holding operation to save honour and buy time while a political way out was found. Speaking right after the meeting with General Wladyslaw Sikorski, Weygand did not hide his despair. France, he said, must now suffer for twenty years of moral looseness. "As a Catholic," Sikorski told him, "you may talk like that, but not as a Commander in Chief."[11]

Full of promises, telling the French that no matter how many might be forced to capitulate – "We must share this loss together as best we can" – Churchill did not argue with the military and naval conclusions that evacuation must end May 31/June 1. Gort was instructed to designate a successor for the moment when he would be ordered home. This officer would cooperate in defence of the perimeter, and when, "in consultation with the senior French commander," he judged organized evacuation and further proportionate damage to the enemy no longer possible, he was to capitulate "to avoid useless slaughter".[12] Informed of this by Gort, Abrial signalled: "Given the state of divisions coming from 1st Army, should insist to British Government that four or five British Divisions participate in Dunkirk defence," and sent a letter that evening asking Gort to designate the units to be placed under Fagalde.[13] Simultaneously, with War Cabinet approval, Dill tried to force Weygand's hand by telegraphing in such terms as effectively to prescribe allied policy and imply that there were limits to the alliance: the BEF would remain to cover maximum possible evacuation, but supply problems alone forbade indefinite resistance. "Policy therefore must be to evacuate and orders to this effect have been given to Lord Gort. I should be glad if you would give similar orders to [Abrial] so that he and Lord Gort may be able to act in complete accord." Still insisting on the phone to the reluctant Gort that equal numbers of French must be taken off, Churchill told him it was a political matter. He himself must return and bring Blanchard and Fagalde also.[14]

Despite mixed signals, contradictory intentions and uncoordinated promises, the Navy had been persuaded to return to the harbour on 31 May, greatly increasing the numbers that could be lifted. Georges assured Swayne that the four or five divisions Abrial requested were to cover embarkation only, *not* remain indefinitely. But Gort insisted it was "folly to try and hang on too long". The Chiefs of Staff pressed for Abrial to be given an evacuation order. And the French naval staff signalled its displeasure to the London Naval Mission: evacuation "is an operation long prepared on the sly and seems to be being carried out to the detriment of good order essential for defence of the fortified camp of Dunkirk." The Naval Attaché, Vice-Admiral Jean Odend'hal, must insist on full air and naval support for *all* embarkations. Reminded that equal numbers of French and British should be lifted, Gort asked Eden, Secretary of State for War, whether British troops were to remain in order to evacuate as many French as possible or to leave when they no longer felt secure. Eden replied, the latter.[15]

At Bastion 32 to arrange for Lieutenant-General Michael Barker's 1 Corps to remain under Fagalde, Gort handed Abrial a cool reply to the previous day's insistent letter. Making a favourable impression nevertheless, he gave "everyone present a rendezvous in France for the continuation of the struggle" and said he could be reached until 9 p.m. at La Panne. Fagalde thanked him, believed he had "complete freedom to use [the three Divisions] as seemed best to me" and set about planning to integrate them with his own 60 and 68 DIs on the perimeter. About 12.30 p.m., however, Gort summoned Major General Harold Alexander, Commander 1st Division, to tell him he must take over 1 Corps. Alexander immediately stated his intention to extricate it and surrender none of it. No one at La Panne seems to have questioned this implicit repudiation of Gort's commitment to Abrial. 1 Corps's departure, the War Office was told, would be "worked out in co-operation with the French".[16]

Nor did the Supreme War Council meeting held at 2.30 that afternoon in Paris clarify matters. Disputing comparative air contributions and losses, Churchill and Dill resisted intense appeals for at least half if not the whole of Fighter Command (620 planes) to take part in the impending battle – "*a question,*" General Joseph Vuillemin, C-in-C French Air Force, had said, "*of life or death.*" Saying the evacuation must end within forty-eight hours, Churchill was warned by Reynaud that if news of the massive disproportion of British to French got out, French opinion would be dangerously upset. When Churchill said he had ordered French troops to have precedence and hoped only a small rearguard would be captured, Weygand retorted that 1 Army divisions trapped in the Lille pocket "would probably be exterminated" but until that was confirmed British forces should remain to give them hope of escape. Saying he would order Abrial to get the British rearguard away first, Darlan famously provoked Churchill: No, he could not accept further French sacrifices: they should go together, "*bras dessus, bras dessous*". Dill quickly stepped in to check this sentimental line. They agreed that "under [Abrial's] orders" the British would remain "as long as possible", French and British commanders making the decisions on the spot. The obvious contradictions of the discussion were intractable.[17]

Meantime, at about 3.30 p.m., while the Council was in progress, a standoff began at Bastion 32. Alexander and Tennant appeared, to find General Fagalde, Rear Admiral Leclerc, Abrial's Chief of Staff, and General René Altmayer, Commander French V Corps, present. Abrial invoked Gort's letter stating that 1 Corps would be "under the orders" of Fagalde, who then sketched how he planned to use it in the perimeter defence. To Alexander the proposals seemed militarily unreasonable. "He listened to me without interrupting," Fagalde wrote: "then, when I had finished, gave a laugh, saying, 'You really must be putting me on'." His orders were not to defend a sector but to withdraw his worn troops and embark. It was no joking matter, Fagalde replied; Gort's letter was specific. He read it, translating as he did so. "So you're acknowledging," he said, "that the French Army alone will cover embarkation of the British Army, while the British Army will not help the French Army in its withdrawal." Alexander said he would like to cooperate, but his verbal orders were to withdraw and embark. He had only 1 and 50 Divisions and a brigade of 42 Division; all would go within twenty-four hours. Abrial noted this would leave 20,000 on the beaches and 50,000 defending the perimeter. Alexander was sorry, but the Germans were at the gates of the town: "If we stay here another twenty-four hours, we'll all be taken prisoner." Abrial's Chief of Staff, Capitaine de Frégate de Lapérouse, spoke up to say that if Gort knew this, he had lied; if not, Alexander must make it right. Everything, Alexander insisted, that can be saved will have been saved. "No, General," Lapérouse continued, "There's still Honour." In the ensuing silence, Alexander seeming not to understand, Altmayer calmly asked him to obey the Admiral. Abrial then proposed that since Gort's letter was contradicted by verbal orders, they should go together to consult him since he would not embark until evening. It was about 4.30 p.m. Alexander said it was useless: Gort had left at 4 o'clock. They concluded he was lying. He added that "as the most senior British General remaining on the Continent, he was henceforth Commander-in-Chief of the BEF, and thus dependent only on the Secretary of State for War, Mr Anthony Eden." Fagalde stressed the gravity of disobeying Gort's written instructions: "This decision will disgrace the British Army." Alexander said he would contact Eden.

Having made his way back to La Panne, he phoned him at 7.15 p.m., saying the French wished to hold for three more nights. He believed no more troops could be embarked by prolonging the evacuation and the BEF was "in extreme danger of being wiped out". He requested an immediate decision. Abrial meantime had sent Doumenc and Weygand "an SOS" (as Weygand noted), asking that they get the War Office to stop Alexander breaking off in the night of June 1, "no matter what happens", thus ending embarkation of French troops and compromising "our military honour". Weygand asked Darlan to have Churchill "put the matter right" while he himself contacted Dill. About this time Gort left French shores with no word of farewell to Weygand, having expressed to the French liaison officer accompanying him his "astonishment" at the French Army's lack of will to fight.[18]

With the agreement of the Defence Operations Committee, chaired by Neville Chamberlain, Eden told Alexander he must embark on a 50/50 basis, aim to finish by 1/2 June and so inform Abrial. "Right!" Alexander said. "I will do that." Halifax and Chamberlain also spoke, telling him to withdraw as soon as possible. "This was a very difficult decision and we may get into trouble over it," Chamberlain noted, "but we felt we had to take it." No one cabled or telephoned Weygand.

Reaching Bastion 32 again about 11 p.m., Alexander informed Abrial, saying he would hold on until one minute to midnight, 1 June. But by then the afternoon's Supreme War Council's decisions had arrived. Shown them, Alexander said he did not serve "under the Prime Minister's orders". More reproaches for abandoning his *camarades de combat* followed, ending with the stinging rebuke, "Your decision to re-embark with your three Divisions dishonours England." There was nothing more to say.

Was it by some 'oversight', an angry Howard-Vyse asked the War Office next day, that this order, contradicting what the French had been told, was communicated neither to him nor to Weygand? If not, he added, it was all "most unfortunate" and "I have no suggestions to offer". "The British lion," Darlan observed, "seems to have wings when it's a matter of getting back to the sea." Perhaps the large numbers of French evacuated that day alleviated the tension, as did the excellent, even hazardous, traffic control work on the beaches by French and British officers. The coastal roads being impassable that night, Alexander and Tennant remained at Bastion 32, sitting out for a while on its roof. In the darkness British soldiers were coming in from the periphery. "The beach is that way," they were told. "It's every man for himself; stop for nobody."[19]

When at 8 a.m. next morning, 1 June, Alexander handed in his telegraphed instructions, Abrial again protested that he could not complete evacuation before the evening of 2 June. On the Quai Félix Faure British sailors turned away most of the one hundred officers and nurses of 3 DLM's hospital group. "I'm really sorry, Colonel," said the pier director, "the British are ruthless. You can let only twenty or so go aboard." Alexander was now instructed: "Aim at getting off maximum number French today and withdrawing remainder and covering party night of 1/2 June."[20] Very severe losses had decided the Navy to suspend daylight operations as too costly.

In London and Paris (where news of the capitulation in the Lille pocket arrived) confrontations flared. Disregarding having just accepted Abrial's command, Churchill informed Reynaud that the Admiral could not properly judge matters from Bastion 32. Evacuation, he told the War Cabinet, must end that night: "There was no hope for any French troops that were still outside the perimeter". Admiral Sir Dudley Pound, First Sea Lord, criticized the Marine's procedures and failures. Gort, having returned in the night, regaled the ministers with an attack on Blanchard ("the professorial type"), General Gaston Billotte ("completely flabby"), King Leopold's ADC, General Raoul van Overstraeten ("a courtier"), Abrial, Fagalde, René Altmayer and the French Army ("The French troops, when they saw the Germans advancing, were apt to retire").[21] In Paris Weygand protested at Alexander's instructions from Dill. The open-ended promise on French evacuation ("Impossible to say how long this will take but Alexander force remains until last") was a dead letter. Noting that Abrial's unified command had lasted twenty-four hours, Reynaud said Gort "had fought only when it suited the purpose of his own Army". Brigadier E. L. Spears, Churchill's personal emissary to Reynaud, blamed Abrial, Weygand and the High Command for letting him down. Accusing the BEF of preparing "to leave the French in the lurch," Koeltz complained about the few French evacuees, the small number of British ships available to French divisions and the paucity of RAF squadrons in France. Stood off by Air Marshal Sir Arthur Barratt, Commander British Air Forces France, Vuillemin became increasingly importunate. Politicians indignantly echoed these demands, determined to have documentary proof that, in the event of defeat, responsibility lay not with the French Army but with the RAF.[22]

Very heavy casualties occurred off the coast and great suffering in the burning town and on the beaches as the tense exchanges flew back and forth. Backed by Eden, the Chiefs of Staff and Gort, Dill pressed for Abrial to end it that night "in the interests of our two Armies". General Albert Lelong, French Military Attaché in London, "in a great state of excitement", put Abrial's case forcefully to Dill: it was one thing for Frenchmen to be driven out of Dunkirk by the enemy, quite another to be ordered out by London: "Such an order might have disastrous results on the Alliance." Doubting the instructions would change, he left the War Office "absolutely shaking with anger". Then Churchill, resisting Gort, Pound and others at a Chiefs of Staff meeting, changed his mind again, fearing the French might be nudged to give up. Alexander was told, "We do not order any fixed moment for evacuation". Thus, instructed to remain as long as possible in order to save the maximum number of French and British, Alexander was left with the same contradiction: "In close cooperation with Admiral Abrial you must act in this matter on your own judgement." Deciding he would after all have "certain reserves here tomorrow [2 June] to assist the French", he said he would complete "by midnight [2/3 June]". Embarrassed by the confusion, having assured Koeltz that "Alexander would stay to the end", Howard-Vyse suggested Dill write to Weygand to sort out it all out – an impossible task.[23]

The Dunkirk bridgehead remained a crucial element of Weygand's overall strategy. Countermanding Georges' 29 May instruction to General Antoine Besson foreseeing a fighting retreat from the Somme, he had insisted on his own 26 May Instruction #19, "unequivocally" defining the armies' mission of "a determined resistance on the present position". Deep strategic withdrawal was impossible: "Let us not lose the battle of the Somme in the hope of winning the battle of Paris."

Conferring on 2 June with Generals Gaston Prételat (GA2) and Charles Huntziger (GA4), he checked them also: "The decision has been taken, we'll fight on the present position which covers almost all our remaining factories. The risks are known. The Government has been warned and accepts those risks. It knows that if [the enemy] smashes through us, we'll have to give up coordinated defence of the country and we can count on tanks sweeping on to Paris." Strategic withdrawal aside, he was preaching to the converted. Prételat had put it to the Defence Minister's *Directeur du cabinet* three days before: in a hopeless situation, after everyone had done his duty and honour was safe, was it "necessary to slaughter the whole of French youth and resign themselves to the destruction of the country"? Ought not the Government to "make an effort to save what can still be saved of territory and men? And would it not be wise to try to retain intact the few Divisions in the East possibly to maintain order in France?"[24] Weygand had known this from the beginning. Evacuation in the north was the unwanted final episode in a delaying operation that had been unraveling for almost two weeks.

The Supreme War Council had confirmed on 31 May that massive British land and air help could not be granted. Although a small new BEF would go to France, the War Cabinet opposed further transfer of RAF fighters. The Chiefs of Staff were unmoved by the argument that the battle for France seemed certain to occur before a battle for Britain. This was not, Weygand remarked to Reynaud, "the way to treat an ally in time of war". Though Odend'hal asked for understanding of RN exhaustion ("Can you not increase French means for tomorrow [2/3 June] night?"), Darlan, admitting France had been slow to act, was disgruntled about the smaller numbers of French lifted, the discordance between Churchill's promise and the reality of the rearguard's composition: "We have to hang on to our friends across the way," he wrote to his wife, "to convince them to fight while evacuating."[25] With Alexander more than ever sure that evacuation must stop, the War Office dismissed Abrial's request for full assistance throughout 3/4 June "in order to evacuate French who by remaining have made possible final British withdrawal". Chamberlain and Halifax were similarly impatient. The War Cabinet, however, accepted Churchill's arguments. In the early evening of 2 June French Ambassador Charles Corbin was promised they would do as Abrial asked.[26] But the BEF was leaving. As if to play the game one last time, Churchill had Dill signal Alexander at 8.40 p.m.: "If British troops are entirely evacuated tonight conclude this is with concurrence of Admiral." (Had he received the message, what could he have replied?)

Touring the beaches and harbour with Tennant after 11 p.m., Alexander concluded "that the whole rearguard had got safely away" and sailed to Dover. In fact Navy and merchant ships worked on through this night. Why so many French troops vainly waited near Dunkirk's short west mole for ships they could not see or contact defied clear explanation.[27] Contrary to Abrial's orders and to promises, the British sank blockships at 3.12 a.m. on 3 June – so faultily as not to seal the port. Reaching London, Alexander could not say "how many French troops were left at the bridgehead." To Eden's congratulations, he remarked, "We were not pressed, you know."[28]

Under immense strain, Weygand stormed at the morning meeting on 3 June: Churchill had played a double game since 16 May; obviously Gort had been ordered to withdraw from Arras; the British had ruined his plan and abandoned France. "They cannot resist the call of the ports. Even in March, 1918, they wanted to embark." An air force staff memorandum noted "the bad faith often characterizing Anglo-Saxons". Capitaine Paul de Branthome, assistant Air Attaché, claimed he had literally to follow Air Chief Marshall Sir Hugh Dowding, Commander of RAF Fighter Command, around to get Dunkirk's air cover re-established this day. Weygand endorsed Vuillemin's prediction that without twenty more RAF fighter squadrons in France on the first day of the expected German offensive, the war would be lost for both nations.[29] But the Chiefs of Staff held firm: the French had "lost hope of victory"; anything sent to France "can virtually be written off". Churchill warned Spears, "You should prepare them for favourable response army [two divisions] but disappoint [sic] about air".[30]

With the Dunkirk operations approaching their end, Churchill sent an acerbic message, "We are coming back for your men tonight. Pray make sure that all facilities are used promptly. Last night for three hours many ships waited idly at much cost and danger." Darlan was irate. "I had to have Churchill and the Admiralty 'bawled out'," he noted, "to get them to continue to the night of 3/4 June. The Admiralty declares its men worn out and bewails its lost destroyers. Well, what about us?" Even Pound sent a "disagreeable telegram". The British, Darlan complained to Odend'hal, had escaped only because the French had held and were still holding. Naturally, places went unfilled: it was not easy to break off and get away. Evacuations were "not as methodical as Dover would like them to be". If the British were worn out, "the Frenchmen of Dunkirk are still more so". Operations must continue "for as many days and nights as will be needed to supply and evacuate the fighters of Dunkirk". Stung by all this, Odend'hal tele-typed back to Admiral Maurice Le Luc, "It is quite useless to exchange bad-tempered telegrams, what matters is to succeed in the operations in progress." If Darlan, having said earlier that evacuation must end on 1/2 June, wished to continue, "Paris must say so plainly". Abrial must inform Ramsay. "There is no bad temper here," Le Luc replied, "but a little weariness with having to call for cooperation so often." As for policy change, "This morning people here wanted to continue contemplating evacuation as long as there was anyone to evacuate, but since then!!" Since then Abrial had indicated communications failing, the enemy closing in. Darlan and Weygand were, as Le Luc knew, "resigned to admitting that the coming night will be the last."[31]

Near chaos reigned when Abrial was ordered at 1.34 p.m. to leave. The beaches were under fire; the town, gutted or aflame, was still being pillaged by soldiers, sailors, civilians. Wrecks, flotsam and bodies filled the port. In return for "the British effort on behalf of the French Army" Ramsay requested evacuation of "the largest possible number of British wounded".[32] The last code burnt, Abrial left about 10 p.m., remaining with Fagalde, Laurencie and others off the port and beaches until 2 a.m. before sailing to Dover. Hour after hour in the darkness, a pushing, cursing throng of men boarded the tugs, motorboats, launches, Channel steamers and destroyers that had made their way to the moles. In the early hours 68 DI, under General Barthélemy, commanding the *Secteur fortifié de Flandres*, disengaged and retired on the port; they did not all get away. A horde, "an immense river", of men who had hidden out for days, deserters, pillagers, the detritus of the northern armies, emerged from the shattered town, streaming toward the last ships, blocking Barthélemy's fighters. This time the harbour was successfully sealed. Some commanders sent their men to the dunes for protection, but when the Germans appeared in the morning the Dunkirk quays were packed. On the beaches was the enormous litter of rifles, tin hats, gas masks, boots, clothing, bicycles, smashed and burnt-out vehicles, like the monstrous aftermath of some fantastic military picnic. Offshore the hulks of sunken vessels rose mutely above the surface, bearing their cargoes of dead soldiers.

By 10.30 a.m. on 4 June, when Generals Beaufrère and Tessyres made formal surrender to General von Krantz at the Hôtel de Ville and then Bastion 32, Maintenon had telegraphed Weygand: "There is nothing more to attempt. . . . Admiral Abrial considers operation of the English this night magnificent." Darlan expressed gratitude to Pound and sent congratulations to Ramsay on the "masterly operation" that proved "the fraternal and tenacious spirit of co-operation" binding the two navies. Abrial was received at Buckingham Palace. In all, nearly half as many French as British had been brought out. Many thousands marched away to captivity, with time to consider the remark of at least one German officer at Dunkirk: "Where are the Tommies? Tommies gone and you here; you crazy."[33] Early on 5 June, the Germans struck hard along the Somme–Aisne line.

Well might Darlan tell his wife, "I did not hope to save half the lads" who were got away. Having expected higher losses, he was not less hostile for having been opposed to evacuation from the moment of Gamelin's first inquiry. In London Odend'hal damped down ill-feeling as best he could, emphasizing that there would have been no evacuation without the British, and that more of General René Prioux's First Army would have got away had the Generals been more imaginative. "It is useless to recriminate. We must look to the future: in this case, the two peoples must remain united or perish. We have no choice." To Darlan's personal reproaches he replied, "No, I have not gone over into the British camp and I should be cut to the heart if you thought so." He had had painful encounters with General Sir Edmund Ironside and Pound, "but what is the use of rehearsing or exaggerating them? I believe that in an alliance . . . you must draw a veil over outbursts of temper or disagreements when they are not irreparable." Pound may have telegraphed disagreeably, but had nevertheless spent his ships heavily to rescue Frenchmen. "Whatever the British wrongs may have been, the Dunkirk events must not leave us bitter." Ill-will could also be dangerous: "Great Britain is now haunted by the fear of invasion; she is thinking only of defending herself against this peril and she will not easily agree to send divisions to France or, still more serious, the fighter planes of which we nonetheless have great need."[34]

'Dunkirk' is shorthand for operations about which there can be no consensus. It occurred in a general context of uncertainty about Allied strategy and prospects: humiliating withdrawal from the enterprise in Norway; apparent menace from Italy; United States willingness to be chiefly a supplier of war materiel; unfriendly Soviet reserve; intense German propaganda to divide the Allies; a brief sharp struggle in the British War Cabinet determining whether to seek terms or fight on. In

France this last urgent issue was pitched into a political truce so fragile that it shattered in a matter of weeks. Paul Reynaud had put his finger on it on 16 May: the Allies had two different scenarios in mind. French decision-makers believed the war was virtually lost; with their Army "doomed", as Gamelin had said, they could not conceive of a successful military outcome. Whatever the co-operation and successes of the great evacuation, as seen from France, the BEF's actions, prepared and directed "on the sly" from London, had ruined the possibility of prolonging Dunkirk's *camp retranché*. Holding up his soldier's mask, Weygand had hidden his conviction and intent, and Churchill, even Dill, if not Gort, had responded again and again. Hence Weygand's anger with Reynaud for failing on 26 May to put the question forcefully in London. The last thing he wanted was to have political '*crétins*' exaggerate his pessimism. "In any event, will people stop panicking the British," he had said, "for I need them in order to fight on."[35] He needed the whole of Britain's forces in France, north and south, not to fight on endlessly but to put up such a defence as would win an acceptable negotiated peace for *both* nations. Unable himself to say this, he had failed to induce Reynaud to do so. In the catastrophic aftermath, falling heir to political responsibility in June, he was compelled to accept a dictated armistice.

"We who live in a small island," Sir John Swayne reflected long afterwards, "regard the sea as a high road." For the French it is "the limit of their country." Thus it seemed to them that "to take to the sea would be to abandon their country and would be disgraceful". They regarded British plans as "preparations for deserting them and, on occasions, did not hesitate to say so". Storm Jameson remembered Dunkirk occasioning "a pitch of exultation no one could expect to feel more than once in a lifetime". No such feeling marked the lifting of French troops. As for the men left in the burning port, in the ruined hospital at Zuydcoote or along the littered dunes, they "would have needed a superhuman dose of charity", in Marc Bloch's words, "not to feel bitter as they saw ship after ship drawing away from the shore, carrying their foreign companions in arms to safety. Heroes they may have been, but they were not saints."[36]

'Dunkirk' would not be exorcized in the weeks or even the years to come, although the distinguished military historian, Pierre Lyet, would say it was "to a certain extent *an Allied victory*". At the time Ambassador Corbin remarked hopefully that perhaps it was the combined Franco-British tendencies that "permitted saving so many men". But he was devastated by Churchill's offering in the Commons on 4 June "only a brief word about the valiant resistance of French troops", many of whom had fought a stiffer battle than the BEF; some of whom had held the perimeter to the last. Units had broken, mobs on the beaches behaved badly, but the exploits of others were "passed over more or less unremarked". And why it had come to that was a matter almost too sensitive to touch. Tough young commanders, such as the future Marshal Juin (choosing capture with his men), believed to the end of their days that Gort's actions condemned Weygand's plan. At the time they too deplored the 'insular reflex' of British concentration on what they deemed the chimaera of 'defence of the Islands' when the great French Army itself had not held. The British, Pétain concluded, would let the French fight on unassisted, "until the last available drop of French blood" had been shed, before saving themselves with a negotiated peace. In that case "the French Government would do its utmost to come to terms immediately with Germany whatever might happen to England."[37] His statement reflected anger and despair in the armed services and the political milieu. Soon, amidst a vast military rout, the national perception of being abandoned made it a programme and a fact.

Notes

1   Captaine A.G. Méric, to Voruz, June 8, SHAT 1K130/12; Marceau to Arcole, 28 Mai #7181 [received 15h05], 27N78/2; Weygand, Cahier #16, 1K1430/15; Grand Quartier Général Nord-Est (GQG NE), Journal de Marche (JdM), May 28; Aurore to Alouette and Abrial, May 28 10h00, 1K130/7; Note to Georges, May 28, #1222 3/FT 10h30, ibid.; Amirauté to MNFL (for Abrial), May 28 #454 17h05, SHM II BB⁷3. Darlan, contemptuous of Army and Air Force and seeing how things were going, contemplated a massive gamble should terms be accepted requiring surrender of the fleet, "*I do not intend to obey that order*". He gave precise instructions for the ships, on receipt of a codeword, to sail to Halifax, scuttle, or fight on with the British. Note pour L'Amiral Le Luc [copy], 28 Mai 1940, 1 BB² 187.
2   #2 Military Mission, May 28, PRO WO167/41; Marshall-Cornwall, Notes on a Verbal Report by General Koeltz . . . at 1.30 p.m., May 28, WO216/113 [Koeltz would say events overtook his mission of inquiry (interview, June 2, 1966)]; Report of a talk with Colonel Henri Gauché, head of the 2e Bureau, in Lieutenant-Colonel de Chair to Howard-Vyse,

28 May, WO208/619; Woodall, Military Situation in France as at 2000 hours, 28/5/40, AHS AC75/28/5.

3   François Delpla, Ed., *Les Papiers secret du Général Doumenc (1939–1940)*, Paris 1992 (Doumenc), p. 283; Martin Gilbert, *Winston S. Churchill*, 8 vols., London 1966–1988, (Gilbert), 7:422; Charles Petrie (Ed), *The Private Diaries (March 1940–January 1941) of Paul Baudouin*, London 1948 (Baudouin), p. 64. Indicative of wild speculations in Paris was Jean Monnet's proposal that No. 10 Downing Street try "to discover whether General Weygand had a real war plan. If he had, then General Weygand must without delay be made Prime Minister of France and Minister of Defence. . . . This could be done and political support obtained." Desmond Morton to Prime Minister, 28 May, PRO Prem 7/2.

4   Sir John Swayne to author, June 25, 1961; GQG NE JdeM, May 29; Advance Brassard to Troopers, May 29, 0800 hrs, WO167/5/1; #2 Military Mission, May 29, WO167/41; Doumenc, p. 283; SNO telegram from Swayne Mission, May 29, 1900 hrs, WO106/1692; Carnets du Général Mendigal, May 29, SHAA, 2 DI; Amirauté to Arcole, May 30, #1092, 27N78/2; Rapport du chef d'Escadron A. Zeller, 28N6/12. "This General Champon," Vice Admiral Jean Odend'hal commented to Capitaine de Vaisseau Paul Auphan, "talks too much on the telephone, which perhaps is not secure." May 29, Correspondence Odend'hal–Auphan (hereafter CO–A) (communicated by Hervé Cras).

5   GQG NE JdeM, May 30; Alouette to Annibal, May 29, #1229 0/3, 03h36, 27N81/3; Admiralty to War Office, May 29 (from SNO Dunkirk), WO106/1695; Swayne to War Office, May 29, 12h10, WO106/1698; No. 2 Military Mission Diary, May 29, WO167/41.

6   Arcole to Alouette, May 29 May, 1237 3/FT, 27N3; Weygand to Darlan, May 29, 09h48, 1K130/7; Blanchard CR, May 29; Brian Bond (Ed), *Chief of Staff: the Diaries of Lieutenant General Sir Henry Pownall*, 2 vols, London 1972–1973, (Pownall), p. 353; Troopers from Brassard, May 29, WO106.1613; Howard-Vyse Note for Colonel Bourget, May 29, WO202/5 [French translation in 27N81/31]; Pownall, p. 353; René Cailloux, "Vicissitudes de la collaboration franco-britannique 1940" in *Bulletin trimestrial de l'Association des Amis de l'Ecole Superieure de la Guerre*, 30 January 1966, (Cailloux, 'Vicissitudes'), p. 54; Compte Rendu (hereafter CR) du Général Blanchard, 28 June, and attached CR du Colonel Humbert, 27 N5; Lund to Howard-Vyse, June 2, WO202/5; telephone message to the CIGS from C in C, BEF, 1715hrs, May 29, WO106/1682; Churchill to Eden, Ismay, Dill, May 20, Percival to Ismay, May 29, Ismay to Churchill, May 30, PRO Prem 3/175; Gilbert, 7: 424. The long and fiercely debated question of Gort's instructions in the War Cabinet that morning is in WM146(40) CAB 65/7 & 13.

7   Arthur Bryant, *The Turn of the Tide 1939–1943*, London 1957 (Bryant), pp. 147–8; Méric to Cardes, 27N188; Lieutenant Romagny, Paul . . . to Monsieur le Général Commandant les T.M., August 2, 1K130/11; Somerville, Report on Operation Dynamo. Dover Despatch A14/0/876/40, June 18, Churchill College SMVL 7/2; Adam to writer, March 22, 1956; Osborne War Diary, May 29, WO167/275.

8   Rapport de l'Amiral Abrial sur le Rôle joué par les Forces Maritimes du Nord dans la Bataille de France, p. 66 (signed and probably drafted by Capitaine de Frégate de Lapérouse) [hereafter Abrial Rapport], SHM 1BB² 186, also 1BB² 207. Amirauté to Amiral Nord (for Blanchard), May 29, #1249, 20h10, SHAT ACH#1; B.L. de la Laurencie, *Les Opérations du IIIe C.A. en 1939–1940* (Paris, 1948), p. 84; Blanchard quoted in Maurice Frézouls, *Les derniers combats pour la défense de Dunkerque* . . . (Les Salvages, 1962), p. 25; Arcole to Annibal, May 30, 03h10, SHAA 61P151; Hervé Cras, *Les Forces Maritime du Nord*, Paris, 1955 (Cras, Forces maritimes), p. 110.

9   Telephone talk, Gort to Dill, May 29, 1715 hours, WO167/5/1; Fagalde, Notes, May 29; Dill minute for Eden, May 29, WO106/1750. Cf. Major-General Hastings Ismay's odd view: "Had we not delayed in the hope that Weygand would stage a counter-attack, northwards, the BEF could have got away with its equipment." Ismay minute for Colonel Jacob, July 30, 1940, PRO CAB120/246.

10 P.A. Bourget, "Une année dans l'ombre de Weygand", *Revue des Deux Mondes* (May 1, 1965), p. 29; Darlan to Arcole, May 30, #7321, 13h55, 27N78/2 [the War Office had wind of Abrial's criticism of Maintenon: Troopers to Madelon, no 199, May 30 WO106/1742]. Almost on receipt of Abrial's message, Darlan telegraphed promotions in the Légion d'Honneur to him and Platon (Amirauté to Abrial, May 30, 07327, 15h58, II BB⁷ MN3); some hours later Weygand sent Blanchard and Prioux President Lebrun's "*salut reconnaissant de la Patrie*" [Amirauté to Abrial (from Weygand), May 30, 2130, AHC#1]. Hervé Coutau-Bégarie and Claude Huan's valuable *Darlan* (Paris, 1989), is uncritical and meagre on this affair.

11 Alouette to Annibal, May 29, 03h36, #1229 0/3, 27N81; Baudouin, pp. 60–6; Reynaud, Réponse à la Note . . . Weygand . . . , May 29 (MS), 1 K130/28; Weygand, Cahier 16, May 29, 1K130/15; Sikorski quoted [Weygand's agenda for May 29 provides time and date] in Hugh Dalton, Diary, December 25, 1940, Dalton Papers, LSE.

12 DO(40) 11 & 12, May 30, CAB69/1; Churchill to Spears, for Reynaud, Weygand and Georges, May 30 in WM147(40), CAB 65/7; Telephone talk, Major Vogel to Sinclair, May 30, 1200 hrs, War Office to Gort, May 30, 1400 hrs, in Joslen, CAB44/68.

13 Cras, *Forces maritimes*, pp. 246–7; Abrial, Rapport, p. 57; Weygand,

Cahiers/16/15; Notes on La Panne [Corps Commanders] Conference, evening May 30, WO167/124/3.

14 Dill telegram to Weygand, May 30, in PRO WM148(40), CAB65/7; Major Vogel telephone talk to Sinclair, May 30, 1200 hrs, War Office to Gort, May 30, 1400 hrs, in H. F. Joslen, "The BEF in France and Flanders, 10–25 May 1940" (hereafter Joslen), CAB44/68; Dill, Gort, Churchill telephone talk, May 30, midnight, WO167/5/1. Some of his subordinates evidently thought Gort was 'finished', incapable of issuing 'clear orders': Nigel Hamilton, *Monty: The Making of a General, 1887–1942* (London), pp. 387–90; on defective GHQ organisation, Leese testimony, Bartholomew Committee, June 12, 1940, WO106/1775.

15 Howard-Vyse to War Office, May 31, 0530 hrs, WO106/1742; Swayne to War Office, May 31, 0945, Joslen, CAB44/68; Gort–Percival telephone talk, May 31, 0650 hrs, WO167/5/1; No. 2 Military Mission Diary, May 31, WO167/41; Howard-Vyse to DMO, June 2, WO202/5; Cras, *Forces maritimes*, 248, 255–6; Darlan to Abrial (Weygand to Blanchard), May 31, in Humbert CR, annexe; Abrial, Rapport, p. 57; Eden, Percival, Leese, Gort telephone talk, May 31, 0900 hrs, WO167/5/1; Eden in WM149(40), May 31, 11 a.m., CAB65/7.

16 Lieutenant-General W. G. Lindsell, Narrative of Events, May 31, LHC, Lindsell I/c; Lelong to Guerre, May 31, 13h10, 7N2821; Abrial, Rapport, May 31; Blanchard CR; Lt Col de Cardes's observations, in Voruz to Weygand and Georges, June 5–6, #8764 DES/3, 27N81/3; Notes due Général Fagalde, Commandant le XVIe Corps d'Armée sur les agissements anglais à Dunkerque en mai et juin 1940 [May 31], AN 3W289/218–30; Amirauté to Arcole, May 31, 13h25, SHAT 61P151; Hamilton, p. 390; Gort, Secret and Personal, to Alexander, May 31, WO167/5/2.

17 Vuillemin to Weygand, May 31, No. 3906/3/os, PRO Air8/287, 1D37; SWC, May 31, 2.30 p.m., CAB99/3; Conseil Supérieur du 31 Mai 1940. Discussion relative à l'évacuation de l'armée de Flandres, Archives Nationales 74AP22; Baudouin, pp. 68–74; Edward Spears, *Assignment to Catastrophe*, 2 volumes, London 1954, (Spears), 1: 294–319; Paul de Villelume, *Journal d'une defaite (23 août 1939–16 juin 1940)*, Paris 1976, pp. 360–70; Darlan, Exposé des motifs qui ont conduit le Gouvernement Français à demander une armistice à l'Allemagne et à l'Italie, AN 74AP22.

18 Commandant Lehr, Compte Rendu (de mémoire) des entretiens: Amiral Abrial-Général Fagalde–General Alexander [May 31], 15hr30, Bastion 32, 27N5; Fagalde, Notes, May 31 [he misdates Alexander's second visit]; Voruz to Georges, June 28, 1940, No. 8935/DES/S, 1K130/1Z [hereafter Voruz Rapport], May 31; Abrial Rapport, 57–8, Gort's May

31 letter is annexed; Darlan to Abrial, May 31, Ministerie des Affaires Etranjeres Papiers 40, GB, vol 12, Dossier Dejean; De Cardes, quoted in Voruz to Weygand and Georges, June 5–6, 27N81/3; Amirauté to Arcole, May 31 [received 20h45] #7460, and Koeltz's note on it, 27N81/3; Cras, *Forces maritimes*, pp. 249–50, 336; Weygand, Cahiers 16/15, May 31; Report by Major-General H.R.L.G. Alexander . . . on the Operations of 1st Corps BEF from 1200 hours 31st May till Midnight 2/3 June 1940 (June 10, 1940), WO167/5/2 (silent on this controversy). Darlan's angry comment was that "from the very moment this great war leader [Alexander] arrived at Dunkirk" he wanted to leave for England (Exposé des motifs, 74AP22). Gort, if still at La Panne, must have known of the contretemps.

19 PRO DO(40)13, May 31, 7.45 p.m., CAB69/1; [Harold] Alexander, *The Alexander Memoirs, 1940–1945* (London, 1962), pp. 78–9; Chamberlain Diary, May 31, Neville Chamberlain Papers, University of Birmingham Library; War Office to Brassard, May 31, WO167/5/2; Joslen, May 31, CAB44/69; Lindsell, Narrative, May 31; Howard-Vyse to DMO, June 2, WO202/5; Alain Darlan, *L'Amiral Darlan parle*, Paris, 1952 (hereafter Alain Darlan), p. 56; Captain A.G. Méric to General Voruz, June 8, 1K130/12; Marc Bloch, trans. Gerard Hopkins, *Strange Defeat: A Statement of evidence written in 1940*, New York, 1968, (Bloch), pp. 18–19; Captain W.G. Tennant, Address to Dunkirk 1940 Veterans Association, May 1961, LHC, TEN/21; Nicholas Harman, *Dunkirk: The Patriotic Myth*, New York, 1980, p. 199.

20 The mass of War Office and other relevant telegrams and notes for June 1 are in WO167/41, WO106/1693, 1697, 1742, WO202/4 and 5, CAB104/241, CAB21/1184, Prem3/175; Joslen, June 1, CAB44/68; the French telegrams are in 27N78/3, 27N81, 1K130/7; Rapport du Capitaine du Pontavice . . . sur les événements survenus du 31 Mai 1940 au 4 Juin 1940 [10 June], 28N6/12; Chiefs of Staff meeting, June 1, COS(40)162, CAB79/4; G. Delater, *Avec la 3ᵉ DLM et le Corps de Cavalerie* (Grenoble, 1946), pp. 158–9.

21 WM151(40), June 1, CAB65/7 ("a lamentable story," Chamberlain commented on Gort's account, "of French incompetence and lack of direction," [Diary, June 1]; "a thrilling account," he told his sister, "There seems to have been hardly any mistake that the French did not make. . . . Their generals were beneath contempt and with some notable exceptions the soldiers would not fight and would not even march. The Belgians were better but not steady and in short as usual the brunt of all the hard fighting and the hard work fell upon the British." [Letter to Hilda, June 1, University of Birmingham, Neville Chamberlain Papers]).

22 COS(40) 162, CAB79/4; Spears to Ismay, June 2, CAB21/1282; Spears, Notes: Winston on Phone, Saturday, 1 [June], late afternoon, Churchill

College, Spears papers; Spears, 2: 2–10; Churchill to Weygand, June 1 Prem3/175; Barratt to Newall, June 1, AIR8/287; Lamoureux, Notes de guerre, June 1, unpublished MS.

23 Lelong to Weygand telegrams, June 1, 27N78/3; Odend'hal to Auphan, June 5, CO–A; Cras, *Forces maritimes*, p. 251; Madelon to Troopers, June 1, 1910 Hours, WO106/1742; Howard-Vyse to Redman, June 1, WO202/5 and CAB104/241; Weygand, Cahiers 1K130/15/16.

24 Baudouin, p. 75; Extraits . . . Notes en particulier du GA3 montrant que la possession de la ligue de la Somme a été l'une des préoccupations constantes du General Weygand en Mai 1940, May 30, 27N4/2; Doumenc, p. 289, fn 152 (Doumenc, much more than a mere executant, favoured a fighting withdrawal); [Weygand] Note pour . . . [Georges], May 31, 1280 3/FT; [Georges], Réunion à Chalons le 2 juin 1940 avec le Général Prételat et le Général Huntziger et le Général Weygand, in Alphonse Georges, Carnets, 2 June, SHAT 1K95, and 1K130/7; Banet-Rivet to Dautry, May 30, annex I in Raoul Dautry, Deposition, 16 May 1945, AN 3W280.

25 Spears to Ismay, Ismay to Spears, June 2, Spears Papers and CAB21/1282; Spears, 2: 11–16; Bryant, pp. 159–61; Baudouin, p. 75; Reynaud to Churchill, June 2, Papiers 40, GB, vol 12, Dossier Dejean; War Cabinet, WM152(40), June 2, CAB65/7; War Office telephone call to Howard-Vyse, June 2, 1915 hours, WO106/1692; Odend'hal to Guerre, June 2, 2320/D/CEMI, 27N7/7; MNF to Amirauté, June 2, 22h30, #543, II BB⁷ MN4; Cras, *Forces maritimes*, pp. 337–8; Alain Darlan, p. 57. Darlan had never been a true believer. "If we get English support, our maritime situation will certainly be improved," he wrote before the war. "But we must never forget that British interests in the whole world are immense, that if England goes to war her interests will be threatened everywhere, and that England will defend them before defending ours." Note, July 16, 1937, 1BB²187.

26 ACIGS to CIGS, June 2, WO106/1613; Koeltz note for Howard-Vyse, June 2, 1700 hours, WO202/4; Troopers from Madelon, June 2, no. 203, 1900 hrs, WO106/1742; WM152(40), Conf. annex, June 2, CAB69/13; Corbin to Daladier, June 2, tel 2296, 19h30, MAE 22 Papiers Londres A; Cras, *Forces maritimes*, pp. 338–9.

27 Landed on the long East Mole at 0045 hours, Admiral Wake-Walker noted: "There were no troops on the jetty so I went to the inner end. There I found a French Colonel with about 3000 men waiting to be told where to go. I had to stand at the end telling them that their Colonel was in my ship before they would follow." Dover Despatch A14/0/876/40, June 18, Churchill College, Somerville Papers, SMVL 7/2.

28 War Office to Vice-Admiral, Dover [for Alexander at Dunkirk], No. 140 MO4, June 2, 2040 hours, WO106/1693; Cras, *Forces maritimes*,

pp. 337–8; L. F. Ellis, *The War in France and Flanders 1939–1940*, London, 1953, pp. 240–6; Alexander, p. 79; Alexander quoted by Churchill, WM153(40), June 3, CAB65/7; La Laurencie, pp. 87–9; Fagalde, 'La bataille de Dunkerque mai–juin 1940', *Revue Militaire Suisse*, 97 (July 1952), pp. 323–41; Spears. 2: 33–41; Earl of Avon, *The Eden Memoirs*, 3 vols. (London, 1960–1965), 2:112–13.

29 Baudouin, p. 76; Vuillemin to Weygand, #3987 3/os, June 3, 1D37; [Berthelot?] Note pour le Général Tarnier, 4 June, 74AP22, also in Villelume, pp. 386–7; Paul de Branthome, 'Londres, juin – juillet 1940', *Ecrits de Paris* (July–August 1980), p. 38; Weygand to Reynaud, June 3, #582 Cab/DN, MAE Papiers Dejean/6.

30 'Western Front – British Military Policy', June 3, WP.40.189, CAB66/8; WM153(40), Conf. Annex, June 3, CAB65/13; COS(40)165, June 3, CAB79/4; Redman to Clarke, June 3, CAB104/241; Churchill to Spears, in Halifax to Campbell, June 4, 1.46 a.m., no. 288DIPP, FO371/24382.

31 Clarke to Redman, June 3, CAB104/241; COS 165(40), CAB79/4; WM153(40), June 3, CAB 65/7; Darlan, Journal, June 2–3, I BB^2 208; Cras, *Forces maritimes*, p. 340; Odend'hal to Auphan, June 5, CO–A.

32 On conditions prevailing in 1 Army hospital at Zuydcoote, hit by a 105 mm shell, June 2, Jean Lacaux, *Ambulance chirurgicale No . . .* (Grenoble, 1945), pp. 118–19.

33 Abrial Rapport; Cras, *Forces maritimes*, pp. 340–1, 407–9; Hervé Cras, *Dunkerque*, Paris 1960, (Cras, *Dunkerque*), pp. 467–79; Odend'hal to Darlan, June 5, CO–A; Frézouls, pp. 59–65; COS(40)167, June 4, CAB79/4; Ramsay to Admiralty, June 4, Lloyd to War Office, June 4, WO106/1613; *Haute Cour de Justice . . . contre Amiraux Abrial et Marquis*, 3 parts (Paris-Lyon, 1946), 3: 53; Leo Leixner, *Von Lemberg bis Bordeaux: Fronterlebnisse eines Kriegsberichters* (Munich, 1941), pp. 226–40; Edmond Perron, *Journal d'un Dunkerquois*, Dunkerque, 1977, pp. 64–8. The German officer's remark is in Régis Capponi, *Dunkerque ou la confiance trahie: chronique d'une bataille perdue, 1939–1940* (Nice, 1997), p. 7.

34 Alain Darlan, p. 57; Odend'hal to Darlan, June 5, CO–A. The Chief of Fighter Command, as Ironside noted June 4, was "much inclined to regard himself as completely outside the operations in France, which is quite impossible." *The Ironside Diaries 1937–1940*, eds. Roderick Macleod & Denis Kelly, London, 1962, p. 351.

35 Jacques Weygand, *Weygand mon père*, Paris, 1970, pp. 361–2. "I have seen Weygand twice," Dill wrote, May 27, "a great little man!" (Letter to Wavell, in John Connell, *Wavell*, 2 vols. (London, 1964), 1: 231) The notion that Weygand merely sought a scapegoat, current at the time, survives in the literature (e.g., the excellent study by Eleanor M. Gates, *End of the Affair: the Collapse of the Anglo-French Alliance, 1939–40*

[London, 1981], pp. 132–3). Pertinax, who knew so much, almost certainly misjudged the man and the motive in believing that Weygand "did not scruple to involve [Britain] in a suicide pact". Pertinax (Andre Géraud) *The Gravediggers of France*, New York, 1944, (*Gravediggers*), p. 222.

36 Swayne to author, June 25, 1961; Storm Jameson, *Journey from the North: Autobiography of Storm Jameson*, 2 vols. (London, 1969–1970), 2: 56–7; cf. the report on depressed opinion in PRO INF 1/264, June 5; Bloch, p. 71.

37 Pierre Lyet, *La Bataille de France mai–juin 1940* (Paris, 1947), p. 113; Corbin to de Margerie, 5 June, MAE, Hoppenot Papers/17 (Cf. Lord Perth's comments in this vein about Eden's failure to give credit to the French, Policy Committee, June 3, PRO INF 1/848); Alphonse Juin, *Je suis soldat* (Paris, 1960), pp. 90–1. Doumenc, though consciously presenting a more neutral account in his *Dunkerque* (Paris, 1946), p. 223, believed Franklyn's withdrawal from the Arras pocket settled the fate of the northern armies (*Papiers secrets*, p. 261); Lamoureux, Notes de guerre, June 2; Bullitt to Secretary of State, June 4, *For the President, Personal and Secret*, ed. Orville H. Bullitt, Boston, 1972, pp. 449–51.

THE AIR WAR IN FRANCE

JOHN BUCKLEY

The Western Europe campaign of 1940 stands as the pivotal and defining moment of the Second World War. The Germans achieved in May and June of that year exactly what their Imperial predecessors had failed to bring about in over four years of bloody and attritional effort. Not only did the defeat of the western Allies dramatically shape the course of the war, perhaps more so than any other campaign, it also provoked a radical and far-reaching reassessment of military operations, particularly within the humiliated British armed forces, but also in the Wehrmacht, for in many ways they were as stunned by their success as their opponents.

The air war during the summer of 1940 was decided by many factors, short- and long-term, and although some new elements were brutally and starkly demonstrated in those few weeks in May and June, the failure of Allied air power and the success of the Luftwaffe was rooted deep in the past as much as in recent revolutionary tactical and doctrinal developments. It is clear that air power provided a particular image of the summer of 1940. The popular view is of massed Luftwaffe strike forces surprising and decimating the RAF and *L'Armée de l'Air* on the ground, then spearheading the armoured columns of the Wehrmacht as they drove across France to the Channel, and always, but always, we are presented with the inevitable photographs of the Junkers Ju 87 Stuka dive-bombers. This aircraft's popular image has done more to obscure the realities of the air war over France than any other single factor and it distorted not only the popular view but also official military opinion, notably Allied. If anything defines the modern and indeed contemporary view of France 1940, it is of the partnership of Stukas and Panzers working in perfect harmony.

Naturally, the reality is far removed from this. The air war over France in 1940 and its impact on the campaign as a whole was decided

111

firstly by very limited German innovation, which was crucial on just a handful of occasions, and secondly by Allied inefficiency and inadequate long- and short-term planning. This was underscored more generally by German operational and tactical flexibility and the Allies' ossified strategic and operational state of mind. In the air as well as on the ground, the German victory was one of practical and realistic thinking and a more successful application of available resources to achieve operational aims. In contrast, Allied air power was shackled by strategic dogma, a widespread unwillingness to adapt to the circumstances of the war with which the RAF and *L'Armée de l'Air* were confronted, and patchy and uneven modernization programmes, that were to be exposed more ruthlessly than corresponding inadequacies in the Luftwaffe's force structure.

Organization and Planning

The opposing air forces in May 1940 had radically differing views of how an air campaign was likely to unfold. Their organization reflected such thinking to a limited degree, but in all cases the RAF, *L'Armée de l'Air* and the Luftwaffe went into battle in May 1940 with aircraft of mixed capabilities. The revolution in aircraft technology in the mid-to-late 1930s had prompted major re-equipment programmes with the Luftwaffe leading the way, closely followed by the RAF, with *L'Armée de l'Air* in their wake.[1]

Nevertheless, all three air forces had been pressured into accepting aircraft types considered unfit for their purpose, political and economic pressures prevailing. This fused by 1940 with differing levels of modernization and integration of new equipment. *L'Armée de l'Air* was to be caught out most clearly by this process, and in the summer of that year suffered from untested equipment and lack of training with available new aircraft types. The RAF too was unwilling to commit the latest fighter, the Spitfire, to the continent, and both they and the Luftwaffe were well aware that a number of their operational aircraft types were barely, if at all, adequate for the task in hand.

The Luftwaffe
The German air forces were and are widely regarded as being the pace-setters in doctrine and innovation in the late 1930s and early 1940s,

though principally because of their success and less because of hard evidence of revolutionary thinking. Indeed, the Luftwaffe was perhaps the one key area in which the Germans enjoyed superiority in equipment at both quantitative and qualitative levels. However, this was not so marked as is often made out and, in any case, the success of the Wehrmacht lay in its use of equipment, not the equipment itself. Notably, the Germans enjoyed no great advantage in numbers of tanks, but utilized what they had far more effectively.[2]

The strategic background and doctrinal make-up of the Luftwaffe in 1940 is one that is still swaddled in myth and misconception. Despite many highly effective works over the last two decades, the Luftwaffe is often still viewed as a mere appendage to the Army. This view cannot be sustained by the evidence.[3] The Luftwaffe was as interested and motivated by visions of strategic bombing and independent operations as the RAF, the USAAF and even *L'Armée de l'Air*. The twin-engined bombers of the late 1930s were ultimately in theory to be superseded by four-engined designs in the following decade. Indeed, early work on large strategic bombers had been abandoned not because of a change of philosophy but because of resource implications, technological shortcomings and Göring's realization that twin-engined bombers were cheaper and thus in the short-term more cost effective than four-engined designs.[4]

However, the strategic situation of the late 1930s and problems encountered in procuring strategic level air forces forced the Luftwaffe to accept an air strategy in the short-to-medium term that more closely mirrored the integrated strategic vision of Major-General Walther Wever. Wever had advocated until his death in 1936 a view of air warfare that supposedly reflected Hitler's notion of a united nation aiming for one common goal and that not to do so was contrary to the principles of national socialism. This translated to the concept of the armed forces working closely together to be successful.[5] Wever's vision ultimately resulted in the concept of the 'Operational Air War' as a means of utilizing air power to defeat an enemy state by vanquishing its armed forces. Such thinking was laid down in *The Conduct of the Air War*, published in 1935, which encapsulated the notion of the operational air war. It was to form the basis of Luftwaffe doctrine in the Second World War. It stated:

9.   The task of the Wehrmacht in war is to break the will of the enemy. The Wehrmacht is the strongest embodiment of the will

of the nation. The defeat of the enemy armed forces is therefore the most important goal in a war.

10. The task of the Luftwaffe is to serve this aim by its conduct of the air war within the framework of the grand strategy.[6]

It went on to argue that the Luftwaffe should take a wide-ranging role, supporting the army and navy as and when necessary, but also to seek ways of attacking the enemy state – its centres of industry and strength – direct. This view of how an air war would be conducted, essentially a fluid and flexible model, suited the Luftwaffe of the late 1930s well. Clearly, it allowed notions of strategic air war to be preserved and on occasion this prevailing thread surfaced, detrimentally so in the case of the willingness to switch to city bombing in September 1940 over Britain. It also fitted with the nature of Luftwaffe technology and capability in the years leading up to and during the early phase of the Second World War. The Luftwaffe was not to become a slave of doctrine in the way that perhaps we can view the RAF, but the lack of a clearly stated defining theory of war was to be their undoing when army demands escalated enormously from Barbarossa onwards. Nevertheless, the broader approach to air strategy was to serve Germany well in the operational and campaign environment of 1939–1941.

The image of the Luftwaffe as a close air support (CAS) force, nevertheless, prevails. In part this emerged from the effective deployment of small amounts of air forces at critical moments in 1940. Indeed, there is little doubt that the Luftwaffe was more proficient at CAS than the RAF and *L'Armée de l'Air* during the French campaign. The roots of these successes have perhaps two sources.

Firstly, the flexible doctrine of the Luftwaffe was demonstrated in its willingness to co-operate effectively with the army when required. Unlike the RAF, which was openly hostile to air force–army links, the Luftwaffe, though always determined to ensure its independent profile, was far more amenable to such inter-service co-operation.[7]

Secondly, the impact of the Spanish Civil War was to precipitate some limited and highly specialized and focused innovation within the Luftwaffe. Though the importance of the Civil War has been exaggerated, there is evidence that certain elements within the Luftwaffe, and indeed the Army, took on board specific lessons and proceeded to apply them in the early years of the Second World War. During the 1936–1939 period little was discovered in Spain that the Luftwaffe was not aware of, but they began to accept the value of practical experience, which in part emphasized already understood concepts of CAS dating back to 1918 and the post-World War One era.[8]

In fact, the Luftwaffe had gone to Spain hoping to test out strategic bombing theories, but circumstances dictated otherwise. Wolfram von Richthofen, initially an opponent of CAS[9] who saw little value in dive-bombing,[10] came to recognize its importance in Spain and was a prime mover in developing techniques and dealing with operational difficulties. Much of this work was begun unofficially and without sanction and was first deployed in support of Franco's Bilbao offensive. Although theoretically understood, none of the practical aspects of CAS were in place in the Luftwaffe prior to Franco's Basque campaign.[11] Problems in air-to-ground communications and vice versa were exposed. Links were put in place to deal with this, along with air liaison officers (*Fliegerverbindungsoffiziere* or 'Flivos'). Techniques in CAS bombing and targeting were developed and the crucial requirement of inter-service co-operation fully emphasized.[12] On return from Spain, Richthofen was ordered to set up Fliegerkorps z.b.V (Special Duties Air Corps) to examine CAS, and this formation was to become the famous Fliegerkorps VIII.[13]

Spain, however, prompted no major reorganization of the Luftwaffe and the impact of CAS operations was limited. Many officers mirrored their counterparts in Britain, France and the USA and believed Spain to be an interesting but hardly relevant sideshow.[14] In 1939 the Luftwaffe possessed only one flying unit dedicated to CAS, Lehrgeschwader 2, equipped with ageing Henschel Hs 123s.[15] Even the much celebrated Junkers Ju 87 Stukas were intended for wider operations than just CAS.[16] Thus, the much quoted figure of 15% of the Luftwaffe being given over to direct army support in the early stages of World War Two is somewhat misleading, as this figures includes the Ju 87s.[17] Some principles of CAS had been set down in a *Truppenfuhrung* 'Operations' manual in February 1939, and a small tactical experience unit, *Gruppe Taktische Erfahrungen*, was established to disseminate new ideas throughout the air force, but its influence was limited, and once again the Luftwaffe was to develop its CAS skills in the early stages of the Second World War by practical experience and improvisation rather than received doctrine.[18] On the eve of the war Luftwaffe Chief of Staff Hans Jeschonnek passed judgement on CAS, emphasizing its dangers and high attrition rates, particularly if the enemy enjoyed even localised air superiority. The Luftwaffe was to serve the broader aims of a campaign and CAS operations should only be undertaken in very particular circumstances when the benefits would be considerable, if not decisive.[19] It is clear that the Luftwaffe's CAS capability in 1939–1940 was limited and focused, but it was enough to be effective in the French campaign and to provide the Germans with a crucial edge over the Allies.

Other lessons of the Spanish Civil War were taken on board by the Luftwaffe and helped to shape strategy. Question marks were placed against the ability of even experienced crews to locate and hit targets in cloud or at night, and the need for seizing air superiority was clearly proven when the ratio of fighter to bombers was increased from one to three to one to two.[20] Moreover, the Luftwaffe came to believe that civil defence measures could be utilized to sustain morale during air bombardment.[21] At the very least such concerns began a process of questioning the concepts of strategic air war. Nevertheless, the Luftwaffe of 1939 was still very much predisposed to a higher view of air warfare than is commonly conceived. In the wake of the victory over Poland many within the Luftwaffe, most notably Chief of Intelligence 'Beppo' Schmid, argued for a concerted air and naval campaign against Britain rather than a head-on collision with the French army.[22] The much-discussed autumn campaign plans were also partly focused on air strategy with the desire to seize territory in the Low Countries considered essential to stymie RAF raids on the Ruhr.[23] Generally, however, the Luftwaffe was more concerned, as indeed most of the German armed forces were, in avoiding a major conflict in the autumn and winter of 1939, despite Hitler's bullying.[24]

The OKH plan of operations for the late spring and summer of 1940, which called for Army Group A to punch through the Ardennes, altered radically the role and place of air power within German planning. The Luftwaffe would now be required to play the kind of role laid down in Wever's operational air war concept. Although the Luftwaffe was still not to be tied to the army's needs, it was to play a role in shaping and influencing ground operations, be it through seizing air superiority, CAS, battlefield interdiction or morale-sapping air raids.

There is little doubt that the nature and doctrine of the Luftwaffe was better suited to the strategic environment of 1940. Its multipurpose and pragmatic approach proved to be inherently flexible and adaptable to the style of campaign thrust upon it. However, the type of operations undertaken over France and the Low Countries were not what was desired by the Luftwaffe. Despite enhanced capabilities and experience, and generally more modern equipment, the German air force was proved to be weak in a multitude of ways, and, other than in application of air resources in certain areas and circumstances, the Luftwaffe was only moderately better prepared for the style of campaign in France than its adversaries.

Allied Air Power – The RAF and L'Armée de l'Air

In 1940 Allied air power was supposedly exposed as weak, poorly equipped and inadequately constituted for modern warfare. *L'Armée de l'Air* is usually portrayed as shambolic and often hardly merits a mention in comparison with the RAF. Not that the RAF escapes lightly, as the emphasis here is all too often based on heroism in the face of overwhelming odds, the inefficiencies of aircraft, and agonizing and soul-searching over the lost years of the interwar period. However, even though there are elements of accuracy in all of these generalizations, disentangling the myths from the realities is involved. Many of the Allies' problems were self-inflicted through inappropriate strategic planning, poorly conceived doctrine and inadequate equipment, but also to blame was a general malaise in Allied leadership and an inability to use the available resources available effectively. Moreover, the overstated importance of air power in explaining the defeat of the Allies and emphasis on German tactical and operational dynamism both in the air and on the ground has concealed other issues. It is always worth noting that if the war had come a year to eighteen months earlier the RAF and even the Luftwaffe would have been caught out in the same manner as *L'Armée de l'Air*. Additionally, it should also be recalled that the RAF had spent the previous twenty years planning to fight a war quite different to that forced upon it in the summer of 1940.

These factors should not deflect any attention away from what was a disaster for *L'Armée de l'Air* and the RAF. Indeed, some have taken the view that the RAF was never fully committed to the French campaign and thus exonerated itself from too much blame. In fact, the RAF attempted to intervene and influence the campaign as best it could, in the only way it knew how. Unfortunately, its methods, doctrine and force structure were largely inappropriate for the continental commitment that Britain had undertaken.

French air power was clearly in a state of flux in the summer of 1940 and was still caught in the midst of the kind of re-equipment and modernization programmes that had prompted both the British and French Chiefs of Staff in Britain to plead, during the Munich crisis of 1938, for more time to prepare for war.[25] The French were not to be afforded that luxury.

Doctrinal wrangling was a significant factor in the disaster that awaited French air power in 1940. Throughout the interwar period, and especially after *L'Armée de l'Air* had become an independent force in 1933, army and air force leaders squabbled over how air power might be best developed to support service requirements, not that French strategy was always best served by such deliberations. The army unsurprisingly emphasized the use of air forces to screen reconnaissance aircraft and French ground forces in a manner akin to the First World War. The value of bombing operations was also being studied, but the scope envisaged was limited. In contrast, the air force attempted to emphasize the value of the air superiority battle, and in this the bomber would be the key. An aggressive air campaign would be waged against the sources of enemy air power in order to secure control of the air space over which the land battle would be fought.[26]

The confusion over the direction of French air power spilled over into procurement policy. One particular result was the disastrous BCR (Bombardment Combat Reconnaissance) aircraft, which was supposed to fulfil a variety of air power requirements, but instead led French planning and design up a cul-de-sac.[27] The adage that a horse designed by a committee would turn out as a camel is particularly apposite and the BCR has been described as a "two-engine, eight-ton, underarmed and underpowered dinosaur".[28] In general terms, without a clear goal and with an aero-industry still steeped in the practices and thinking of the past, the French were left with far too much to do by the late 1930s.

In 1937 Pierre Cot, the air minister, intervened in an attempt to bring some form of order to French air doctrine. The army's view, that *L'Armée de l'Air* should be used to deny use of French air space to the enemy, prevailed, largely because it fitted well with French national strategy. Consequently Plan V was initiated to expand fighter strength. This was still incomplete by 1940, though the fruits were beginning to become apparent. Although the essence of Plan V was not in itself misguided, it did illustrate all too vividly the defensive and reactive nature of French thinking. *L'Armée de l'Air*'s belief that the battle for air superiority required aggressive and offensive action akin to the Luftwaffe was also not without merit, though it is quite possible that it masked the French air force's desire to build a truly independent strategic air arm in the long term.[29]

Undoubtedly French air doctrine did not to serve the needs of the campaign of 1940 effectively. Its reactive stance and its notion of parcelling air units out in small quantities to provide localized air cover across the front was untenable in the face of the Luftwaffe's concentrated approach. But it was a deployment that reflected French strategic thought, one based on defence and prevention, and one that was detrimentally influenced by the army to a significant extent. The problems of the army's lack of understanding compounded with the air force's endeavours to wriggle out of the army's clutches to precipitate an unwieldy and clumsy command system that precluded effective inter-service co-operation, and it was upon the ability of the French to react to German initiatives that France's security depended.[30] These problems were hardly helped by the French Chief of Air Staff, General Vuillemin, who is described in one source as "an elderly bomber pilot not over-endowed with dynamism".[31] His conservative approach reflected the general malaise evident in much of the French military.

The RAF was better prepared for war in 1940 than its French counterpart, but not for the nature of the continental war that developed in that year. The RAF had been preoccupied with many issues in the interwar period, but thinking deeply about army support, and in particular how to influence a major campaign on the continent, had not been high on the agenda. It is clear that in judging the failure of the RAF to deal with the Luftwaffe onslaught in May 1940 it should be noted that the RAF neither sought nor expected to fight such a campaign until mere months before the outbreak of war.[32]

The RAF had established itself in the interwar years as essentially a strategic bomber force and expected a future war to be conducted without the need for ground support operations. Only a very small fraction of resources was given over to army co-operation and precisely how the RAF might influence ground operations directly was marginalized as an irrelevance – Air Staff policy maintained that the war would be decided by air strikes before ground operations became pressing. In an environment of colonial policing, financial stringency and the lack of a desire at a political level ever again to countenance a continental commitment akin to the Great War, CAS in the RAF stagnated.

To a degree this was shaped in the RAF, as in many air forces, by the 1914–1918 experience. The First World War had witnessed heavy attrition rates during CAS operations and the RAF was determined not to endure such losses of valuable aircraft and pilots in the future. The Air Ministry argued that the benefits of CAS had been outweighed by the loss.[33] By 1932 the War Office manual *The Employment of Air Forces with the Army in the Field* argued that CAS operations should be strictly limited in view of the attrition rates to be expected. However, the manual did display some prescience in stating that dedicated CAS aircraft were too vulnerable and that strafing attacks by fighters equipped with light bombs was the most effective way of carrying out ground attack operations. Such attacks, it was argued, had a debilitating effect on ground troops' morale. Fighters could of course be used in attaining air superiority and this was to remain the first call on air assets in supporting land operations.[34] In these cases the manual was to be proven correct in the Second World War. Specialized CAS aircraft were too vulnerable to enemy fighters and the swing-role fighter-bomber was to be the most effective means of offering army support. Perhaps most pertinently for the 1940 campaign the argument about air superiority seems particularly ironic.

In March 1939, in view of Britain's possible commitment to fighting on the continent again, the War Office pressed for army support air forces numbering in excess of 100 squadrons.[35] This was wholly unrealistic in the circumstances, but, when one considers the level of air support afforded to the Overlord operations, was not too wide of the mark. By November 1939 CAS policy was still drifting. The Air Ministry argued that it could find no evidence of CAS operations against a prepared enemy being effective, though what it made of the German 1918 spring offensive and the Hundred Days was not made clear.[36] It went on to argue infamously that CAS should only be applied in cases of attacking a retreating enemy, to stymie an enemy breakthrough, to cover a retreat or, in very rare cases, against a prepared enemy position.[37]

The official policy of the RAF by May 1940 was, therefore, to avoid direct air support, but it was also to underestimate the crucial nature of, at the very least, contesting air superiority. One RAF officer commented that in the interwar period "the RAF forgot how to support the army,"[38] And General Wavell noted in March 1939 that "the RAF had given little or no thought to the problem of close support of ground operations".[39] It was even claimed by the RAF that attempts to improve army–air force liaison were violating the purity of air force doctrine.[40]

How, therefore, did the RAF expect to be able to influence events on the continent? The thrust of Air Staff thinking was that the bomber force should be used to attack Germany itself, particularly the Ruhr, as 60% of Hitler's vital war plant was concentrated in that region. The French and British chiefs of staff debated this at some length in the months leading up to May 1940. The British Air Staff argued that Bomber Command should attack the Ruhr as soon as the Wehrmacht invaded the Low Countries, notably before the Luftwaffe could establish itself in Belgium and thus be in a position to intercept the RAF's bombers. They further argued that such raids would draw Germany's air assets into protecting the Ruhr and thus would support Allied ground forces. The French were unconvinced. They claimed that more immediate support was required and that attacking German industry would only be effective in the long run. Moreover, they were concerned by the prospect of retaliatory strikes by the Luftwaffe against inadequately defended French cities.[41] French fear of Luftwaffe raids had already manifested itself at the time of Munich, with the French Chief of Air Staff claiming that *L'Armée de l'Air* could offer resistance for only two weeks.[42] Additionally, a French general told the British military attaché in Paris that France's cities would be laid in ruins as they had no means of defence against concerted air assault.[43] Such concerns were still prevalent in 1939–1940. Indeed, only in April of 1940 did the French agree to the use of Bomber Command against the Ruhr, and then only against oil refineries and marshalling yards.[44] Even at this stage, the British War Cabinet continued to express concerns and retained the right to permit or block the bombing of the Ruhr.

It is worth noting that the RAF's deployment in France of the Advanced Air Striking Force (AASF) was not to support the army as much as to allow its short-ranged light bombers – Fairey Battles and Bristol Blenheims – to be able to reach Germany itself. It was considered no more than a short-term measure until longer-ranged bombers could replace them and facilitate operations direct from Britain. Consequently, the dedicated army support air forces supporting the BEF directly consisted of five squadrons of Lysanders, four squadrons of long-range reconnaissance Blenheims and four squadrons of Hurricanes (to be expanded to six on the outbreak of German aggression).[45]

It is clear that the RAF's contribution to the continental campaign was shaped by its views on the primacy and versatility of the bomber force. Bomber Command would aid the efforts of the army, but indirectly through attacking Germany, and on occasion, and if absolutely necessary, by direct air attack. Charles Portal, who became AOCinC Bomber Command on 3 April 1940, was already a fierce opponent of direct army support. He had been active in blocking the transfer of No. 2 Group (Bomber Command) to the AASF, claiming that fifty Blenheims acting on out of date information and against a well defended advancing enemy would not provide results worthy of the losses to be expected.[46] In such views he was largely supported by the CAS, Cyril Newall.

As for Fighter Command, this force, which was capable of offering considerable support to the army by contesting air superiority with the Luftwaffe, was again guided by the notions and philosophy of strategic bombing. Dowding was always concerned that his forces would be drawn into salvaging the situation in France and would be bled white by such operations, thus leaving Britain helpless should the French campaign be lost. Strategic air defence was his priority and he blocked repeatedly efforts to deploy ever greater fighter strength to the continent. Nevertheless, much of Fighter Command did find itself in combat over France, and by the close of the campaign few squadrons had not seen at least some action in support of the army, and in particular its extrication from the continent.[47]

Allied air strategy in May 1940 was therefore based on the principles of zonal air superiority fighters, long-range bombing against strategic targets and limited direct army support. Perhaps most importantly, it was for the most part reactive to German initiative, whilst lacking the ability to react quickly or decisively. The RAF had its notions of using the bomber fleet to influence the war on the ground, but was internally lacking conviction in its ability to do so, saddled as it was with much equipment that was unfit for the grand designs of the Air Staff. Moreover, the RAF had distanced itself from the practicalities of war on the continent in 1940. Admittedly, it had not had the advantage of testing its theories in the Spanish Civil War, but it is doubtful that even if it had it would have begun to question seriously its views on strategic bombing and air power in general.

Consequences – The Air Campaign
The three major air forces therefore went into battle in May 1940 with a good deal of baggage in tow. The French were still in a state of re-equipping and were shackled with an inappropriate concept of

modern air war; the British were locked into a view of air war that was to prove ultimately effective, though after much greater investment than they imagined, and the Germans, with a more limited concept of air war in the prevailing environment of 1940, were moderately better equipped to deal with the forthcoming campaign.

In terms of actual air assets on 10 May 1940, the Luftwaffe began operations with some 3500 aircraft available, including roughly 1700 bombers, of which 380 or so were dive-bombers, supported by 1200 fighters, Bf 109s and Bf 110s.[48] In addition, and for the airborne assault on the Low Countries, the Luftwaffe had some 530 transport aircraft, Junkers Ju 52s.[49] What then of the Luftwaffe's supposedly crucial and perhaps decisive role? Clearly, the first aim of the 'operational air war' doctrine, seizure of air superiority, was important and by engaging the fighter strength of the Allies in attritional battle the Luftwaffe consigned the attempts by the Allied bombers to disaster, though many losses were due to flak rather than German fighters. It should be noted, however, that the Allied air forces were not in the main caught on the ground, as was, and is, often made out. Just as in Poland, they were destroyed when they tried to intervene in the ground war.

There is no doubt that the Luftwaffe's suppression of the French 55th Division as Guderian's troops struggled across the Meuse was critically important, most obviously in panicking the French artillery. However, this was hardly representative of the Luftwaffe's CAS effort generally. Guderian had co-operated effectively with Loerzer, commanding Fliegerkorps II, and had been supported by Richthofen's specialist Fliegerkorps VIII, but, beyond the Sedan crossings, Luftwaffe CAS was sporadic and limited in effectiveness. Indeed, Rommel's 7th Panzers crossed the Meuse without air support at all. Notably, the value of CAS diminished rapidly once the war of mobility and manoeuvre began, and this epitomized the campaign after 15 May. Junkers Ju 87s were not generally used as roving artillery, as is often perceived, and when caught by Allied fighters were savagely mauled. In one incident twelve Ju 87s were downed by five French fighters for no loss.[50] Moreover, co-ordination of air and ground troops was problematic. Friendly fire incidents were not uncommon and Guderian reported how his troops, dismayed at being bombed by their own aircraft again, fired back and downed a Luftwaffe aircraft. He described this as "perhaps an unfriendly act".[51] In addition, the Luftwaffe had not been able to prevent the Allies from observing from the air the movement of troops through the Ardennes – it was fortunate for the Germans that the Allied high command failed to recognize its significance quickly enough. Finally, the air assault on the Low Countries was a disaster for the Luftwaffe with air transport assets there suffering 80% attrition.[52]

Nevertheless, the Luftwaffe had contributed to the downfall of the Allies. It had not occurred in exactly the manner envisaged by the Luftwaffe, but the seizure of air superiority had been achieved and the support offered to the Meuse crossing had been invaluable. In addition, transport aircraft helped to maintain the advantage of the breakthrough by ferrying in supplies to the spearhead troops, airbases being established to the west of the Meuse by 16/17 April.[53] Much of this fitted, to a greater or lesser extent depending on action, with the Luftwaffe's view of air operations and strategy. But the limits of German air power were soon to be exposed around Dunkirk and, later, over Britain. The flexible air doctrine was effective against poorly prepared opponents but RAF Fighter Command had been designed to defeat an attack by the Luftwaffe and was to demonstrate the Luftwaffe's shortcomings. Even in victory in France the Luftwaffe had suffered badly, enduring a 36% loss rate,[54] though this was not a dissimilar rate to that of the panzer arm, which itself lost 30%.[55] Importantly, this was a rate Göring's force could not sustain and the defeat over Britain should be viewed as the final part of a five-month campaign conducted by the Luftwaffe.

For the French campaign, the British could call upon, in addition to the BEF Air Component, the ten squadrons of Battles and Blenheims of the AASF supported by four squadrons of Hurricanes.[56] L'Armée de l'Air could in theory call upon upwards of 5000 aircraft, but the vast majority were obsolete and unusable in the frontline. The French fighter arm may have achieved a total of around 750–800 modern types, although the majority were still Morane-Saulnier 406s, described as underpowered and underarmed in one source.[57] In bombers, however, the French could muster only some 150 modern types, although the quality of such aircraft was competitive with Luftwaffe models. Perhaps the most significant failing of French air units was in operational readiness and logistical support, for sortie rates in units lagged well behind their British and German contemporaries. Daily sortie rate per fighter per day was 0.9, while Luftwaffe and RAF fighters were flying on average 4.0 sorties per day per aircraft.[58] The French modernization programme was in part responsible and ready rates in squadrons in transition ran at only 40%.[59]

The essential problem for the Allies was that their effective air units were rapidly swamped. RAF Hurricanes were simply outnumbered and were constantly kept in action by the Luftwaffe to prevent their use elsewhere. Losses soon mounted, however, and the axiom of modern air war that attrition rates are always excessive was soon being hammered home. The greatest losses came during the Allies' attempts to intervene against the Germans' Meuse crossings. A wave of RAF and L'Armée de l'Air attacks came to nothing and suffered appalling casualties, largely due to low-level attack runs, lack of fighter escorts, heavy flak defences and the inadequacies of the bombers employed, particularly the Fairey Battle. The RAF suffered its heaviest single major operational loss rate ever over Sedan, some 62%.[60] The RAF soon switched to higher-altitude bombing and in the case of the AASF to night bombing. This reduced loss rates dramatically. During daylight operations from 10 to 14 May the AASF suffered 50% loss rates; during nighttime operations from 20 May to 4 June losses fell away to 0.5%, though accuracy and effectiveness decreased also.[61] The enforced relocation of the AASF south of the Aisne did nothing to help and from the 16 to 19 May the AASF played only a limited role. The Air Component was withdrawn from the continent effectively by the 21st, leaving almost 200 Hurricanes to be abandoned. Indeed, only seventy-five were destroyed or written off during the fighting on the continent.[62]

What then of Allied planning? There is little doubt that the RAF's vision of how the continental air war would unfold had been exposed as deeply flawed. Efforts to use Bomber Command from Britain to attack the Ruhr and divert German air forces from the front had singularly failed. Not one German aircraft was so distracted. Moreover, such raids had achieved little if any material damage. The inability of the RAF, or indeed L'Armée de l'Air to contest air superiority for any length of time was a critical failure. Not surrendering air superiority was far more important to the Allies than winning it in 1940, but by under-resourcing this effort the RAF and L'Armée de l'Air handed the initiative to the Luftwaffe and were never in a position to wrestle it back.

It is clear, therefore, that a variety of long-term influences were at work in shaping the air campaign of 1940. A number of Allied and German operational decisions were important in those few weeks, it is true, but the nature of how the air war was going to unfold had been decided long before the Luftwaffe launched itself against the Allies. The Luftwaffe's limited capabilities were enough to see it home, but this was mostly because the Allies arrayed against them were weaker still in doctrine, resources and ambition.

Notes

1 See R. Overy's introduction to H. Boog (ed.), *The Conduct of the Air War in the Second World War – An International Comparison*, (Oxford, 1992).
2 R.A. Doughty, *The Breaking Point: Sedan and the Fall of France 1940* (Hamden, Connecticut, 1990), pp. 1–3.
3 See W. Murray, *Luftwaffe: Strategy for Defeat*, (New York, 1985); R.J. Overy, *The Air War 1939–1945*, (London, 1980).
4 W. Murray, *Luftwaffe*, p. 19.
5 K.A. Maier et al., *Germany and the Second World War – vol. II*, (Oxford, 1999), pp. 34–5.
6 Luftwaffe Dienstvorschrift 16, *Luftkriegfuhrung*, (Berlin, 1936), paragraphs 9 and 10. Altered in March 1940, but not substantially so. See also J.S. Corum, 'From Biplanes to Blitzkrieg: The Development of German Air Doctrine between the wars', *War in History*, vol. 3, no. 1, p. 97.
7 Guderian's discussions with Loerzer, commanding Fleigerkorps II, prior to the Meuse crossings are a case in point.
8 W. Murray, "The Luftwaffe Experience" in B. Cooling (Ed.), *Case Studies in the Development of Close Air Support*, (Washington, 1990), p. 76. (See Muller notes p. 3 for full ref.)
9 W. Murray, *Luftwaffe*, p. 15.
10 P. Deichmann, *Spearhead for Blitzkrieg: Luftwaffe Operations in Support of the Army 1939–1945*, (London, 1996), p. 42; E. Heinkel, *Sturmisches Leben*, (Stuttgart, 1953), pp. 331–3.
11 W. Murray, *Luftwaffe*, p. 15.
12 Air Ministry, *The Rise and Fall of the German Air Force*, (London, 1948), pp. 16–17.
13 K.H. Schulz, 'The Collaboration between the German Army and Luftwaffe: Support of the Army by the Luftwaffe on the Battlefield', *US Army MS B-791a*, p. 3.
14 R. Muller, 'Close Air Support: The German, British and American experiences 1918–1941', in W. Murray and A.R. Millett, *Military Innovation in the Interwar Period*, (Cambridge, 1996), p. 162.
15 Generalstab 8. Abteilung, 'The Development of the German Ground Attack Arm and Principles governing its Operations to the End of 1944',

December 1944, Air Historical Branch translation, No. VII/14, p. 4.

16 H. Boog, *Die deutsche Luftwaffenfuhrung 1935–1945*, (Stuttgart, 1982), p. 578.

17 K.H. Volker, Die Deutsche Luftwaffe 1933–1939, (Stuttgart, 1967), p. 189.

18 P. Deichmann, *op. cit.*, p. 54.

19 R. Muller, *op. cit.*, p. 163.

20 W. Murray, *Luftwaffe*, p. 16.

21 Intelligence report by Major F.L. Fraser based on trip to Berlin, Air Raid Precautions Department, 19/7/37, CAB 63/14.

22 'Proposal for Conduct of Air War Against Britain', German Air Force Operations Staff (Intelligence), 22/11/39, Air Historical Branch (AHB) translation, no. VII/30.

23 H. Trevor Roper, *Blitzkrieg to Defeat: Hitler's War Directives*, (London, 1965), p. 13 – Directive No. 6, 9/10/39.

24 Maier et al, *Germany and the Second World War* – volume II, p. 242.

25 P. Facon, 'The High Command of the French Air Force and the problem of rearmament 1938–9 – A Technical and Industrial Approach', in H. Boog (ed.), *The Conduct of the Air War in the Second World War – An International Comparison*, (Oxford, 1992), pp. 154–8.

26 M. Forget, 'Co-operation between Air Force and Army in the French and German Air Forces during the Second World War" in H. Boog (ed.), *The Conduct of the Air War in the Second World War*, pp. 422–4.

27 P. Vennesson, 'Institution and Air Power: The Making of the French Air Force', in J. Gooch, (ed.), *Airpower: Theory and Practice*, (London, 1995), pp. 49–51.

28 E. Cohen and J. Gooch, *Military Misfortune: The Anatomy of Failure in War*, (London, 1990), p. 227.

29 See P. Vennesson, *op. cit.* for more on this.

30 J. Terraine, *The Right of the Line – The RAF in the Second World War*, (London, 1985), p. 120.

31 A. Horne, *To Lose a Battle*, (London, 1969), p. 71.

32 W. Murray and A.R. Millett, *Military Effectiveness*, vol. II, (London, 1988), p. 99.

33 Air Ministry, *The Second World War 1939–45, RAF, Air Support*, (London, 1955), p. 9 in Muller p. 165.

34 War Office, *The Employment of Air Forces with the Army in the Field*, (London, 1932).

35 AHB Narrative II/117/5(A), pp. 72–3.

36 Air Ministry, *op. cit.*, p. 10.

37 Ibid.

38 J. Terraine, *op. cit.*, p. 383.

39 J. Connell, *Wavell: Scholar and Soldier*, (New York, 1965), p. 204.

40 J.M. House, *Towards Combined Arms Warfare: A survey of 20th century tactics, doctrine and organization*, (Fort Leavenworth, 1984), p. 47.

41 D. Richards, *The Royal Air Force 1939–1945 – volume I: The Fight at Odds*, (London, 1953), pp. 110–12.

42 P. Stehlin, *Temoignage pour l'Histoire*, (Paris, 1964), pp. 86–91.

43 Col. Fraser to Phipps, 23/9/38, CAB 24/279.

44 D. Richards, *op. cit.*, p. 112.

45 J. Terraine, *op. cit.*, pp. 123–4.

46 AHB Narrative II/117/(5)A, pp. 173–4.

47 See R. Wright, *Dowding and the Battle of Britain*, (London, 1969), for a full account of Dowding's role, though temper it with Terraine's more balanced version in *The Right of the Line*.

48 AHB Translation No. VII/107, "Luftwaffe strength and serviceability tables Aug 1938 to April 1945", derived from records of VI Abteilung Quartermaster General's Department of German Air Ministry; R. Hallion, *Strike from the Sky: The History of Battlefield Air Attack 1912–1945*, (Washington, 1989), p. 136.

49 W. Murray, *Luftwaffe*, p. 54.

50 R. Hallion, *op. cit.*, p. 146.

51 H. Guderian, *Panzer Leader*, (London, 1952), p. 113.

52 W. Murray and A.R. Millett, *A War to be Won – Fighting the Second World War*, (Cambridge and London, 2000), p. 68.

53 General Halder's diary entry for 16/5/40, *Kriegstagebuch*, volume I, edited by Hans-Adolf Jacobsen, (Stuttgart, 1964).

54 W. Murray, *Luftwaffe*, p. 40.

55 H. Guderian, *op. cit.*, p. 75; Maier et al., *Germany in the Second World War*, c.p. 294.

56 D. Richards, *op. cit.*, p. 108.

57 W. Gunston, *Encyclopaedia of Combat Aircraft*, (London, 1976), p. 166.

58 R. Hallion, *op. cit.*, p. 144.

59 P. Buffolt and J. Ogier, 'L'Armée de l'Air Française dans la campagne de France (10 Mai to 25 Juin 1940), *Revue Historique des Armées*, volume II, no. 3, pp. 88–117.

60 D. Richards, p. 120.

61 D. Richards, p. 127.

62 D. Richards, p. 126.

THE ROYAL NAVY'S ROLE
IN THE CAMPAIGN

ROBIN BRODHURST

If you were to ask the average schoolchild what the role of the Royal Navy was in the Battle of France in 1940 I suspect that you would get a rather surprised look and after a deal of thought the word "Dunkirk" would come up. That, of course, would be all, and anyway "it was all done by civilians in little boats" and the Royal Navy had made little contribution. Like all such comments there is a grain of truth in this, and I suspect that if Sellar and Yeatman had progressed beyond the "full stop" of 1918 when America became Top Nation, then their account of 1940 would have been something like that of my pupils. I would *not* suggest that the Royal Navy played a key role in the battle of 1940, except in the evacuation from Dunkirk, but I *would* suggest that it played a more important role than that for which most historians usually give it credit. It is important to remember that the Royal Navy was fighting a war from 3 September 1939, whereas the RAF was for much of the time dropping propaganda leaflets and refusing to bomb private property, and the Army was not involved in any fighting until the spring of 1940.

One of the first things that the Royal Navy had to do in the war was to deliver the Expeditionary Force across the Channel to France. The W Plan, devised by Lieutenant Colonel Hawes after Munich[1] and put into effect on 3 September 1939, must rank as one of the most successful operations in the whole war. As the Official History tells us "By 27th September the Royal Navy with shipping of the Mercantile Marine under their control had moved to France, without the loss of a single life,

152,031 army personnel
9,392 air force personnel

21,424 army vehicles
 2,470 air force vehicles
36,000 tons of ammunition
25,000 tons of motor spirit
60,000 tons of frozen meat

in addition to other stores, equipment and supplies."[2] The success of this has often been overlooked and Roskill is even more blasé about it, giving it little more than a paragraph in his Official History.[3] However, if German U-boats and/or minefields had interfered with the movement it could have had disastrous consequences. Throughout the period of the Phoney War the Royal Navy was busy convoying supplies and reinforcements across the Channel, usually to Brest, St. Nazaire and Nantes, which became the principal supply bases of the BEF, while using Calais, Boulogne etc. for leave movements, which started in December.

Despite the ease and success of this initial movement the Royal Navy had, as previously noted, actually been fighting since 3 September 1939 and involved in a major campaign since 8 April in Norway. The Norway campaign is important in that it resulted in damage to major units of the German Navy. Neither of their battleships was yet ready for service and their two battlecruisers had both been damaged and were out of action for at least six months. Their cruiser force was reduced to two ready for service and there was a maximum of only ten destroyers. U-boat strength was between forty and fifty. This was not a sufficient strength to interfere in either our lines of communications to France or in the evacuation from France. It meant that the Home Fleet did not have to deploy its main strike force in the southern waters of the North Sea where they would almost certainly have been vulnerable to German airpower. The Norwegian campaign had two other important effects. Firstly, it brought home to the Royal Navy (at least to those afloat) the vulnerability of their ships to enemy air attack, in particular in the enclosed waters of the Norwegian fiords. Secondly, as we all know, it precipitated the Parliamentary debate that forced Chamberlain out of office and propelled Churchill across Horse Guards from the Admiralty to 10 Downing Street.

Having introduced Churchill to centre stage it is important to look both at him and at the other key personnel in the Royal Navy who people this episode. With Churchill at No. 10, although still living at the Admiralty, there was a new First Lord from 10 May: A.V. Alexander. Albert Victor is a much maligned individual, not least by the new biographer of the First Sea Lord, but he did a stout job in looking after the interests of the Royal Navy, and in backing up his Sea Lords. He was not interested in the operational matters, or at least he was not allowed to become involved in them as the more forceful Churchill had done with such controversial results in the Norwegian campaign. The professional head of the Royal Navy was Admiral of the Fleet Sir Dudley Pound, not the first choice for this demanding post, but in June 1939 the only realistic choice. He had had a brilliant career, culminating in the command of the Mediterranean Fleet from March 1936 to June 1939, when he had delivered over to Andrew Cunningham as well-tuned a weapon of war as it was possible to find. He was used to the corridors of Whitehall, having served there in every rank since being a Commander in 1909, alternating with sea-going appointments. He had been Assistant Director of Plans, Director of Operations, Director of Plans, Assistant Chief of Naval Staff and Second Sea Lord, and was recognized as an outstanding staff officer.

The second key naval officer was the Flag Officer, Dover, Vice Admiral Bertram Ramsay. He had had an equally outstanding career as a young officer, culminating in the excellent posting in 1935 as Chief of Staff to the C-in-C Home Fleet, Sir Roger Backhouse. Sir Roger, who became First Sea Lord in 1938, before dying in June 1939, was an inveterate centralizer and in 1935, after three months, Ramsay resigned rather than continue in what he saw as an impossible and useless job. He went on to the retired list and was occasionally used by the Admiralty to do odd jobs. One of these had been after the mobilization of the Royal Navy during the Munich crisis in 1938 to report on the condition of Dover as an operational base, which led to a large programme of re-equipment and the earmarking of Ramsay for the command of Dover in wartime. He was appointed to Dover in September 1939, although still on the retired list and, while initially subordinate to C-in-C Nore, by October he was reporting directly to the Admiralty. He was an austere Scot, of very high professionalism and great personal warmth once an initial reserve was penetrated, who was to become, by most accounts, the outstanding Admiral of the Royal Navy in the war, before tragically dying in 1945 in an air crash.

Early on during the war, in fact as early as October 1939, when an

131

attack on the Low Countries had seemed imminent, the Royal Navy had prepared plans for operations off the coast of Holland and Belgium. The aim of these plans was clearing allied shipping from the threatened ports and bringing home diplomatic staffs and other important people, while preventing the enemy capturing the port installations intact. These plans were put into effect as early as 10 May when the Dutch gold reserves and diamond stocks were embarked for passage to England. By 14 May the entire Dutch government had also been embarked and all allied shipping cleared away, while oil reserves had been destroyed. Similar actions were taken in Antwerp by 17 May. The Royal Navy in the persons of the Royal Marines had also taken part in OPERATION ROYAL MARINE in which, starting on 10 May, 2,300 floating mines were streamed into the Rhine, Moselle and Meuse rivers, causing some damage to enemy shipping. However, these were minor footnotes to the main campaign.

It was not until 20 May that plans were started for a possible evacuation of the BEF from the continent. Ramsay on that day took all possible advance steps to organize the necessary personnel ships. Boulogne was evacuated on the night of 23–24 May by destroyers, and an extraordinary action took place with the destroyers *Wild Swan*, *Venemous* and *Venetia*, each carrying 1,000 men, backing out of the port while engaging German tanks, guns and machine-guns over open sights at a range of only a few hundred yards. Ramsay and his command learned a number of crucial lessons from the Boulogne evacuation. Firstly that discipline ashore was critical for an orderly evacuation. (The performance of the Welsh and Irish Guards here was immaculate.) Secondly that darkness was also critical to blunt German air power and blind their gunners, so allowing more men to be got away. Lastly, as had been learned in Norway, the need for air cover had been again demonstrated.

On 26 May at 6.57 p.m. Pound gave the order for OPERATION DYNAMO to begin. The aim was to lift 45,000 men in two days. Pound sent his own Chief Staff Officer, Captain William Tennant, to work under Ramsay as Senior Naval Officer, Dunkirk, and Tennant and the newly appointed Rear Admiral, Dover, W.F. Wake-Walker, were the two key men on the spot who ran the organization of the evacuation. There is no need to tell the story of the Dunkirk evacuation, it has been told often enough recently, and I commend to you the 1958 Ealing Studios film *Dunkirk*[4], with Corporal John Mills of the Royal Engineers being on the beach with the civilians Dickie

Attenborough and Bernard Lee, but then being evacuated from the South Mole by the Royal Navy.

There are five factors that explain the success of the evacuation. Firstly the weather. Any form of choppy weather would have stopped many of the small boats working at all and evacuation from the beaches in a heavy surf would have been well nigh impossible, but almost throughout the course of OPERATION DYNAMO the sea was calm. In 1588 "God blew and they were scattered"; in 1940 God did not blow and they were saved. Secondly was simply a question of lifting capacity. The final figures of lifted personnel are still remarkable reading: 366,162 men. To carry these men nearly 900 ships passed under Ramsay's control, of which 230 were trawlers and drifters, and 203 private motor boats, the famed "little ships". However, it was the fifty-six destroyers who lifted one third of the personnel evacuated. Pound gave Ramsay thirty-nine extra destroyers, one fifth of the Royal Navy's remaining destroyer strength. Given Britain's worldwide commitments, this was a brave decision and one that Pound obviously worried over. On 29 May he withdrew all the fleet destroyers from the Dover Command, as they were essential for the protection of the Atlantic convoys, leaving Ramsay with mainly 1914–1918 vintage ships. In fact he rescinded this order after very strong representations from Ramsay the next day, but it shows the difficulty the Admiralty faced in balancing commitments. Pound could well feel justified in his worries, as the final results from a naval point of view were much the same as in a major engagement: nine destroyers sunk and nineteen badly damaged. The Royal Navy destroyer strength world-wide was reduced to seventy-four.

The third factor was the work of Tennant and Wake-Walker. Tennant made the critical decision that the major point of embarkation was not to be the beaches but the port, and he also made the decision to use the East Mole, and so increased the nightly lift capacity. Wake-Walker commanded afloat and had two flagships sunk under him. He provided the link between Ramsay and Tennant when radio failed, as it often did. Both Tennant and Wake-Walker went on to have extremely good wars and command cruiser squadrons, Tennant after having *Repulse* sunk under him in December 1941. They were nobly supported by the naval shore parties who took control both in the harbour and on the beaches, and who brought a measure of discipline to what on occasion was an undisciplined rabble, occasionally at the point of a pistol.

Fourthly was the role of Vice Admiral Sir James Somerville, whose part in the Dunkirk saga is so often ignored. Somerville had been mistakenly retired from the Royal Navy in 1939 with suspected tuberculosis. He had been appointed to the Admiralty to the gloriously named job of Inspector of Miscellaneous Weapons and Devices. He had gone over to Calais on 25 May in response to a demand from Churchill. Brigadier Nicholson had reported that his anti-tank guns could not stop the German tanks and Churchill had directed that naval 12-pounders should be mounted on lorries at Portsmouth and sent over to Calais by train ferries from Folkestone.[5] On his return to Dover he met up with his old friend Ramsay and relieved him for the forenoon of 26 May, allowing Ramsay to get some sleep. On return to the Admiralty he suggested to Pound that he return to Dover to alternate with the desperately overworked Ramsay in taking command of the evacuation. Pound agreed and Somerville

> managed that most difficult of things, taking over the running of an unplanned and frantic operation at odd hours without ever threatening the authority of the commander, or allowing any break in the pattern or style of orders to be seen.[6]

Ramsay, in his Report on DYNAMO wrote:

> The attributes of this officer for initiative and resource are well known throughout the Service, but I venture to suggest the opinion that never in the course of his long and distinguished career have they been put to better use than during the operations for the evacuation of the Allied Armies from Dunkirk.[7]

Lastly, there was Ramsay himself, who towers over the history of the Royal Navy in the Second World War alongside Pound and Cunningham. Indeed his performance here ranks alongside Cunningham's at Crete where they held their commands together by sheer force of personality, taking, as it were, the whole weight of the worries and agonies on to their own shoulders and sending back out again ships that were desperately tired. To give an example of Ramsay's mind, here is a quotation from a letter to his wife written at 0100 on 27 May:

> I have on at the moment one of the most difficult and hazardous operations ever conceived and unless *le bon Dieu* is very kind

there will be certain to be many tragedies attached to it. I hardly dare to think about it & what the day is going to bring with it. . . . How I would love to cast off the mantle of responsibility which is mine & become just peaceful & retired once again. . . . Poor Morgan [his Chief of Staff] is terribly strained & badly needs a rest. Flags looks like a ghost. . . . All my staff are completely worn out & yet I see no prospect at all of any let up. . . . As for my ships they have not a moment's rest unless they are damaged badly.[8]

Ramsay's performance at Dover from 1939 to 1942 ensured that he was chosen to plan the invasion of North Africa and then command the forces that successfully invaded Italy and eventually Normandy. He is, in the view of many naval historians, the greatest all-round admiral in the Royal Navy of the Second World War. Many would like to see a bust of him in Trafalgar Square alongside Jellicoe, Beatty and Cunningham.

There is one other matter that ought to detain us, if only briefly, and that is discussion of the RAF and their performance over the beaches. Many personal accounts of the evacuation make some reference to the lack of air cover provided[9] and there was much ill feeling at the time. Ramsay even mentioned it in his own official despatch. However, that is a simplistic view and it needs to be placed in its proper perspective. Careful study of the figures and of the losses suffered by the Luftwaffe shows that the contribution of Fighter Command to the success of the evacuation was considerable. Between 26 May and 4 June fighter aircraft flew a total of 4,822 hours over Dunkirk and 106 of their number were lost. Fifty-eight enemy aircraft were shot down over Dunkirk, and seventy-five more in areas affecting the evacuation. The Air Ministry's comment on Ramsay's despatch that "It was not to be expected that all air action would be visible from points on the coast" must be accepted as a fair answer to all those who felt that too little had been done to protect them from German bombers.[10]

It is usually forgotten that there was a large number of troops of the BEF still in France after the Dunkirk evacuation. There were two fighting divisions south of the Somme, 1st Armoured and 51st Highland, as well as 150,000 men and women employed on bases and lines of communication. OPERATION ARIEL is less well known than OPERATION DYNAMO, but was no less effective if less dramatic. It rescued nearly 200,000 British and Allied troops along with a considerable quantity of equipment and transport. The black spot for British arms here was at St. Valery where Rommel's 7th Panzer Division caught the 51st Highland Division as it awaited embarkation from the beaches and the port throughout the night of 10–11 June. Sadly no ships appeared and the division went into captivity, the only occasion in this campaign where a considerable body of troops fell back to the sea but could not be rescued. In fact over 200 vessels of all sizes were assembled, but fog made it impossible to control them as most had no wireless. Only at the eastern end of the perimeter, at Veules les Roses, were any number successfully evacuated, and then under heavy shellfire. 2,137 British and 1,184 French troops were rescued, but the bitter feeling remains, however ill-justified, that they were sacrificed. As late as June 2000 there was an article in *The Times* claiming that Churchill sacrificed the division in order to keep France fighting.[11]

The various evacuations were directed by Admiral James, the Commander-in-Chief at Portsmouth, and Admiral Dunbar-Nasmith, commanding Western Approaches at Plymouth. The northern ports of Cherbourg, Caen, Le Havre and St Malo were all successfully evacuated by 17 June, but there was one disaster in the otherwise successful events on the western coast. On 17 June troops were shifted by lighters out to the shipping in Quiberon Bay, from where three liners had sailed the day before, all full of troops. At 3.35 p.m. the *Lancastria* was bombed and sank, taking with her over 3,000 men. So hideous was the news that it was never made public. Churchill forbade any publication of the event, saying, "The newspapers have got quite enough disaster for today at least."[12]

The evacuations from the Biscay ports, Brest, St Nazaire, La Pallice, Nantes, Rochefort and La Rochelle, were all very hurried affairs, and more time could have been spent on the removal of stores and equipment. However, intelligence about the speed of the German advance was often exaggerated and this led to wrong decisions being made on the spot for perfectly understandable reasons. For example, on 18 June Admiral Dunbar-Nasmith was told that there were 8,000 Polish troops approaching St Nazaire, who had to be evacuated, with the Germans in close pursuit. So he despatched six destroyers and seven transporters to fetch them. In fact only 2,000 appeared and the Germans were not close behind them. Thus much shipping was needlessly risked.[13] There were also many civilian refugees evacuated from southern French ports, mainly to Gibraltar and then back to the UK. A further 22,656 persons were evacuated safely from the Channel Islands between 19 and 23 June. Adding all these figures together it is possible to come to a figure of 368,491 British troops and 189,541 Allied troops evacuated and somewhere between 30 and 40,000 other British subjects as well. Furthermore, though much equipment was needlessly abandoned, no less than 310 guns, 2,292 vehicles and 1,800 tons of stores were also saved.[14]

It is fair to ask why the Germans did not interfere more effectively with these later evacuations. Certainly well-deployed submarines could have played havoc with many of the unescorted troopships leaving the Biscay ports. The Luftwaffe did perform quite well, the *Lancastria* being their biggest victim. However, the fact remains that a large number of unescorted transports did reach safety in British ports which the Germans should have sunk, and much of the Biscay coast was out of the range of RAF fighter cover. It is an early example of the inability of the Germans to co-ordinate their aircraft and their naval forces effectively.

In searching for a conclusion to all this I cannot do better than to quote the official historian of the *War At Sea*, Captain Stephen Roskill:

> But it was not only for the rescue of the soldiers that these operations deserve to be remembered. The psychological impact upon the free peoples was immense, for it had been shown that Hitler's all-conquering armies could be denied the full fruits of their land victories by the skilful and determined application of maritime power. In the United States, whose President and people had been watching with breathless absorption the progress of the struggle in Europe, the effects were profound and undoubtedly contributed to the readiness with which great and generous help was soon to be given to a sorely pressed but wholly determined Britain.[15]

The success of the evacuations was primarily due to the professionalism of the Royal Navy, the decision-making of their middle management in the persons of Ramsay, Tennant and Wake-Walker, and the undoubted bravery of the crews of the small ships, both regular navy and civilian, who again and again put their lives in danger and hazarded their ships in order to evacuate the Army. It is no wonder that politicians so often appeal to the Dunkirk spirit.

137

Notes

1 Major General L.A. Hawes, CBE, DSO, MC, The Story of the "W" Plan, *Army Quarterly*, Vol. 101, No. 4, July 1971.
2 Major L.F. Ellis, *The War in France and Flanders, 1939–1940*, HMSO, 1953, p. 15.
3 Captain S.W. Roskill, *The War At Sea, 1939–45*, Vol. I, HMSO, 1954, p. 63.
4 *Dunkirk*, 1958, Ealing Studios, co-financed by MGM, screenplay by W.P. Lipscomb and David Divine, music by Malcolm Arnold.
5 M. Simpson (Ed.), *Somerville Papers*, Naval Records Society, 1995, pp. 28–9.
6 M. Stephen, *The Fighting Admirals*, Leo Cooper, 1991, p. 60.
7 Somerville Papers, p. 33.
8 RMSY 8/10, Churchill College, Cambridge.
9 For example, Anthony Rhodes, *Sword of Bone*, Faber & Faber, 1942 and John Horsfall, *Say not the Struggle*, The Roundwood Press, 1977.
10 Roskill, p. 218.
11 *The Times*, 4 June 2000.
12 W.S. Churchill, *The Second World War* (1949), Vol. II, p. 172.
13 Ellis, p. 304.
14 Roskill, p. 239.
15 Roskill, p. 240.

BRITISH HIGH COMMAND AND THE REPORTING OF THE CAMPAIGN

STEPHEN BADSEY

British Press reporting of the dramatic events of 10 May to 4 June 1940 provided the opportunity for myths to flourish which coloured the British view of the battle for some years. In turn, this was a direct result of the very confused policy of the Chamberlain government towards the Press during the 'Phoney War'. A Ministry of Information (MoI), in preparation for four years, was activated in September 1939, only for Chamberlain to appoint the ineffectual Lord Macmillan as minister.[1] Consequently, as the BEF deployed to France in early September 1939, the MoI caused chaos among British newspapers by vacillating on whether this move could be reported, including a police raid on Fleet Street on 12 September to hold up newspaper distribution. "The rage and fury of the newsmen passes all bounds," noted Harold Nicolson.[2] Despite two changes of minister within the next eight months, the MoI would not recover from this bad start for another two years.

Clause 21 of the Licence and Agreement between His Majesty's Postmaster General and the BBC allowed for the stations of the BBC "to be taken possession of in the name and on behalf of His Majesty" in case of emergency.[3] Chamberlain was credited, at least among journalists, with the more extreme view that "broadcasting had no part to play in modern war, and should cease as soon as war broke out".[4] Instead, the BBC retained its notional independence, while in practice coming under greater government control.[5] Far from having no place in the war, radio broadcasting became the dominant British news medium, the BBC 9 o'clock evening news reaching between 43 and 50 per cent of the population, and far outstripping any newspaper.[6] Twice-weekly cinema newsreels also remained popular, although more as a form of entertainment than news.

On the war's outbreak the BBC closed down its television service and the nation's cinemas, theatres and concert halls were also briefly closed down for fear of air raids, although rapidly re-opened. To avoid providing homing beams for enemy aircraft the BBC consolidated its regional radio transmissions into a single Home Service. As a sign of its new importance, a single radio receiver was allowed for the first time within Parliament itself, located in Committee Room 11.[7] For overseas listeners an Empire Service had been running since 1932, described by the BBC itself as intended for those "more Blimpish than Colonel Blimp himself", and definitely unsuitable for Americans.[8] A European Service in a variety of languages began broadcasting in January 1940.

The Chamberlain government was generally reluctant to communicate any information to anyone, including its own people, and was deeply committed to the idea that Britain should not engage in propaganda.[9] What exactly this meant was not clear, except that 'propaganda' was distinctly un-British and included having properly organized war reporting. *The New Statesman and Nation* (the weekly journal of middlebrow Socialism) in May 1940 condemned the German practice of having "writers and journalists with military training formed into Propaganda Companies to accompany the troops" as the very antithesis of British values.[10]

War reporting, whether from the BEF or from Britain and other countries, was a low priority compared with maintaining the right tone in the media. The MoI guidelines, drawn up on 18 September 1939, were that for the period of the Phoney War they must "fill the French and English papers, but particularly the French papers, with fraternization stories and human interest stories about the English in France. Only in that way will the awkward period be covered."[11] Senior British officers were deeply pessimistic about the chances of victory should the Germans attack.[12] Among their biggest fears was that the morale of British troops overseas or civilians at home might succumb either to German propaganda or to sheer boredom, and they viewed the media's role as to keep that morale as high as possible by providing good news.[13]

As a consequence of this attitude, the BEF left for France with no war correspondents accompanying it, and not until mid-October did it create a Directorate of Public Relations.[14] At BEF General

Headquarters (GHQ) in Arras the correspondents who followed were lodged in various hotels, with a Press Centre established at the Hôtel de l'Universe. This former 18th Century convent was remembered by Bernard Gray of the *Daily Mirror* as noteworthy for its "extraordinarily bad service and extraordinarily good looks of a young waitress" (her name was Yvonne), with "its bedrooms as cold as the attitude of the management".[15] Copying First World War practice, Public Relations came under the Intelligence Branch of the BEF, headed by the Director of Military Intelligence (DMI) Major-General Noel Mason-Macfarlane (known to all as 'Mason-Mac'). The brother-in-law of Lieutenant-General Sir Ronald Adam (who commanded III Corps of the BEF), Mason-Macfarlane was a highly political soldier who had spent the pre-war years as a military attaché in several European countries including Germany, and had once offered personally to shoot Hitler. One of his staff officers, Major Ewan Butler, has left a deeply admiring pen-portrait of the 50-year-old general as convivial, hospitable, outspoken, near-crippled and probably impotent from old sporting and war injuries, and compensating by excessive indulgence in Armagnac, tobacco and temper. Naturally, Butler adds that "his relations with the Press were particularly cordial".[16]

While it was unusual for the DMI to be so directly involved with the Press, Mason-Macfarlane does seem to have built up a genuine rapport with some journalists; Charles Graves of the *Daily Mail* and Bernard Gray of the *Daily Mirror* were both admirers. He also helped the BBC (as did Field Marshal Lord Gort, the BEF's commander) with the creation in January 1940 of a Forces Service.[17] Prior to this many soldiers had tuned to a French station run by Radio Luxembourg (which had itself closed down at the war's start) called *Fécamp Radio International*, advised by a 'BEF Wireless Entertainment Committee' chaired by Field Marshal Lord Birdwood, the veteran First World War army commander.[18]

War correspondents at Arras held the honorary rank of captain and were provided with batmen. They wore officer's uniform without rank insignia, with a Press brassard that many preferred to discard and a green-and-gold cap-badge with the letter 'C' for 'correspondent' that led to them being confused with the Church Army, or uncouth suggestions that the initials should be for 'War Correspondent'. Regulations for correspondents issued in September 1939 were essentially the same as those of 1926 (issued to take account of radio), which in turn had not changed significantly since 1918.[19] Other than Lord Birdwood, several of those involved with the Press were also First World War veterans returned to service, including the Chief Censor at the War Office, Major-General John Hay Beith (better known as 'Ian Hay', author in 1915 of *The First Hundred Thousand*). On the reporters' side was another First World War legend, the now elderly Sir Philip Gibbs, who replaced his son Anthony as war correspondent for the *Daily Sketch*; and also Evelyn Montague, son of C.E. Montague, reporting for the *Manchester Guardian*.

Arras usually had a contingent of more than twenty correspondents and about sixty came and went in the course of the Phoney War. Other than the British and Dominion journalists, those from the United States were allowed a special standing from the war's start. American legislation made it illegal for any belligerent country to engage in propaganda within the United States or directed at it, and British policy circumvented this by co-opting United States' reporters as official war correspondents.[20] Six French newspapers also had journalists with the BEF.[21] The BBC was represented at first by Richard Dimbleby, with David Howarth as producer and Harvey Sarney as sound engineer. There were also newsreel cameramen from the five major British companies, later joined by a cameraman and assistant working directly for the Army,[22] and an Army still photographer. A second, smaller group of correspondents joined the headquarters of the RAF's Advanced Air Striking Force at Rheims, based at the Lion d'Or Hôtel. These included Charles Gardner for the BBC, two newsreel cameramen, at least eight reporters from British newspapers or news services and a number of Americans, including Bill Henry of CBS.[23] There were also arrangements for small numbers of British correspondents to join the various French armies in the event of a major German offensive.

Journalists were not allowed outside Arras without a 'conducting officer', also with captain's or major's rank. These included a number of decorated First World War veterans and also the impressively wealthy Captain the Hon Harry Tufton, who was popular with reporters through having his own suite at the Ritz in Paris.[24] Military order was imposed by the Deputy Assistant Director of Public Relations, Major (later Lieutenant-Colonel) J.V. McCormack, a diminutive, competent gamecock of a man who seems to have stunned most of the reporters into accepting him as their leader. A daily Press briefing took place at the Hôtel de l'Univers, sometimes given by

Mason-Macfarlane, more usually by McCormack. As the months progressed, some of the reporters also obtained at least one interview each with Lord Gort and his senior officers.[25] Stories were cleared at the Censor's Office and telephoned through under supervision at the Post Office, until a direct-line teleprinter was supplied by the Newspaper Proprietors' Association.

Many of the correspondents complained that the British at first, and the French all the time, treated them almost as spies. Unfortunately, in one case it was true. The correspondent for *The Times* was H.A.R. 'Kim' Philby, already recruited by Soviet intelligence. According to another journalist, Philby as *The Times'* man was uniquely favoured by a weekly luncheon *à deux* with Mason-Macfarlane in person.[26] Whether Philby supplied any useful information to the Soviet Union, and whether this was passed to Nazi Germany, is not known.

Throughout the period of the Phoney War the correspondents developed a reasonable working relationship with their conducting officers. But the major problem was the French censorship. Relationships between the French Army and their own national media were considerably more hostile than in Britain and the French censors took a perverse delight in imposing arbitrary or infuriating restrictions.[27] The British organized in December 1939 a visit by their correspondents to British and French troops in the Saar region, but Dimbleby later claimed that a French conducting officer would not allow him to report that the troops he had interviewed were actually in France.[28] Particularly notorious were the daily French official communiqués and Press briefings, given at the Hôtel Continental in Paris by a Colonel Thomas, remembered by British journalists as "supported by a number of hard-faced ladies" with "small imitation scissors in their hats".[29]

Caught between British demands for good news stories and French obstinacy, the reporters either moved or were sent elsewhere, or sulkily did their jobs. Philip Gibbs even contrasted his comparative freedom in the First World War with the existing level of censorship, which he condemned as "rigid, frustrating and ridiculous", as well as protesting against reporters not being allowed to visit the front lines.[30] Philby also argued that censorship had killed his interest in war correspondence, "Besides, the idea of writing endlessly about the morale of the British Army apalled me".[31] Dimbleby and his radio team abandoned news for light entertainment, holding interviews with celebrities who visited

143

the troops. In March Dimbleby decided that he "had run out of anything to say about the war" and asked for a transfer. He was sent to Cairo in April, being replaced by Bernard Stubbs.[32] On 10 May both Philip Gibbs and the British United Press correspondent, Richard Macmillan, were in London; while Philby was elsewhere for two days, probably in Paris.[33]

Given the confusion of the reporters when the German attack came and the almost surreal world in which they found themselves for the next few days, it is convenient to review the actual sequence of events. On 10 May the German attack began on the Netherlands and Belgium with air and ground forces, and both countries abandoned their neutrality. The BEF, together with French First Army and the rest of the First Group of Armies, moved to its pre-planned positions in Belgium, completing the move by 12 May. Next day the battle took an utterly unexpected turn for the Allies as German armoured forces in strength crossed the River Meuse into French territory between Sedan and Dinant, having passed through the Ardennes forest of Luxembourg and southern Belgium meeting little resistance. This was the beginning of the main German attack, driving westward across France. On the morning of 15 May the Netherlands surrendered and Winston Churchill (who had become Prime Minister on 10 May) was telephoned by French Prime Minister Paul Reynaud, who informed him that the battle was lost. On 17 May the BEF, together with the French forces in Belgium, began an orderly retreat under pressure from the Germans to their front, but it was never subect to a major German attack. The leading German armoured forces to the South reached the English Channel at Abbeville on 20 May, cutting the BEF off from its reserve supplies, fuel and ammunition. On 25 May Lord Gort made a critical decision to give up any idea of attacking and to withdraw the BEF to what was to become the Dunkirk perimeter. On 27 May Belgium surrendered to the Germans and the Dunkirk evacuation began. British fears that this would be followed by an immediate German attack across the English Channel proved groundless, but so did British hopes that France could be kept in the war after suffering such a major defeat. The Germans began their attack southwards on 4 June, British forces continued to evacuate through ports in Normandy and Brittany, and France surrendered on 22 June.

The impression gained by the correspondents of the battle was very different. Shortly after dawn on Friday 10 May a single German bomb

144

hit the Hôtel de l'Univers. By mid-morning the correspondents, like the rest of the BEF, had already been alerted that the move into Belgium would take place that afternoon.[34] Rather than travelling with the front-line divisions, they moved with the main headquarters to Lille, where a new Press Centre was established at the Hôtel Carlton. Lord Gort left his Intelligence staff at BEF rear headquarters in Arras and established his advanced command post in a village close to Lille, one of a number of small villages that he used for this purpose. Only Mason-Macfarlane as DMI moved up, together with two staff officers, Major Ewan Butler and Lieutenant-Colonel Gerald Templer (plus one aide).[35] An important clue to Gort's behaviour appears in the brief which he gave in person to the War Cabinet on the morning of Saturday 1 June, on his return from France. Gort's reasons for the BEF's predicament were that he had been let down by the fighting qualities of his allies:

> The resistance of the Belgian forces opposite the Maestricht peninsula [recte: Maastricht appendix] had collapsed almost at once. The speed of the German advance had coincided almost exactly with the estimate of the GHQ Intelligence staff. . . . [But] the French [First] Army on his right under General Blanchard had not the powers of resistance anticipated.[36]

This accords with information given to the BBC and newspapers in London (presumably in confidential or unofficial briefings) that up to about 15 May operations in Flanders had gone very much as expected.[37] Taken at face value, it means that even before the moves of 10 May Gort, with Mason-Macfarlane's guidance, had expected a Belgian collapse on the frontiers and that the BEF would be in immediate peril. Gort had no need of an Intelligence staff once the battle started, since its grim and pessimistic job was already done. Indeed, Mason-Macfarlane, who was no admirer of Gort, had hinted as much to Philip Gibbs.[38] It was only the precipitate collapse of French First Army, coupled with the collapse of the Dutch, that had come as a surprise.

Despite his own account of having to drive between the British front line divisions, Gort's headquarters, Brussels, Lille and Arras,[39] Mason-Macfarlane took an unusually active role in Press affairs during the next week. As with much else about events between 10 May and 4 June, there is a problem with reliable sources for the Press, not least because the Intelligence war diaries for BEF GHQ and for all three Corps were destroyed in the retreat. The most detailed contemporary account is the memoirs of Bernard Gray of the *Daily Mirror*, published in 1942 following his death while reporting the Middle East in the previous year. Correspondents with the BEF were not allowed to keep diaries in case of capture and some of Gray's details also cannot be corobborated. But, while they seldom duplicate each other, sources for the Press in the campaign generally agree on the course of events.

Once established at Lille, the war correspondents were allowed to drive around next day, with two or three reporters and a conducting officer to each car. Gray's car trip took his party into Brussels and then back to Arras to file stories of what they had seen. Subsequent trips took the correspondents, with Mason-Macfarlane's approval, closer to the front line, as far as Louvain and Wavre, before returning to Brussels or Lille depending on the time. The correpondents were not allowed to visit the front line troops, but got close enough at least for the newsreel cameramen to film field artillery. Many of them had portable wireless sets on which they would listen to the BBC while motoring along.[40]

For the first few days of the battle the focus of British media and public interest was almost entirely on the fighting in the Netherlands and northern Belgium. German advances elsewhere were disregarded or simply unknown, particularly as the French official communiqué for the evening of 13 May (the day of the critical river crossing over the Meuse at Sedan) stated that all German attacks had been repulsed. It is not clear whether the practice of daily Press briefings continued at Lille, although it seems likely, and within a few days of the reporters' arrival Mason-Macfarlane gave them startling news. He announced that the battle in front of the BEF was going badly, with Dutch and Belgian forces giving ground. German forces had also broken through in the Sedan sector and the French had given way. According to Mason-Macfarlane's own account, he then added a polititcal comment on the situation:

> I remember saying to the assembled war correspondents that history provides many examples of a British Army being asked to operate under appalling handicaps by the politicians responsible for British policy, but I doubted that the British Army had ever found itself in a graver position than that in which the governments of the last twenty years had placed it.[41]

Mason-Macfarlane, and Butler who helped draft the statement, give the plausible date of about the evening of 15 May for this briefing. Bernard Gray gives the evening of Sunday 12 May, which seems too early for the obvious reason that the Germans did not cross the Meuse at Sedan until the following day. Although both Lieutenant General Pownall and General Ironside recorded their anxieties about Belgian forces in front of the BEF on 12 May, there is no mention of a threat to Sedan.[42] But there is a piece of indirect corroborative evidence. War correspondents with the Advanced Air Striking Force at Rheims could keep diaries and Charles Gardner of the BBC recorded that on 12 May he and his colleagues were also briefed that "the Germans are reported to be getting through in the Sedan area". This reflects accurately the information coming from the RAF Photographic Development Unit (later the Photographic Reconnaissance Unit or PRU) that the German armoured columns were already on the River Semois and that the French had failed to hold them in the Belgian Ardennes.[43]

Even so, if Gray and his colleagues were briefed by Mason-Macfarlane that evening as he describes, then this was a very pessimistic position for the British Army to take so early. But Mason-Macfarlane was to give at least two further versions of this briefing and speaks of 15 May as being "my last Press conference at Lille".[44] It is possible that both Gray and Butler were mistaken as to the exact contents, or that they and Mason-Macfarlane mixed up two separate briefings three days apart.

It is certain that this briefing in Lille took place before 17 May, when Mason-Macfarlane was appointed by Gort to command the improvised 'Macforce' as a guard to the exposed Southern flank of the BEF, taking Templer with him and leaving Butler as the sole Intelligence officer with Gort's headquarters. Its message certainly got through to the newspapers and to the BBC, where the midnight Home Service News broadcast on 17 May quoted an anonymous source in London to the effect that the situation was the most dangerous that Britain and France had faced since the German offensive of March 1918.[45]

From 16 May onwards there was a sudden falling off in news from the BEF reaching Britain, with stories about the RAF and even the Royal Navy filling the resulting spaces. On 17 May the war correspondents were ordered to move back to Arras by Lieutenant-Colonel McCormack. In the absence of other evidence, the principal motive for this move seems to have been to secure the correspondents' safety, in the belief that they had done their job by maintaining British morale through the Phoney War and now had no other useful function. They left Arras on 18 May for Amiens, and then for Boulogne, losing most of their belongings including their typewriters when the Hôtel de l'Univers was heavily bombed. Once the Arras teleprinter was destroyed it was virtually impossible for them to get reports out, since the only communication from Boulogne to London was the King's Messenger.[46] From 19 May, when German bombers destroyed most of the port area of Boulogne, including the newly established Press Centre, the war correspondents were in no position to report anything and took refuge in various local hostelries. "So here we were, the world's Press," the newsreel camerman Ronnie Noble remembered, "all really being kicked out when I suppose the biggest story in our history up to that time was there to be covered."[47]

British journalists sent to the French armies had, if anything, even less fortune in trying to report the war. Those reporting with the Second Army were allowed no closer to the front than Vouziers (40 kilometres south of Charleville-Mezières, the centre of the main German armour's crossings), given one inadequate briefing and then put on a train for Paris as the retreat began.[48] The experience of the journalists with the Advanced Air Striking Force followed a similar pattern. After broadcasting daily from Rheims from 10 May to 15 May Charles Gardner moved to Paris next day and took his wife to safety at Le Havre on 17 May. Back in Paris, Gardner found that by 19 May "the Press officer system had broken down",[49] and that he was unable to continue broadcasting. He flew to Cherbourg shortly afterwards, and so to Poole and London. Some journalists who had missed the start of the battle tried to get back out to France while it was being fought. Philip Gibbs, together with Geoffrey Harmsworth, flew from London to Paris with the intention of travelling by train through Amiens back to Arras. As their train was about to leave they were told that Amiens had already fallen to the Germans. Unwilling to return to Britain, they remained in Paris until ordered to fly out by the British military authorities, arriving back in Britain at about the time of Dunkirk.[50]

At Boulogne on 21 May the conducting officers put the war correspondents on ships back to Britain, burnt their office archive on the quayside and raided the officers' club bar for drinks before themselves departing.[51] Philby remembered that "In London, I had written two or three pieces for *The Times*," but "I have no idea what I wrote."[52]

Indeed, since reporters were not usually given individual by-lines and were often heavily sub-edited, it is impossible to track reports by specific journalists appearing in newspapers. A MoI report of 27 May confirmed that all newsreel cameramen had also left France by that date.[53] Once back in Britain Charles Martin of British Pathé volunteered as a Royal Navy cameraman. Sailing on a warship from Harwich to Dunkirk, he took the only film of the evacuation from the British side, although spending much of his time helping the survivors.[54]

One important effect of the early evacuation of the war correspondents was that it deprived the soldiers of the BEF of accurate news of their own wider circumstances. On 25 May the French military authorities put out a request that, given the very confused nature of the fighting, newsreaders and reporters should not mention specific locations or formations for fear of the enemy making use of the information, making reporting the campaign virtually impossible. Newspapers and the time to read them were both in short supply, but the BBC Forces Service remained an important link with the outside world. It has been quaintly suggested that the first that most troops knew of their predicament was on Sunday 26 May, the 'National Day of Prayer', when the BBC carried the services from Westminster Abbey and the Archbishop of Canterbury prayed before a congregation, including King George VI and Churchill, "for our soldiers in dire peril in France".[55] More probably most soldiers of the BEF, which had been retreating for eight days, were already quite aware of the threat.

Churchill's government had far more immediate concerns than Press presentation, which was certainly not the greatest problem that it had inherited from Chamberlain. But it was at this time losing the propaganda battle and with it the credibility that it needed for its own survival. If little news came from the war correspondents, there was no shortage from other sources, including daily communiqués from BEF GHQ, from Paris, Brussels, and from Amsterdam where a brand new Reuters' teleprinter had finally begun operation on 9 May,[56] and above all from Berlin. The inadequately staffed BBC Monitoring Service was overwhelmed trying to keep track of German radio announcements.[57] By 15 May the British Press was reporting German claims to have crossed the Meuse and three days later both the newspapers and the BBC announced that the BEF had started to retreat.

These statements were hard to reconcile with French official communiqués that up to 17 May insisted that the German bridgehead at Sedan had been counter-attacked and contained for a gain of only a few miles.

In Britain itself Parliament had been in Whitsun recess when the German attack had begun. It had been recalled on 13 May to recognize the new government, but after Churchill's 'blood, toil, tears and sweat' speech to the Commons it had adjourned for a further eight days. The only remaining vehicle for British official pronouncements was the MoI, including frequent statements on BBC radio by Alfred Duff Cooper, Churchill's new Minister of Information. On the evening of Trinity Sunday, 19 May, Churchill gave his first ever radio broadcast as Prime Minister, 'Be Ye Men of Valour'. Carried on all BBC services, this offered a grim but positive message, including the claim that "we may look with confidence to the stabilization of the front in France".[58] Two days later a broadcast on the 9 o'clock news by Duff Cooper repeated this line. "The war news today is grave; it is no good pretending that it is not," Duff Cooper began, but added that, "The Army of Great Britain and the far greater Army of France are still there: they are neither in retreat, nor have they suffered heavy losses."[59] This was when German sources were – truthfully – reporting their troops at Abbeville, even BEF Intelligence placed them west of Amiens, and more than a week after Mason-Macfarlane's briefing to the war correspondents that the battle was already lost.[60]

At the morning War Cabinet on 23 May Duff Cooper first requested a new brief for the Press, only to be told that he should take his guidance from Churchill's statement in the Commons that afternoon. Carrying on the ideas of the Phoney War, government policy was to avoid telling the public the full extent of the military collapse in France, through fear of causing national panic. It was into this delicate situation that the Army once more intervened with its own firm line for the British people. Early on 25 May 'Macforce' handed its last troops to other formations and Mason-Macfarlane was ordered to report to GHQ. He sent Templer on ahead and was himself probably present for Gort's critical briefing that evening when the decision was taken to withdraw to Dunkirk.[61]

Next day Mason-Macfarlane was back in Britain with both his staff officers, having conferred with General Sir John Dill – who was about to take over as CIGS – either at BEF GHQ, or at the War Office, or both. On 27 May the War Office DMI, Major-General F.G.

Beaumont-Nesbitt, took Mason-Macfarlane to see Harold Nicolson, now Parliamentary Under-Secretary at the MoI and Duff Cooper's deputy. Mason-Macfarlane told Nicolson that the BEF was in a desperate situation with ammunition only for another three days, was about to suffer a catastrophic defeat and that the blame should be placed "partly on the Belgians and French and partly upon our own politicians".[62] Nicolson called Duff Cooper into the meeting and the MoI began to prepare for a British military disaster, although refusing to apportion blame.

At that evening's War Cabinet Duff Cooper again raised the issue that "the public were, at the moment, quite unprepared for the shock of realization of the position". Even the French official communiqués had by now conceded that the Germans had reached the coast, but statements and hints to the Press from the Allies continued to give the impression that these were isolated units that were about to be counter-attacked strongly. Churchill's response to Duff Cooper was that the Belgian armistice, due to be announced next day, 28 May, "should go a long way to prepare the public for bad news".[63] At the next morning's War Cabinet Duff Cooper was even more insistent, reading a letter from one of his senior officials:

[P]ressing for a frank statement of the desperate situation of the British Expeditionary Force. He feared that, unless this was given out, public confidence would be badly shaken and the civil population would not be ready to accept the assurances of the Government of the chances of our ultimate victory. . . . The Minister suggested that he should make a short statement in [sic] the 1 o'clock news of the BBC.[64]

This time Churchill gave way and Duff Cooper made his broadcast, repeated before the 9 o'clock news. But his main theme was the need to avoid both any falling out among the Allies and any desire to blame the French, which would give the Germans a propaganda victory.[65] That afternoon Duff Cooper also took part in a Commons debate on the MoI, in which he announced a more active role for the Ministry in the future.[66]

Also on 28 May Mason-Macfarlane gave the reassembled BEF war correspondents a further briefing at the Berkeley Hotel in London. This time Bernard Gray of the *Daily Mirror* took detailed notes of Mason-Macfarlane's statement, which began:

"I am afraid that there is going to be a considerable shock for the British public. It is your duty to act as shock absorbers and I have prepared, with my counterpart at the War Office, a statement which can be published, subject to censorship".[67]

Mason-Macfarlane's statement was very similar in tone and content to the Lille briefing two weeks earlier and completely contrary to government and MoI policy: disaster was looming, the fault lay with the inter-war politicians, and the French (and Dutch and Belgians) had let the British down:

> The BEF has fought what has amounted to almost a lone fight against the massed spearhead of German attack, in the shape of vast motorized formations. . . . It is now no secret that on several fronts, the French failed to withstand the assault. Let there be no recriminations.[68]

Next morning's newspapers were full of blame for the French Army's betrayal of the BEF, causing the French Ambassador to write "a passionate letter" of complaint to Nicolson.[69]

For the following evening, 29 May, General Dill secured for Mason-Macfarlane the BBC 'Postscript' slot, a popular series of short talks by invited speakers that followed the Home Service 9 o'clock news. Speaking anonymously as a senior BEF commander, Mason-Macfarlane praised both the BEF and the RAF in its support, and ended in sombre terms:

> I wish I could conclude this talk on the BEF on a more cheerful note, but I cannot, and it's no good mincing matters. My message for you tonight is this: Your BEF, virtually encircled through no fault of its own, has put up and is putting up a show of which the whole of Europe must be proud, and has displayed a level of leadership, efficiency and gallantry rarely equalled in the annals of the British Army. There now remains a vital task, and I say to you all, in the name of your BEF, work as you have never worked before, and see that the new Armies which we are now raising are adequately and rapidly equipped, so that they may continue worthily the great work which those lads have done and are doing for you all in France.[70]

The existing script for this broadcast contains no direct criticism either of the French or past British governments, the criticism was perhaps in its tone. Macfarlane's concluding paragraph was taken up and repeated as an item on the BBC news for its midnight broadcast and for its two early morning broadcasts next day at 7 a.m. and 8 a.m.[71] According to Butler, Mason-Macfarlane was summoned that morning to the MoI by Duff Cooper, who was furious at being ignored. After a stormy exchange of views, Mason-Macfarlane left the meeting utterly unrepentant.[72]

Also on 29 May the BEF received what amounted to a benediction and last rites in the form of a public telegram from King George VI and a reply by Lord Gort, carried by the BBC Home Service and by the national newspapers next day. The King told Gort:

> All your countrymen have been following with pride and admiration the courageous resistance of the British Expeditionary Force during the continuing fighting of the last fortnight. Faced by circumstances outside their control in a position of extreme difficulty, they are displaying a gallantry that has never been surpassed in the annals of the British Army. The hearts of everyone of us at home are with you and your magnificent troops in this hour of peril.[73]

At last the British people were left in no doubt as to the seriousness of the position.

Next evening's BBC news announced that the Dunkirk evacuation was in full swing.[74] Duff Cooper flew to France on 2 June bearing a request from the War Cabinet that his French equivalents should tone down their optimistic pronouncements.[75] It is known that the MoI drew up an emergency plan, based around a radio broadcast to be given by Churchill on 5 June, if a German invasion was imminent or had already taken place.[76] These plans were rendered irrelevant only by the successful evacuation from Dunkirk and the German decision to turn south against France rather than attempt an immediate *coup de main* across the Channel. The correspondents loyally did their job, promoting a view of the Dunkirk evacuation that they had not themselves witnessed as being a British triumph. On Tuesday 4 June, in a speech that was widely reported in the following day's newspapers, Churchill addressed the Commons on the military situation, attributing the success of the evacuation at Dunkirk to the Royal Navy.[77]

The issue of the culpability of inter-war politicians needed no prompting from Mason-Macfarlane or anyone else. On 25 May *The New Statesman and Nation* carried a front-page leader arguing that "For eight months we have been living off legends: instead of fighting this war with weapons and techniques of our own time, we have told each other stories of past triumphs".[78] The argument reached its final form in early July with the publication of the best-selling book *Guilty Men* by Frank Owen, Editor of the *Evening Standard*, Michael Foot, one of his best reporters, and Peter Howard of the *Sunday Express*, writing collectively under the pen-name of 'Cato'.[79]

The most enduring myth of Dunkirk did not come from Churchill or from the newspapers. On Wednesday 5 June a new speaker in the 'Postscript' series, the writer J.B. Priestley, gave his first talk, taking Dunkirk as his subject. "Nothing, I feel," Priestley told his listeners, "could be more English than the battle of Dunkirk, both in its beginning and its end, its folly and its grandeur." It was Priestley, also, who first told "how the little holiday steamers made an excursion to hell and came back glorious."[80] Priestley's genial delivery made him a major success with listeners, establishing for his 'Postscript' broadcasts (mostly made on Sunday evenings through summer and autumn, 1940) what the BBC estimated as "the biggest regular listening audience in the world", including 31 per cent of the British adult population.[81]

Meanwhile, the Battle of France was not actually over. On 11 June a small contingent of war correspondents and cameramen including Bernard Gray, Kim Philby and Ronnie Noble with their conducting officers again left London to return to France, among them a few Americans. Coming in through Cherbourg, they encountered the last survivors of the 51st Highland Division, so beginning another of the small pieces of campaign mythology. They travelled on to Le Mans and even as far as Rouen, but getting a story out was virtually impossible. Gray soon left from St Mâlo for Holyhead; Philby left from Brest.[82] Again, the reporters could only describe what they saw, which was a British Army still functioning, columns of French refugees and no sign of the French Army except for a demoralized rabble.

But even before the Dunkirk evacuation, the main elements of the British myth of the 1940 campaign in France and Flanders were in place – the neglect of military spending in the inter-war years, the 'guilty men' of appeasement, the failure of the French high command about which Britain could do nothing, the failure of France and other countries to fight, the British fighting alone against the strongest German forces.

This was not a spontaneous myth, but a position deliberately promoted by Mason-Macfarlane as DMI of the BEF to the Press and public. A strong clue that Mason-Macfarlane was acting under orders, or at least with Army high command support, is that he was not sacked, but rather sidelined. His next posting was as GOC Gibraltar. He finished the war as a lieutenant-general with a knighthood and in 1945 he stood successfully as a Labour MP. Major Butler went on to a successful career as a lieutenant-colonel with SOE, specializing in propaganda. Templer ended the war as a corps commander and his Army career as a field marshal. At the very least, senior Army officers actively connived at Mason-Macfarlane's behaviour. From an extremely early stage of the Battle of France until its end the British people were given the Army version of events through radio and the newspapers, with a disregard for government wishes and policy that was unprecedented in British civil-military relations.

A more conspiratorial interpretation, but still well within the available facts, is that members of the Army high command had by either mid or late May – or perhaps even much earlier – decided that the BEF was lost and the war with it. Between 10th May and 4th June they released through the Press the Army's own version of a 'stab in the back' myth as a prelude to defeat, just as the German high command had done in August 1918, using Mason-Macfarlane, as their willing mouthpiece. This is not the sort of thing on which generals are obliging enough to leave a written record of their own involvement, if indeed any such involvement took place at all.

Acknowledgements

The BBC Written Archives Centre, Caversham Park, Reading, and particularly Mr James Codd, Senior Document Assistant.
The Trustees of the Imperial War Museum, London, together with the staff of its Department of Documents, Department of Sound Records, and Film and Television Archive.

1   INF 1/1 'Committee of Imperial Defence, Sub-Committee to Prepare Plans for the Establishment of a Ministry of Information, Progress Report for Period Ended January 31st, 1938', Public Record Office, Kew [PRO]; Ian McLaine, *Ministry of Morale: Home Front Morale and the Ministry of Information in World War II* (London: George Allen and Unwin, 1979), pp. 12–40.

2   Nigel Nicolson (ed.) *Harold Nicolson: Diaries and Letters 1939–1945* (London: Collins, 1967), p. 32; Nicholas John Cull, *Selling War: The British Propaganda Campaign Against American 'Neutrality' in World War II* (Oxford: Oxford University Press, 1995), p. 38; McLaine, *Ministry of Morale*, pp. 37–8.

3   INF 1/1 'Committee of Imperial Defence, Sub-Committee to Prepare Plans for the Establishment of a Ministry of Information, Progress Report for Period Ended 31 January, 1938', p. 27, PRO.

4   Jonathan Dimbleby, *Richard Dimbleby: A Biography* (London: Hodder and Stoughton, 1975), p. 96.

5   Asa Briggs, *The War of Words: The History of Broadcasting in the United Kingdom Volume III* (London: Oxford University Press, 1970), pp. 87–91; Nicholas Harman, *Dunkirk: The Necessary Myth* (London: Hodder and Stoughton, 1980), pp. 236–7.

6   Briggs, *The War of Words*, p. 43.

7   E.S. Turner, *The Phoney War on the Home Front* (London: Michael Joseph, 1961), p. 22; Briggs, *The War Of Words*, p. 96.

8   Cull, *Selling the War*, pp. 45–6.

9   Briggs, *The War of Words*, pp. 99–100.

10   *The New Statesman and Nation* Volume XIX Number 481, 11 May 1940, p. 160, quoting the *National Zietung* for 27 April 1940.

11   INF 1/494 'Ministry of Information: Press and Censorship Division: Liaison between British and French censorships 1939–1940', Letter to the Director of the Censorship Division, 18 September 1939, PRO.

12   Martin S. Alexander, '"Fighting to the Last Frenchman"? Reflections on the BEF Deployment to France and the Strains of the Franco-British Alliance, 1939–1940', *Historical Reflections/Reflexions Historiques* Volume 22 Number 1, Winter 1996, pp. 235–62; Brian Bond, *Britain, France and Belgium 1939–1940* (London: Brassey's, 1990), pp. 23–31; 49–51.

13   McLaine, *Ministry of Morale*, pp. 54–5.

14   WO 259/4 'Notes on the Regulations for Press Correspondents Abroad', 5 October 1939, PRO.

15   Bernard Gray, *War Reporter* (London: Robert Hale, 1942), p. 17; Philip Gibbs, *The Pageant of the Years: An Autobiography* (London: William Heinemann, 1946), p. 465.

16 Ewan Butler, *Mason-Mac: The Life of Lieutenant-General Sir Noel Mason-Macfarlane* (London: Macmillan, 1972), pp. 100–7; Gray, *War Reporter*, pp. 57–8.

17 Briggs, *The War Of Words*, pp. 127–8; J.R. Colville, *Man of Valour: The Life of Field Marshal the Viscount Gort VC GCB DSO MVO MC* (London: Collins, 1972), p. 157.

18 Briggs, *The War of Words*, p. 126–8.

19 WO 259/4 'Notes on the Regulations for Press Correspondents Abroad', 5 October 1939, PRO.

20 Cull, *Selling War*, pp. 21–32; 40–4.

21 WO 197/52 'BEF GHQ Press Censorship December 1939 – May 1940', PRO.

22 Dimbleby, *Richard Dimbleby*, p. 91; Transcript of an interview with Ronnie Noble, newsreel cameraman for Universal attached to the BEF 1939–1940 [Hereafter 'Interview with Ronnie Noble'], Accession Number 005392/07, Department of Sound Records, Imperial War Museum, London [IWM] p. 1; INF 1/195 'Ministry of Information: News Reels: General Policy of Companies, 1940', PRO.

23 Charles Gardner, *A.A.S.F.* (London: Hutchinson, 1940), p. 25; Interview with Ronnie Noble, p. 1, IWM; A.H. Narracott, *The Lion Had Wings: A Record of the RAF in France* (London: Frederick Muller, 1941), pp. xv, 123; Cull, *Selling War*, p. 41.

24 Dimbleby, *Richard Dimbleby*, p. 101.

25 Interview with Ronnie Noble, p. 24; Gibbs, *The Pageant of the Years*, p. 471.

26 Interview with Ronnie Noble, p. 7, IWM.

27 INF 1/186 'Press and Censorship Bureau: Liaison between British and French censorship September 1939: July 1940', PRO; Ewan Butler and J. Selby Bradford, *Keep the Memory Green: The First of the Many, France 1940* (London: Hutchinson, 1950), pp. 27–8.

28 Dimbleby, *Richard Dimbleby*, p. 94; WO 197/52 'BEF GHQ Press Censorship December 1939 – May 1940', PRO.

29 Alistair Horne, *The Lose A Battle: France 1940* (London, Macmillan, 1969), p. 337.

30 Gibbs, *The Pageant of the Years*, pp. 460–1, 479.

31 Kim Philby, *My Silent War* (London: MacGibbon and Kee, 1968), p. 2.

32 Dimbleby, *Richard Dimbleby*, p. 102; Charles Gardner, *A.A.S.F.*, pp. 166.

33 Gibbs, *The Pageant of the Years*, p. 480; Gray, *War Reporter*, p 49.

34 Butler, *Mason-Mac*, pp. 111–12; Brian Bond (ed.) *Chief of Staff: The Diaries of Lieutenant-General Sir Henry Pownall Volume One 1933–1940* (London: Leo Cooper, 1972), p. 308; Gray, *War Reporter*, pp. 49–50.

35 F.H. Hinsley *et al*, *British Intelligence in the Second World War: Its Influence on Strategy and Operations, Volume I*, (London, HMSO, 1979), pp. 143–5; Butler, *Mason-Mac*, pp. 112–17; John Cloake, *Templer, Tiger of Malaya: The Life of Field Marshal Sir Gerald Templer* (London: Harrap, 1985), pp. 73–5.

36 CAB 67/7 War Cabinet Minutes 11.30 a.m. Saturday 1st June 1940, PRO.

37 BBC Home Service News broadcast 8 a.m. 15 May 1940, transcript held on Reel HNB 32, BBC Written Archives Centre, Caversham Park, Reading [WAC].

38 Gibbs, *The Pageant of the Years*, p. 475; Colville, *Man of Valour*, p. 235.

39 Papers of Lieutenant-General Sir Frank Noel Mason-Macfarlane DSO KCB, PP/MCR/C5 [hereafter Mason-Macfarlane Papers] Reel 2, Item 29, IWM. This is a typescript draft, believed to have been written after the Second World War, either for a speech or for his memoirs, covering Mason-Macfarlane's involvement in the events of May 1940. It does not include some passages quoted by Butler from this period in his biography of Mason-Macfarlane, and has the appearance of being typed from notes or dictated by someone unfamiliar with the 1940 campaign.

40 Gray, *War Reporter*, p. 56; Interview with Ronnie Noble, p. 11.

41 Butler, *Mason-Mac*, p. 116; Gray, *War Reporter*, p. 57; Mason-Macfarlane Papers, Reel 2, Item 29, IWM.

42 Roderick Macleod and Denis Kelly (eds.) *The Ironside Diaries 1937–1940* (London: Constable, 1962), pp. 303–5; Bond, *Chief of Staff* pp. 311–14.

43 Gardner, *A.A.S.F.*, p. 159.

44 Mason-Macfarlane Papers, Reel 2, Item 29, IWM.

45 BBC Home Service news broadcast, 12 midnight 17 May 1940, Reel HNB 32 WAC.

46 Gray, *War Reporter*, p. 100.

47 Interview with Ronnie Noble, p. 18, IWM; Cull, *Selling War*, p. 70.

48 Horne, *To Lose a Battle*, pp. 337–8.

49 Gardner, *A.A.S.F.*, pp. 164–9, 188.

50 Gibbs, *The Pageant of the Years*, pp. 480–4. Note that Gibbs' dating is very vague, not least in his belief that the German attack started in April.

51 Gray, *War Reporter*, p. 118; Cull, *Selling War*, p. 70.

52 Philby, *My Silent War*, p. 1.

53 INF 1/5 Ministry of Information Progress Report, May 1940, PRO.

54 Interview with Ronnie Noble, p. 19, IWM.

55 Harman, *Dunkirk*, pp. 238–9.

56 INF 1/5 Ministry of Information Progress Report, May 1940, PRO.

57 INF 1/5 Ministry of Information Progress Report, May 1940, PRO.

58 Winston Churchill, *Great War Speeches* (London: Corgi, 1978), pp. 13–16.
59 The text of this speech was reported in *The Times*, 22 May 1940, p. 3c.
60 *The Times*, 22 May 1940, p. 6a; WO 197/86 'BEF Macforce – All Papers in Connection with this Force' Intelligence map from BEF GHQ dated 21 May 1940, PRO.
61 Colville, *Man of Valour*, p. 216; Bond, *Chief of Staff*, p. 39; WO 197/86 'BEF Macforce – All Papers in Connection with this Force', Letter from Lieutenant-Colonel P.M. Hall to C7 (War Diaries), War Office, 22 April 1943, enclosing Mason-Macfarlane's briefing map, PRO; WO 197/188 'BEF GHQ Reports May–June 1940', Summary for the Composition, Moves and Dispositions of Macforce 17–25 May, entry for 25 May and signal message from 'Campus' [BEF GHQ Rear] 23 May, PRO.
62 McLaine, *Ministry of Morale*, p. 74.
63 CAB 65/7 War Cabinet minutes 11.30 a.m. Thursday 23 May 1940 and 10 p.m. Monday 27 May 1940, PRO.
64 CAB 67/7 War Cabinet minutes 11.30 a.m. Tuesday 28 May 1940, PRO.
65 The text of this broadcast appears in *The Times*, 29 May 1940, p. 4c.
66 The text of this statement was reported in *The Times*, 29 May 1940, p. 3b.
67 Gray, *War Reporter*, pp. 120–1; unaccountably, Harman, *Dunkirk*, p. 243, describes this talk as 'strictly off the record'.
68 Gray, *War Reporter*, p. 121.
69 Nicolson, *Harold Nicolson*, p. 91.
70 The typescript text of this broadcast is in the Mason-Macfarlane Papers, Reel 2, Item 12, IWM; this is confirmed by Butler, *Mason-Mac*, p. 119; and Ewan Butler, *Amateur Agent* (London: George G. Harrap, 1963), pp. 22–3. There is no copy of the script held by the WAC, but a Script Index Card in Mason-Macfarlane's name does confirm that he was the anonymous officer, and the quotations from the script in the other BBC News broadcasts mentioned confirm its authenticity.
71 BBC Home Service News broadcasts 12 midnight 29 May 1940, and 7 a.m. 30 May 1940, Reel HBN 33 WAC.
72 Butler, *Amateur Agent*, pp. 23–4; Butler, *Mason-Mac*, p. 120.
73 'The King's Salute to the BEF'; text taken from *The Times*, 30 May 1940, p. 6a–c. See also BBC Home Service News 9 p.m. 29 May 1940, WAC.
74 Harman, *Dunkirk*, pp. 236–7.
75 Alfred Duff Cooper, *Old Men Forget: The Autobiography of Duff Cooper, Viscount Norwich* (London: Rupert Hart Davis, 1953), p. 280–3; CAB 65/7 War Cabinet Minutes 10 p.m. Monday 27 May 1940, PRO.
76 McLaine, *Ministry of Morale*, pp. 66–7.
77 Churchill, *Great War Speeches*, pp. 16–26.

78 *The New Statesman and Nation*, Volume XIX Number 483, 25 May 1940, p. 659.

79 Michael Foot, Preface to the Penguin Edition of 'Cato' [Pseudonym], *Guilty Men* (London, Penguin, 1998).

80 J.B. Priestley, *Postscripts* (London: William Heinemann, 1940), pp. 1–3.

81 Quoted in Angus Calder, *The People's War: Britain 1939–1945* (London: Grenada, 1969), p. 160. Briggs, *The War of Words*, pp. 210–14.

82 Gray, *War Reporter*, pp. 126–47; Philby, *My Silent War*, p. ; Interview with Ronnie Noble, pp. 27–9, IWM.

THE INFLUENCE OF THE BATTLE
OF FRANCE ON BRITISH
MILITARY DOCTRINE

JOHN DREWIENKIEWICZ

Over the majority of the 20th Century the British attitude to establishing and enforcing Military Doctrine has been at best lukewarm. At heart, the British Army is happiest studying and drawing lessons from its own long history of small unit actions, where individual qualities counted for most.[1] When periods of peace intervened and did not produce appropriate lessons, for example in the 1880s, the American Civil War was studied from the point of view that most closely mirrored the British approach. Hence Henderson's close scrutiny of the actions of the Confederates in the Shenandoah Valley, in itself a relatively small piece of the overall conflict.[2]

However, in the course of the First World War the British Army *did* recognize the need for a generally accepted way of doing things, which looks in retrospect quite like what we now call doctrine. It was the process of agreeing organizations that worked, with manageable scales of equipment, manned by soldiers who had learned the relevant basics in individual training and who had practised with the other Arms (Tanks, Infantry and Artillery) to produce the synergy required for all-arms warfare. Above all the Artillery took a unified approach, ensuring a common application of their skills.

The last 100 days of the First World War had seen the blossoming of a tactical system which produced a successful method for isolating and overrunning specific limited areas. This was followed up by swift consolidation, regrouping, restocking logistics, extending communications and repeating the process several days later. It was all-arms warfare, but no proven and consistent formula had been found to break all the way through a firmly held defensive line in one single continuous operation. The prime lesson of the First World War was

161

thus that defensive tactics worked and were feasible for less trained troops, while offensive operations were harder, needing much more training and meticulous staff work to co-ordinate the available resources.[3]

This was the doctrine which was embodied in the Report of the Committee on the Lessons of the First World War in 1932[4] and which was taken to France by the British Expeditionary Force at the start of the Second World War. Such training as was done in early 1940 was done first for "a defensive battle against a German attack supported by strong air forces and armoured and mobile formations".[5] Training in 'mobile warfare', which involved moving to counter any local breakthrough, came next, with 'offensive operations against fortified positions and field defences' as the third priority.

German operations in Poland were analysed, but many of the factors were seen as being specific to Poland, with defences that faced in the wrong direction.[6] Moreover, the main focus of the BEF until late April 1940 was in getting to France, being equipped and learning the basics for static, defensive warfare. Very few units expected to need to be mobile, and those units that were so expected had their work cut out to train themselves.[7] The nearest attempt to all-arms tactics was the Arras Counterstroke, when 'Frankforce' was put together as an ad-hoc assortment of forces. It went well at first, but the tanks outran their infantry and the infantry in turn outran their artillery support. Everyone outran their air support. Throughout the Flanders campaign each unexpected occurrence was met with an ad hoc response. The practice deprived formations of reserves and created inadequate command arrangements for the new groupings.

In the wake of Dunkirk there was a realization that training had been lacking in realism and that the written word of reports on German methods had been insufficient to prepare troops for actual operations.

So, as the first requisite of a 'lessons learnt' process, there were indeed plenty of lessons to learn. A proper process was gone through. General Sir William Bartholomew, a past Commander of the Imperial Defence College[8] and CGS India until 1937, recently retired as GOCinC Northern Command, was appointed to lead the study. His committee considered "lessons of the recent operations in Flanders which can be applied usefully to our present organization and training, and to suggest modifications to organization, training and equipment which should be made to meet the problems with which the British

162

Army will be faced in the event of an attempted enemy invasion of this country."[9] The committee included the Director of Military Training and took verbal evidence from thirty-six individuals from lieutenant general to major, as well as written evidence and 'opinions' from three major generals, including Montgomery.

The report correctly identified the psychological dislocation that the Germans had achieved. "By every means in his power and often with great ingenuity the enemy has concentrated his means of attack on the morale of his opponents. In the application of his weapons, he relies almost as much on terrorization by noise as on material effect. . . . Similar attempts to undermine morale included the dropping of dummy parachutists behind our lines, while ruses such as passing troops through the lines disguised as refugees were also employed. Every conceivable ruse has been employed, and to counter them we must be active both mentally and physically."[10] Nevertheless, the identification of the issue only led to debate as to how to counter it. It did not anywhere suggest that any attempt should be made to do the same to the enemy.

The major issues were seen by Bartholomew as four[11]:

- "The offensive spirit had been blunted by the 6 months devoted to elaborate defensive positions." The solution to this was "to hit him hard at every opportunity. Moreover the German dislikes being attacked, and this may be the weak spot in his armour."
- Next, discipline was lacking. Physical fitness, the ability to live hard and the need for rigid discipline were of paramount importance.
- Next, urgent action was required to place co-operation between the two Services, namely the Air Force and the Army, on a better basis.
- Finally anti-tank defence was key. An increased scale of issue of tanks and anti-tank weapons was "of the first importance . . . All ranks must be taught to adopt aggressive tactics against tanks which succeed in penetrating our positions; they should be hunted and ambushed by day and stalked and harried by night, relentlessly and tirelessly."

In looking at more specific lessons, only adjustment was thought to be needed. "The teaching of our manuals is correct, but the doctrine laid down in our pamphlets must be modified to suit the very wide fronts which were imposed on us."[12] "Positions must have depth, and localities must be capable of holding out though isolated, and must on no account withdraw because they are outflanked, or even surrounded."[13]

The conclusion was reached on anti-tank weapons that the production of the 6 pdr anti-tank gun should be hastened.[14] The German use of air power was admired, notably the ability to concentrate the air effort in one area, the close co-operation between German Army and Air Force, and the value of air attacks as supporting fire to cover ground assaults. Bartholomew felt it imperative to introduce a comparable system into the British Army and Air Force, capable of working down to brigade level.[15]

The use of ad hoc formations was correctly identified as a major cause for concern.[16] This, combined with orders being given at conferences, and as verbal orders not followed up by written confirmatory orders, produced a lack of co-ordination.[17] The 'motor contact officers', or liaison officers, were one way round these difficulties, and the scales of such people was raised. It was noted that steps had already been taken to implement this requirement.[18]

The last section covered the operation and organization of the individual arms – cavalry, gunners, infantry and sappers. By far the most prescient recommendation concerned the way armoured units operated. It was stated: "At night the regiment was always withdrawn to the rear to link up with its maintenance services. It is suggested that we should train to the German system, whereby armoured vehicles 'laager' where they end up at nightfall and the maintenance vehicles are sent to them, in spite of certain obvious risks."[19]

Thus, it can be demonstrated that lessons *were* identified at the top level. Interestingly, little was said of the quality of junior leadership, although an identified need to give potential officers formal training appears to stem from anecdotal tales of some breakdown of leadership in the latter stages of the BEF retreat. Certainly schools for junior officers were established quickly in the aftermath. However, the Bartholomew Committee was considered and staffed in a top-down way, and it disappears from view quickly. There is little trace of subsequent action that hammers the lessons home.[20]

In a similar timeframe an Army Training Memorandum was issued[21] within a few weeks of the end of the Flanders Campaign. This was longer on 'experiences' than on 'analysis', but it provided low-level guidance down to platoon commander. Some of the contents are very mundane – 'How to march', for instance – but there were more useful lessons applicable more widely in 'The time factor in training' and 'Liaison with other arms'. On 'Time' it stated: "The German is fully alive to the importance of time; he takes risks and acts boldly. If we are going to get the better of him, we must speed up our methods, our planning, and the execution of our plans." . . . "It is by forethought, by great organization, by quick thinking, by quick appreciation of the ground, by quick planning, by means of clear and concise orders, and by acquiring a knowledge of all arms that we shall save time."

Thus, while one might have hoped for a more analytical approach, a number of key lessons were identified. Had they been taken into practice and institutionalized in the Western Desert in 1941 many of the reverses might have been avoided. But doctrine was generally seen as theatre-specific, so there is no evidence of the lessons being systematically carried from the UK to Egypt, except by individual commanders.[22]

One might have expected that the Director of Military Training would have featured strongly in the subsequent events, with firm direction emanating from on high and with the equipment production programme being refocused within the War Office to take into account the areas for urgent improvement. But if we study the period June 1940 to September 1942 it is not possible at this distance to make out much of this sort of direction. Very soon after the end of the war a series of monographs on different aspects of military activity was produced; most were well written and emerged as bound volumes in the late 1940s. Young Royal Engineer officers in the 1950s and 1960s were brought up on Military Engineering (Field),[23] which pulled no punches and included colourful examples of 'how not to do it'. A typical example, which relates to the Flanders Campaign, reads[24]: "A sector was taken over by a Belgian division and it was decided that the British field company which had prepared the bridge for demolition be left to blow the bridge under the orders of the Belgian division. . . . A Belgian officer was placed on the bridge to give the necessary order. The commander of the Belgian division, to ensure that the bridge was not blown before necessary, sent a note to the officer on the bridge. On the envelope he wrote, 'Not to be opened until the enemy approaches so close to the bridge that there is a danger of it falling into his hands'. Inside the envelope was an order to blow the bridge forthwith. It appears that the Belgian officer opened the envelope without reading the instructions on the outside. He showed the letter to the RE officer, but not the envelope, and gave the order to blow." This sort of vivid example helped a new generation to understand the reason for procedures which at first sight were formal and bureaucratic.

However, the monograph on 'Training' that was produced as part of this series did not see the light of day. It got to final draft stage, but, in the words on the front of the file in Whitehall, "It has been decided that this Monograph will not be issued on general distribution as it is not up to the standard required."[25] Thus it exists, and its non-publication is itself a testament to the fact that the experience in this area was not a model of 'how to do it'. While lessons were identified, they were not systematically applied, and the Monograph describes the way that lessons had to be relearned painfully, because there was no mechanism for imposing institutional internal change on the organization through doctrine.

The role of the Director of Military Training was the co-ordination of the Military Training of the Army, Regular and Territorial, in Commands and in all educational and training establishments. As such, he answered directly to CIGS and was responsible for all basic training, of which a lot was going on. In the summer of 1940 CinC of GHQ Home Forces was appointed and GHQ Home Forces was given the responsibility for collective training, defined as the training of All Arms Formations, rather than individual units, in the commands. The first CinC, Ironside, did not achieve much in his short tenure and Brooke relieved him in July 1940. The handover appears to have consisted mainly of a discussion on the use of the loaned Rolls Royce!

However, one top-down decision which *was* made for the good was to keep the Staff College open and producing a steady flow of Staff officers. This may seem obvious to us, but it was not the case in the First World War, when the Staff College was closed altogether for the duration. Even so, there was a natural reluctance to spare officers from their units to go on a long course in the middle of the war.

It also proved impossible to redirect the equipment programme. The losses at Dunkirk were simply too great. In artillery the losses amounted to 60% of all the British Artillery 'world stock'[26] and there was no one who was prepared to take the risk, as Robert E. Lee did in the winter of 1862 when he sent his 6-pdrs back to be melted down and recast as 12-pdrs of stopping production. There is evidence that the conversion of at least one factory from 2-pdr anti-tank gun production to 6-pdrs was considered. However, it was estimated that only

100 of the new guns would be obtained instead of 600 of the smaller.[27] Thus, it took until April 1942 for the first 6-pdrs to arrive in the Western Desert, although there were some intermediate improvisations using old 3" anti-aircraft guns mounted on anti-tank carriages.[28] One hundred of these expedients were made, which incidentally gives the lie to the idea that the British did not ever learn the lesson of the usefulness of anti-aircraft guns in the ground role.

Turning to tanks, it was similarly recognized[29] that the British tanks had poor mechanical reliability, needed thicker armour, a better armour-piercing weapon and an HE shell. But again, any significant modification to the production process was not allowed since any major change of design would have slowed down tank production, not least since only twenty-five of the 700 tanks sent to France had returned.

Some top-down direction was given with respect to Army/RAF co-operation. The RAF formed an 'Army Co-operation Command' headed by an Air Marshal (a three-star rank) with an Army Brigadier (a one-star rank). But that and a training school[30] was the sum of it. The main emphasis was on air recce. Alanbrooke in particular pressed hard for closer linkage and tried to do more from GHQ Home Forces, but the RAF was too busy defending Britain from the Luftwaffe to commit itself to any systematic form of Army support. That said, Montgomery achieved as good results as anyone in his time at 5 Corps in the winter of 1940, in setting up pragmatic links through horse-trading.[31] In return for making a high priority of army provision to counter-attack parachute landings on airfields, he got some tactical liaison with the RAF Light Bomber squadrons in his area. This enabled him to include experimentation with the best way of controlling air support at brigade or corps level in his exercises in the winter of 1940.

Returning to Bartholomew, his next point, the 'Offensive Spirit', was probably not susceptible to top-down direction. This was an area which was best left to local commanders. In this case, the answer was 'Battle Schools' and 'Battle Drill'. The first Battle School was set up in Ashdown Forest by Alexander, encouraged by Alanbrooke.[32] Here troops practised the standard field movements so that everyone knew his place in relation to his comrades. The principal use of Battle Drill was in the offensive and 'Fire and Movement' was developed into an art form. To ensure realism live ammunition was used, in conjunction with thunderflashes and guncotton. This realism in training produced casualties, but they were accepted as the necessary price to pay for ensuring that troops were inoculated against the sound and shock of battle.

The innovation was recognized as worthwhile and soon CinC Home Forces adopted and institutionalised the idea, inaugurating divisional Battle Schools and eventually a GHQ Battle School at Barnard Castle, where instructors were trained. But the concept was only adopted officially by the DMT in the War Office in 1942.[33]

Which leads to Bartholomew's fourth point, 'Discipline', and all his other sub-points, such as the need to avoid ad hoc formations, the need for proper orders, for liaison officers, and to be prepared to operate at night. Alanbrooke was able to focus on these through Staff College exercises and Study Periods, and there are plenty of records of his directing such periods. But they were not started until after Christmas of 1940. Until then he was much more involved with the short-term need to get around his forces on the ground. On the other hand Montgomery was more driven, initially as a Divisional Commander, then as a Corps and District Commander. But of course Montgomery was, then and later, left to get on with his own thing. He was not having to sit up until 2 a.m. with Churchill, as Alanbrooke was, after November 1941, trying to prevent the PM from insisting on colourful and imaginative schemes that were beyond the power of the British Forces at that time.

Over the period immediately after the Fall of France it was Montgomery who established a reputation as a thorough trainer and he featured increasingly in the Staff College Study Periods. In the aftermath of Dunkirk he arrived back in 3 Div HQ on 6 June 1940, and on 14 June he issued a 5-page memo on 'Important Lessons' with twenty-two pages of appendices.[34] In them he acknowledged the superiority of German tactics, while identifying their tendency to fight by day and concentrate in defended localities at night. He was early in identifying the effect of concentrated artillery fire. Within weeks he was promoted to Corps Command.

His commander then was Auchinleck. Auchinleck's strategy, in common with the rest of GHQ Forces at the time, for dealing with invasion was to hold the shoreline as though it was the Maginot Line or the Thin Red Line of the Crimea. He felt that he needed armoured divisions to deal with any penetration of his line. Montgomery, on the other hand, wanted to extract his infantry divisions from the shoreline in order to be available as a reserve to deal with any penetration. Montgomery was determined not to allow himself to be got back into the static defence position which had dominated his time in Flanders, but rather wanted to be retraining his corps for a war of movement. This led to him countermanding his superior's order to continue building up coast defences very soon after arriving as 5th Corps Commander. The point here is that the British defence was based on the continuous manning of the best available obstacle, precisely in the same way that the Maginot Line had been defended. What had been overlooked until then was that the French had put their best troops into the best defences, leaving the less good troops to cover the less good obstacles, albeit in the areas that were seen as less likely approaches for the enemy. Montgomery saw that the best trained troops were most useful in responding to crises and could respond most quickly, with the best chance of success. Equally, the less well trained and less well equipped troops were best committed to holding ground where familiarity and prior occupation would count for most.

As a newly appointed Corps Commander he was quite a long way down the food chain, so this approach would have infuriated his military superiors. But he was vindicated when in August 1940 many of the UK Armoured Forces were sent to Egypt, depriving the Army in Southern England of the Armoured reserves that were the basis of Auchinleck's design for battle.

Montgomery's Corps consisted of two divisions, but he also had operational control of the static troops defending Portsmouth. Over the next 12 months he persevered with constant, almost messianic, fervour. He held exercises throughout the winter in a progressive series of evolutions, building on what he had started in 3rd Division. Corps Exercise No. 1 involved 30,000 troops and involved all arms, including the RAF, starting to work together, with the theme of the exercise being the attack.

His constant themes were the need to use divisions as divisions, not fragmenting them into their units, centralized artillery control and operations at night. In late October 1940 he was at the Senior Staff Course at Minley Manor[35] near Fleet, lecturing about 'Training in Wartime'. He declared that "Anything I say is my own personal view and has no official significance. . . . I will tell you what I do myself and how I train my corps. . . . I have had no guidance from above . . . on the subject"[36] This was not entirely true, for he had lots of guidance on the emphasis that was required of him on forward defence. But he had chosen to ignore it! Yet he does seem to have been the only commander engaged in systematic drilling of lessons at this stage, when the threat of invasion was still very high. He went on: "There is nothing new in this – but it is sound occasionally to collect your ideas and put down in concrete form what are the things that really matter in battle."

He could only have got away with this if he was being watched over from on high, and indeed he was, for Alanbrooke as CinC Home Forces was in constant touch with him. In January 1941 Alanbrooke went on the record at a staff college exercise at Camberley in expressing his views on the "present stagnation of higher training".[37] This is clear proof that there was not any worthwhile training taking place at levels above corps at that stage. However, Montgomery's long-suffering 5th Corps was out on exercise throughout the winter months. In late March they had their fifth exercise, which tested night movement, thus moving into an area where the Germans were known not to be good. It cannot have been comfortable. In the words of Field Marshal Templer: "It was Monty's achievement to rebuild the Army in England after Dunkirk. There is no doubt that, however much he was mocked outside 5th Corps, his methods were copied and in time became the accepted doctrine throughout the Army."[38] Alanbrooke's diary entry for 31 March 1941 indicates the overall quality of the senior Army commanders in the UK at the time: "Half our corps and divisional commanders are totally unfit for their appointments; and yet if I were to sack them I could find no better. They lack clarity, imagination, drive and power of leadership."[39]

In the summer of 1941 Montgomery took his Corps through a further series of exercises, BINGE, MOREBINGE and SUPERBINGE, all concentrating on the fighting of divisions as divisions to capitalize on the synergy of all arms. BINGE was of course Montgomery's word for the state of body and mind he was seeking to produce in all his troops. It had quite a different, opposite meaning to its meaning today. "Soldiers must be on their toes. They must have the light of battle in their eyes. They must be full of 'binge'."[40] It is also worth remembering that all this exercising was taking place in wartime Southern England, over private land, and that the rest of the army was trying to do the same, while farmers struggled to coax maximum food production out of the land. So there must have been considerable tensions, between Montgomery and his fellow Corps Commanders on the one hand, and between the Army and the farming community on the other.

Alanbrooke held his first really large exercise, BUMPER, in September 1941 and chose Montgomery to be the chief umpire. BUMPER was recognized to be the most important of all the Second

World War large-scale manoeuvres, not only because of its ambitious size, but because it was the first of its kind and thus the forerunner of the others.[41] It lasted from 27 September to 3 October 1941, with twelve divisions taking part, three armoured and nine infantry, with corps troops, tactical air recce and Army air support squadrons, a total of a quarter of a million men.

The "principle lessons derived"[42] bear a striking resemblance to Montgomery's lessons delivered at Minley twelve months previously. The need for Army Air Support and the need to avoid breaking divisions down to brigade groups often featured strongly; the co-ordinated divisional attack was seen as being more effective, but was rarely attempted. On the credit side the "fighting efficiency and spirit" were said to be of a commendable standard.

The one area where Montgomery does not appear to have exercised any influence was in the Army's internal organization of its basic fighting formations, its Divisions. In early 1942 Sir Bernard Paget, by then CinC Home Forces, having taken over from Alanbrooke when he in turn took over from Dill as CIGS, issued orders for reorganizing Divisions. The Infantry Division swapped its third dismounted infantry brigade for an army tank brigade, while the Armoured Division lost its second armoured brigade and gained one lorried infantry brigade. Nonetheless Montgomery promptly held an exercise, Exercise TIGER, in May 1942, to test out the new divisional organization.

No reference to Montgomery would be complete without some mention of the way he dealt with inadequate people. On arrival as a Corps Commander one of the very first things he did was decide which of the commanders at various levels had to go. Of the Area Commander he wrote: "I have no hesitation in saying that he should be at once removed. He is ineffective, lacks initiative, energy and drive and is obviously extremely idle. He is quite unfit to be a Major General, and should be relieved of his command at once and placed on retired pay." And Montgomery did not even command the man. Of the Commanding Officer of the unit defending the Isle of Wight he wrote: "He is 63, and is a really pathetic sight. He served in South Africa in 1899. He is very old, frail and looks very ill. He should . . . be sent away to end his life in peace somewhere." And the Commander Royal Engineers was "completely and utterly useless. He had served many years in India and was prematurely aged; he has taken to drink. He is unable to explain anything clearly and gives the impression of being mentally deficient."[43]

So whatever else was on Montgomery's notepaper the IIP (Investors in People) logo was probably not.

The other place where lessons learned might have been applied was, of course, the Western Desert. The Training Monograph states that "there was close and constant liaison between the various DMTs and the DMT in the War Office, but the tendency was definitely for the training in each theatre to be run entirely on its own and for its own particular needs."[44]

The Allied forces out in the Western Desert during the BEF campaign were essentially 3½ divisions of pre-war regulars. After Dunkirk it was decided to bring existing units up to strength rather than to send new units out, so the main reinforcement was 2nd Armoured Division in August/September 1940. It is recorded that the main training activity in December 1940, Training Exercise No. 1, used the orthodox methods set out in the pre-war official pamphlet "The Division in the Attack", based on First World War experience. Nonetheless, that training was sufficient, for, as General Bill Jackson writes, "Compass was one of those rare battles that did go according to plan. It was fought with professional standards which were never again achieved by the British in the Western Desert until El Alamein."[45] It is worth recalling the scale of this success, for subsequent events led to it being forgotten. Some 38,000 Italians were captured, with 237 guns and seventy-three tanks, for total Allied losses in killed, wounded and missing of just 624. Such asymmetric victories are rarely a spur for introspection and revision. And because the tactics were not seen as being broken, they were not perceived as needing to be fixed. Nonetheless, the run of success went on until February 1941, when Beda Fomm was won "by sound tactical methods, with close and intimate co-operation between tanks, artillery and infantry".[46] But in retrospect Wavell later described the run of success that ended in March 1941 as "an improvisation after the British fashion of war rather than a setpiece in the German manner.[47]

However, the next months saw the dilution of the regular units with replacements that had had only individual training at a time when the quality of the opposition was greatly improved by the arrival of the Germans in Africa. Earlier successes had led to overconfidence and overextended deployment. The rest of 1942 was remarkable for the succession of Allied setbacks. A lack of all-arms co-operation was evident in all the actions, with a particular lack of mutual confidence arising between the infantry and armoured units. "(T)here was no time

172

for divisional training with new equipment. Regimental commanders had barely enough time to train their own units, let alone train with their supporting infantry and artillery."[48] By Operation Battleaxe in June 1941 the two sides were so closely matched in numbers and equipment that generalship, tactics and training were the deciding factors. As Jackson points out, "In these actions the partially trained British units showed a tendency to which they were to become prone, of attacking too soon without properly co-ordinated artillery support."[49] The reverses and equipment losses of May and June 1941 provided the stimulus that created 'Jock Columns', described as "the momentary panacea in unhappy tactical situations of disorganization following defeat".[50] These units were all-arms groups, but were too small to be effective against any determined enemy. Throughout the rest of 1941 there is no trace of the training that was being conducted in the UK being seen as in any way relevant to events in the desert.

One opportunity the Desert Army had to refocus itself was when Auchinleck arrived over Christmas 1941. Auchinleck must have been aware of what Alanbrooke above him and Montgomery below him had been preaching and teaching throughout the previous twelve months in the United Kingdom on how to deal with German tactical methods. Indeed, he would have taken part in Alanbrooke's Staff College Studies. But it appears not to have convinced him, for very few of Montgomery's twelve principles were being quoted. And Alanbrooke cannot entirely escape censure, for he must have been involved in the decision to select Auchinleck for command in the Middle East. In June 1942, Auchinleck made two major organizational changes, neither of which reflected current thinking in the UK at the time. First, he decreed that the brigade group was the basic fighting formation, rather than the division. And second, he disbanded the Armoured Division Support Group in order to produce the artillery needed for the Brigade Groups.[51] Thus at Gazala, despite a superiority of eight to five in artillery, "the dispersion of the artillery among small bodies not under command of the highest artillery commander who could exercise collective control" was quoted as the prime reason for failure.[52]

Having thus institutionalized the changes that lost the Cauldron Battle, he in June 1942 recentralized the artillery. However, he also created a series of mobile battle groups within the brigades, which further fragmented the available forces into penny packets. Moreover, again in Jackson's words, "The full extent of the Cauldron defeat was never really appreciated by the British higher commanders at the time because other disasters followed in bewildering succession."[53] Procedures for the co-operation of the different arms with one another remained neglected, almost exactly when Montgomery, back in UK, was summing up, in the wake of Exercise TIGER, that "it will be seen that the whole conception of the offensive employment of an armoured division is based on:

> keeping it intact, and ready to operate as a complete division.
> And
> Not allowing the division to drift with the battle piece-meal."[54]

Meanwhile in July 1942, Kippenberger, the NZ infantry brigade commander, was writing: "It was regarded as axiomatic that the tanks would not be where they were wanted on time."[55]

The Allied response to the Cauldron and Gazala defeats was to try another reorganization, this time by splitting divisions up to establish a number of key points as a framework within which the rest of the division would operate. Again, this system was not based on what was known to work, but rather was almost a process of trial and error. Happily though, Auchinleck did then order the centralization of artillery at the highest practical level. This was described as "the first healthy sign of the British artillery being used properly under centralised controls."[56]

As a postscript to the attitude of the British to training, it is instructive to note the debate between the Americans and the British Staffs over the planning for Operation Torch, the Allied landings in Tunisia. The Americans did not think that their contingent would be able to reach an adequate state of training by mid-October 1942 and therefore did not think that the operation could be synchronized with the major offensive planned in the Western Desert. The British Chiefs of Staff felt that training should be sacrificed in favour of early action. Jackson remarks that "the American staffs could not refrain from pointing out the penalties which the British had paid for putting speed before preparation".[57]

Thus it can be seen that the Allied forces in the Western Desert were unable to develop battle-winning tactics once the advantage of the cohesion of the pre-war regulars had been eroded by attrition. It is acknowledged that the training of formations was the responsibility of their commands[58] and it is clear that this training was not very successful until late 1942. It took until Montgomery arrived in Egypt to begin to get it right. Colonel Jacob, writing in August 1942, stated that "no formation ever fought for long under the Commander and staff who had been training it. Brigades were taken from their divisions and pushed into the battle piece-meal. Some cavalry regiments were even broken up, squadron by squadron, and sent to join other regiments. The well-tried principle that the best results from artillery are obtained by its centralized control was forgotten. . . . It is undoubtably true that we showed ourselves incapable of concentrating superior force, and of utilizing the whole of our resources simultaneously. This showed itself in the dismal recurrence of the same event, namely the overruning of brigade after brigade by an enemy in superior force, while the rest of the army appeared powerless to assist."[59]

So to conclude and to return to the original question, it can be shown that valid lessons were drawn from the shattering experience of defeat in Flanders in the summer of 1940. But those lessons were not then impressed on the Army and the other Services in a top-down way, nor was the equipment programme significantly altered. It fell to Alanbrooke to give Montgomery and Alexander their heads – Montgomery in his messianic, driven way, and Alexander in a much less intense, but still effective, mode. The War Office did not address the issue, but rather left it to commanders on the ground to evolve their own methods of trial and error. If we have to give marks to those who drew the lessons, we could give Bartholomew 7/10 for his analysis; but the CIGS/DMT combination only get 2/10 for the way they drove the lessons through; and the Alanbrooke/Alexander/Montgomery combination 8/10, with the greatest credit undoubtably going to Alanbrooke for spotting his winners and backing them through thick and thin.

Notes

1   This paper develops a theme first set out by Mr J. Harding of the Army Historical Branch in an unpublished paper. I am most grateful to him for drawing it to my attention.
2   The British Army's selective use of aspects of the American Civil War is a thread linking officer education of the pre-First World War Army with that of the Inter-war years.
3   For a modern treatment of British army Tactics in the First World War, see *Battle Tactics of the Western Front* by P. Griffith, published by Yale University Press in 1994.

4 Report of the Committee on the Lessons of the Great War – October 1932. WO33/1297.

5 Army Training Memorandum No. 26, dated November 1939, War GS Publication 26 217.

6 Described in 50 (Northumbrian) Div War Diary for November 1939. PRO Ref. WO 166/605.

7 For a fuller treatment of British Army Training in 1939 and 1940, see the 1992 Royal College of Defence Studies Thesis of Brigadier K.J. Drewienkiewicz.

8 The Imperial Defence College was founded in 1927, with the charter of fostering greater understanding between senior military and diplomatic officials in planning the defence of the British Empire. The institution still exists today, having been renamed the Royal College of Defence Studies in 1970.

9 The Bartholomew Report, July 1940. PRO Ref. WO 106/1741.

10 Bartholomew Part I.

11 Bartholomew Part I.

12 Bartholomew Part II, Para 3.1 (c).

13 Bartholomew Part II, Para 3.1 (b).

14 Bartholomew Part II, Para 4 (d).

15 Bartholomew Part II, Para 6 (c).

16 Bartholomew Part II, Para 7 (a).

17 Bartholomew Part II, Para 7 (c).

18 Bartholomew Part II, Para 7 (d).

19 Bartholomew Part II, Para 2A.

20 The Minutes of the Executive Committee of the Army Council for 1940 contain no reference to it.

21 Army Training Memorandum No. 34 of July 1940, scale of issue one per officer.

22 "By and large the training of formations was the responsibility of their commanders. There are regrettably all too few records of the many exercises which took place, particularly during the period from the beginning of the war to the Battle of El Alamein in Oct 42." Training in the Army. The War Office (MT2), undated, Chapter IV, p. 211.

23 Military Engineering (Field), The War Office 1952.

24 ME (Field), p. 239.

25 Training in the Army, WO Ref 20/3 (MT2(a)) Front page. PRO Ref 277/36. (Training Monograph).

26 The Development of Artillery Tactics and Equipment. (Artillery Tactics Monograph). The War Office 1951, p. 41.

27 Artillery Tactics Monograph, p. 67.

28 Artillery Tactics Monograph, p. 127.

29 Quoted in *The North African Campaign 1940–43*, by W.G.F. Jackson, Batsford 1975, p. 30.

30 Training Monograph, Chapter XIII, p. 344.

31 *Monty, The Making of a General*, Nigel Hamilton, 1981, (Hamilton), p. 450.

32 Training Monograph, Chapter III, p. 199.

33 Training Monograph, Chapter I, p. 4.

34 Hamilton, p. 408.

35 Minley Manor was purchased as a training area in 1938, and became the home of the Senior Staff College in 1940. It remained a part of the Army Staff College until the late 1960s when it was offered to the Royal Naval staff College. They declined and the real estate was transferred to the Royal Engineers Training Brigade. The Royal Engineers are still in residence and the Engineer in Chief of the Army currently works from the location.

36 Hamilton, p. 440.

37 Hamilton, p. 453.

38 Hamilton, p. 469.

39 Quoted in Hamilton, p. 523.

40 Hamilton, p. 441.

41 Training Monograph, Chapter III, p. 191.

42 Training Monograph, Chapter III, p. 191.

43 Hamilton, p. 425.

44 Training Monograph, p. 203.

45 Jackson, p. 42.

46 Jackson, p. 68.

47 Wavell Despatches 10 July 1946, quoted in Jackson, p. 47.

48 Jackson, p. 124.

49 Jackson, p. 129.

50 Jackson, p. 130.

51 Jackson, p. 199.

52 Artillery Tactics Monograph, p. 135.

53 Jackson, p. 221.

54 Hamilton, p. 535.

55 Quoted in Jackson, p. 260.

56 Jackson, p. 257.

57 Jackson, p. 263.

58 Training Monograph, p. 211.

59 Quoted in Hamilton, p. 578.

REPERCUSSIONS:
THE BATTLE OF
FRANCE IN
HISTORY AND
HISTORIOGRAPHY

THE FRENCH VIEW

MARTIN S. ALEXANDER

Part I: Some History

The campaign of France and Flanders in 1940 was, to adapt Winston Churchill's words about the Battle of El Alamein in 1942, only a beginning, not an end. Despite the significance of the campaign and the resulting Allied defeat, the series of military operations in France and Flanders from 10 May to 22 June 1940 has not greatly interested the French over the last sixty years. Indeed, it still does not interest them much.

The important issues and events in the Second World War for the French occurred *after* the French agreed to German armistice terms on 22 June 1940. They chiefly concern the formation and the policies of the Vichy régime established on 10 July 1940 in the eponymous spa town in central France, a completely new government and state led by Marshal Philippe Pétain, the victor of Verdun and commander-in-chief of the French armies on the Western Front in 1917–18. What interests the French most of all, because it mattered so much to them in looking back on the years from 1940 to 1944, was what began in October 1940. This was the occasion of Pétain's one and only meeting with Hitler, at Montoire in south-west France, when the Marshal agreed to "enter into the way of collaboration" with Germany. The contested histories and memories, and therefore the historiographical battles, in France have chiefly raged over the French record of collaboration after June 1940. Opposition or resistance to that collaboration with the victorious Germans *after* France's defeat is what has really mattered to the French, continues to matter and will probably continue to matter for all time as the French strive to 'historicize' what occurred in their country during the Second World War.[1]

These are factors that Anglo-Saxon scholars need to recognize. Without such recognition it is impossible to comprehend otherwise

181

inexplicable oversights, blank spaces, blind spots and omissions in the French historiographical record of the 1940 campaign. For, undeniably, there are a large number of themes that in French writing have not been well treated to date, or not treated at all. We shall return to some of these later in this essay.

What about the 'history', in so far as we can say there is one, what about some of the controversies from the French point of view? First, it must be admitted that the French armed forces in general performed rather poorly in operational terms in 1940. This collection of essays has considered various aspects of the BEF's performance and the performance of the Belgian army too. This is proper, keeping in mind that what happened in France and Flanders was an Allied defeat, as the American-Israeli historian Jeffery A. Gunsburg properly emphasized some twenty years ago.[2]

However, the point made in his essay by Mungo Melvin – that excellent operational methods alongside poor strategy and grand strategy will ultimately cost you the war – can be turned on its head in regard to the French in 1940. For in the French case shortcomings at the operational level in 1940 should not obscure the fact that the French – and British – essentially got the blueprint right for the conduct of the Second World War. Their grand strategy embodied a successful formula to bring about eventual Allied victory and overthrow both Hitler's Germany and its European ally, Mussolini's Italy. Of course, serious initial setbacks dogged the 1940 campaign (and were evident, too, in Norway in 1940 and in Greece and Crete in May 1941). These delayed the Allied victory by a couple of years.[3] The Allied leaders had planned for Germany's defeat in 1943 or 1944. It did not occur till mid-1945. This was more a miscalculation than a sign of a fundamentally flawed grand strategy. We should not unduly criticize Franco-British political/military plans for the course and conduct of the Second World War merely because the initial clash of arms brought France's unexpected defeat.[4]

To employ an extended metaphor, the opening phase and ultimate course of the Second World War calls to mind the soccer World Cup tournament in England in 1966. This, for English football supporters of the day, began with a huge disappointment as a downcast nation awoke after England's tedious, drawn opening match with Uruguay at the 'home of football', Wembley's Empire Stadium. The match possessed neither drama nor attacking flair. It was a far cry from the showcase for soccer skills that English enthusiasts, gathered round their television sets, had eagerly anticipated. Alf Ramsey, the England team manager, had issued a bold (some immediately said foolhardy) pre-tournament prediction that England would win the World Cup on home turf. Yet in July 1966, as the matches that mattered began, the team was unable even to win the first game. This carried an echo of a notorious Allied propaganda poster whose slogan was attributed to France's prime minister of the summer of 1940, Paul Reynaud: "We'll win because we're the stronger!"

Ironically, Ramsey and Reynaud were both right. Yet the English soccer-loving public no more believed Ramsey on the gloomy morrow after the World Cup opener than did shocked, downcast French people when on 18 June 1940 a junior general, Charles de Gaulle, reiterated Reynaud's bouncy optimism by declaring in a BBC radio broadcast from London that in France and Flanders "France had lost a battle, but has not lost the war!" The English football players proved unable to get their team and nation off to a winning start in the campaign for the World Cup. And in 1940, too, a victory with which to begin the campaign proved beyond the Allies. To conclude the sporting analogy, one might say that the French lost the first game of the 'group phase' of the Second World War in 1940; yet they still finished as a member of the team lifting the winner's trophy in 1945.

Thus the overall pattern taken by the Second World War confirmed pre-war Allied strategic plans. From 1937–1938 the French and British politicians and civil servants understood that establishing policy-making machinery and bureaucracy for effective Anglo-French strategic, economic and financial coordination, along with joint missions for arms purchase in the USA, could not be left until three years into another major war, as it had been in 1914–1918. To the credit of Daladier, Chamberlain and their officials, crucial features of a sustainable, rationally-organized war effort and war economy were not only in place but were running smoothly before 1940. A strong cast of rising stars and capable technocrats were employed in these inter-Allied institutions on the eve of the débâcle: people like the later founder of the European Economic Community, Jean Monnet, despatched to the USA in 1938–1940 to buy 1,000 Curtiss fighter aircraft for France, and René Mayer, a serious and highly competent French politician of the post-war Fourth Republic, sent to head the French economic mission to London in 1940.

These were men who would proceed to the front rank of French leaders in business and political life at the close of the Second World

War and in the later 1940s and 1950s. In 1940 they were in key places, doing important but unsung and unglamorous work at the hub of the machinery of the Franco-British war effort, and particularly in the engine-rooms of the coalition's war economy. These points are too often neglected by historians sixty years after the defeat of 1940, just as they were too readily neglected by the over-confident, cocky German leaders who felt sure they had won, bar the shouting, in June and July 1940.[5]

What about the Dunkirk episode and the Allied performance in histories of 1940? Much depends on one's perspective. From that of the French, Dunkirk was almost ripe for caricature within a tradition of knavish, self-serving acts by 'perfidious Albion'.[6] Perhaps the retreat and evacuation was almost a prefiguring of Tommy Atkins as Billy Ocean, something along the lines of "When the going gets tough, the Brits get going." The legend of Dunkirk as a cowardly British sell-out of embattled France is probably ineradicable from French popular mythology. There was no really full-scale British commitment to defence on the European continent in 1939–1940, no pledge that the defensive battle there really had to halt the Germans.

There was a sense in France that the British had selfishly looked to themselves, exploiting their island status and withdrawing across the moat of the English Channel to fight another defensive battle. The British were, in this bitter French interpretation, ready to trade French soil, indeed French sovereignty, in order that the British Empire could live to fight another day. The myth has proved seductive for many French people. Berating the British for making only a half-hearted commitment to saving France has not disappeared in the six decades since the tragic parting of the entente in June 1940.[7]

Yet there was a British counter-myth to set against this singularly French outlook on Operation Dynamo. It was surely most pithily expressed in the uncompromising remark by the commander of the British AASF (Advanced Air Striking Force) deployed in France in 1940, Air Marshal Arthur Barratt, "that the RAF could not win the war if the French infantry had lost it".[8]

On the Dunkirk evacuation it seems unlikely that a synthesis will be established on which all can agree, French and British historians, newspaper feature writers, the man in the pub or café. On a personal note, I no longer hold out the hopes (or illusions) for a meeting of minds that I held as the fortieth anniversary of the campaign approached in 1980. Indeed, that anniversary itself was, from a historiographical

184

point of view, a disappointment. The year before saw publication of Jeffery Gunsburg's important *Divided and Conquered*, and Jean-Baptiste Duroselle's wider study of pre-war French foreign policy, *La Décadence*. A year after the anniversary Eleanor Gates' *End of the Affair* appeared, a detailed account of the Anglo-French rupture. There were belated French memoirs, inevitably from second-tier actors (given the passage of time), but shedding light nonetheless. But 1980 occasioned little new, archive-based scholarship. Characteristically, it saw Alistair Horne's popular book *To Lose A Battle* republished with no changes, to catch a tide of book-buying interest in the campaign, in Dunkirk and in the subsequent Battle of Britain.[9] The French archives had been closed when Horne first wrote, in the late 1960s. That was no longer the case by 1980. I also hoped, as the 1980 anniversary approached, that academic historians in France would start to take the campaign and the politics surrounding it with more rigour and serious-ness. Perhaps, after forty years, there was a chance for some scholarly convergence and understanding – a shared view. In fact, however, 1980 saw little except further hagiography around the rise of Charles de Gaulle and evidence of the growing fixation of the French with the dark secrets of the Occupation and *les collabos*.[10]

After sixty years, then, it seems unlikely that a synthesis will eventuate. Indeed, a synthesis appears culturally unattainable. The French saw themselves as abandoned at Dunkirk by the British – the lasting legend and big myth from the French standpoint. Many French people felt that the British had never accepted in their heart-of-hearts that the battle to stop Hitler's expected spring offensive *had* to be won on French and Belgian soil. According to this French myth, the British *always* had their eye on a fall-back position, a retreat across the Channel to their 'island-fortress'. Indeed there were even premonitory signs of this nightmarish scenario before the Battle of France and Flanders. The French air and military attachés in London noticed the priority of RAF rearmament production and air ministry orders shift in the winter of 1937–1938 away from bombers to fighters. By 1938 a few sharp-eyed French observers had detected that the new aircraft refitting RAF Fighter Command had a very short operational radius and might well remain stationed on air bases in the British Isles. In 1938–1939 the French authorities wished Britain to re-equip her forces with weapons systems such as modern tanks, field artillery and bomber aircraft that would lend themselves to forward deployment on the Continent. The French wished to see Britain's principal defences positioned in the same geographical sectors as France's own principal line of resistance.[11] Rather as with the financing of the Concorde supersonic aircraft joint project in the 1960s, the French wanted to see Britain become so deeply invested in the joint enterprise – 'Anglo-French War Effort Inc.' – on the soil of continental Europe that the British, too, would be compelled to regard the Battle of France as decisive.

In French legend the British enacted a self-fulfilling logic and abandoned Continental Europe, reverting to 18th or 19th Century type. With their policy of commando raids on the Lofoten Islands, Bruneval and St Nazaire, they seemed to be reverting to a traditional 'British Way in War'. This involved taking as much or as little of the fighting as they wished (to paraphrase the Elizabethan statesman and advocate of sea power, Sir Francis Bacon).[12] Indeed, the anglophobia of many French people shocked by Dunkirk was deepened by the affair of Mers el-Kébir of 3 July 1940. However good the reasons for carrying out the destruction of the French North African battle squadron from the British Admiralty's point of view, the terms and conditions presented to Admiral Gensoul were unnaceptable to an honourable and proud French naval officer. From misunderstanding to tragedy, Franco-British relations thus rapidly went from bad to appalling in that desperate summer of 1940.[13]

Consequently, there seems scant prospect of a shared, objective, historicized interpretation of the events of 1940. Their course was too different, their consequences too contrasting for the two entente nations. France was partially occupied as soon as the Battle of France was over. The Armistice terms of 22 June 1940 placed German soldiers, police and administrators in 60 per cent of France. The demarcation line approximately followed the high-tide mark of the Werhmacht's advance by the moment of the ceasefire, except that the German presence stretched all the way down the west coast of France to the Franco-Spanish frontier. This provision made the Biscay ports available to the German navy and air force. Brest, Lorient, La Rochelle and St Nazaire became bases from which the Kriegsmarine mounted a more aggressive and potent onslaught against British and Commonwealth merchant shipping plying the Atlantic sea-lanes. In British myth, therefore, the sudden French collapse and the particularities of the Armistice terms were also a kind of betrayal, one that deepened the peril into which another bout of 'Continental commitment' had dragged the British people. King George VI may have spoken for many of his subjects when he opined that Britain was better off "going it alone".

Part II: Some French Historiography on 1940

Occupation by the victorious Germans mattered not just for wartime strategy but also for the first wave of writing about the defeat itself. This was because, from the outset, even the French army officers who were not continuing to serve in Pétain's 100,000-man 'Armistice Army' (a total that deliberately replicated the terms imposed on the German army in the Treaty of Versailles in 1919) were not immediately able to set about writing their memoirs. Placing on record their versions of what had happened in the Battle of France and Flanders demanded paper, typewriters, publishers, printing presses. All were hard to come by, except for those who enlisted as propagandists for Pétain's Vichy régime and its singular slant on the causes of the débâcle, or as journalists on collaborationist newspapers. Most French officers lacked the physical means to set about fighting the battles of the memoirs. The dislocation in France in summer and autumn 1940 was unimaginable – dislocation of routine economic life, of families and of government departments, including the war, naval and air ministries. Administrators, along with their files and archives, were chaotically scattered and dispersed.

Nevertheless, though usually written without access to official papers, the production of memoirs did begin during the war. The German occupation and the continuation of hostilities, to the surprise of Pétain as much as Hitler, in 1940 and into 1941 upset many plans. It meant that some leading French protagonists, and many of lesser rank, still had key parts to play in French public life. Many military officers from May and June 1940 became Vichy ministers or led Vichy's army and air force in North Africa, Syria and the Lebanon. One thinks of General Georges Bridoux, General Charles Huntziger and General Henri Dentz. Others served in the residual forces allowed to Pétain's régime within metropolitan France. About 1.6 million French military personnel of all ranks became prisoners-of-war in Germany.[14] Only a few hundred French people heard de Gaulle's appeal of 18 June 1940 from London to continue the fight at Britain's side.

The rigours of Occupation ensured that dealing with 1940 as history

187

was not something that until 1945 greatly concerned many of the French. Had Britain surrendered to Germany in July, or in September, 1940, presumably some rather different things would have happened even within the perspective concerning us here. One thing might have been an earlier historicizing of the war of 1939–1940 – what a book by John Lukacs once called *The War Hitler Won*. The installation of a collaborationist government, more collaborationist the longer the war went on, was an injury to France. To this was added the insult of an extension of German control to all France, in response to Operation Torch in November 1942. This meant that a German military and police presence on French territory was omnipresent in the second half of the war. It drastically revised national priorities. Pétain's ability to present a semblance of normality and to shield 40 per cent of France from direct occupation weakened and then vanished. But so too did concern about what had caused the débâcle in 1940. By the time of the summer of Liberation in August–September 1944 the summer of Blitzkrieg was a very dim memory indeed. Albeit only three or four years in the past, by 1943–1944 it already had the remote feel of a bygone age and a lost world.

In many ways, therefore, French historiography about the Battle of France lacked a head of steam until after the war's end in 1945. The following year saw the appearance of *Strange Defeat*, the posthumous and soon-legendary personal account by the medieval historian and Resistance martyr, Marc Bloch.[15] General Maurice Gamelin, the commander-in-chief of French land forces in 1939–1940, had used his wartime incarceration to write his memoirs. These appeared in three volumes in 1946–1947 under the collective title *Servir* ('To Serve').[16] Gamelin was not the only senior French military figure determined to publish swiftly and 'get his retaliation in first'. Among others who did were Major Jacques Minart, who had been on Gamelin's general head-quarters staff (*Grand Quartier Général*) at Vincennes in 1939–1940. Minart produced a very revealing and under-utilized two-volume account in 1945 entitled *P.C. Vincennes: Secteur 4*.[17] He had kept a diary at the war's outset and his books uncover much about politics and morale at French GQG in the Phoney War. Various publications from operational commanders also appeared. Among those of note was a volume by General Charles Grandsard, the 10th corps commander, and diaries by General Arlabosse, commander of the 11th Infantry Division (nicknamed 'The Iron Division') and General Jules Prioux, commander of the armoured cavalry corps that halted

General Hoepner's two panzer divisions at the Battle of the Gembloux Gap. Other tomes published in the years from 1945 to 1950 included the memoirs of army commanders such as General Edouard Requin (IVth Army) and General Victor Bourret (Vth Army), and a plea for an understanding of the role and fate of the oft-maligned and out-flanked Maginot Line by Gaston Prételat (Second Army Group).[18]

Thus several significant volumes had seen the light of day by 1947, comprising the first wave of French historiography on the campaign in France and Flanders. During the immediate post-war years, however, French people were generally otherwise preoccupied. There was a chronic economic crisis at home, serious industrial unrest, the menace of Communism and bitter political controversy over the constitution for a new governing régime, the Fourth Republic. Abroad the period saw the onset of a fresh war, against Ho Chi Minh and the National Liberation Front, in Indochina.

Between 1940 and 1942 the Vichy régime had sought the French equivalent of Michael Foot and Frank Owen's *Guilty Men*, the culprits for the lost campaign. Pétain had thus placed Gamelin and five other erstwhile Third Republic leaders on trial at Riom. In a watered-down imitation of this spirit of vengeance and scapegoatism, the Fourth Republic held a parliamentary inquiry from 1947 to 1950 that examined the events in France between 1933 and 1945. It interviewed a selection of French political, military and administrative leaders and published its findings as a two-volume report supported by nine volumes of evidence and documents in 1951–1952. The appearance of this mass of testimony prompted further officers to produce their memoirs in the early-to-mid 1950s. Especially noteworthy were those by two former chiefs of French military intelligence (the *2e Bureau*), General Maurice Gauché and his predecessor, General Louis Koeltz (the latter serving as a corps commander in the 1939–1940 campaign).[19]

More significant in terms of arguments about the causes and responsibilities for the French defeat was the publication of General Maxime Weygand's memoirs, in three volumes, in 1952–55. The first volume was devoted to Weygand's youth in the French army before 1914 and to his functions in the First World War (which he completed as chief of staff to the Allied generalissimo, Marshal Ferdinand Foch). The second volume focused on the inter-war years and particularly on Weygand's period as French army commander-in-chief designate between 1931 and 1935. The last volume was the only one to be

189

published in an English translation. This appeared in 1954 under the title *Recalled to Service* (an exact translation of the French original).[20]

Weygand was an ultra-conservative officer who had long been highly critical of France's republican institutions and political culture. *Recalled to Service* offered a trenchant critique of the inadequacies of French military readiness in 1939–1940 (implicitly blaming some of this on Gamelin, who had succeeded Weygand as chief of the French general staff in 1935). It presented an even more biting attack on allegedly decadent and unpatriotic Republican political leaders and the nation's allegedly 'sectarian' parliamentary parties. These were, for Weygand, the real causes of France's military defeat. He spent little time scrutinizing the army's training, doctrine, weapons or commanders (not surprisingly, since he himself had been one of the most senior). Weygand's memoirs also found space to point an accusatory finger at French allies. These, including Britain, had been complacent about the German menace, too few in number and had not, he claimed, sufficiently paid tribute to the self-sacrificing way that France in 1940 immolated herself as the advance guard to shield and save the ill-prepared Western democracies (i.e. Britain and the USA). In the Weygand version of 1940 the French bought crucial time for the British to complete full-scale mobilization and for the USA and USSR to take the measure of Hitler's Germany and come around to active involvement in the anti-Nazi crusade.

This first wave of French military writing as a phenomenon mainly of the early and middle 1950s can be easily situated in its contemporary context. For this was the one period of apparent stability under the much-maligned Fourth Republic, France's ruling régime from 1944 to 1958. The years from 1951 to about 1956 were the 'golden age' of the régime, akin to the years from 1925 to 1929 in Germany's Weimar Republic (a régime similarly criticized for irredeemable governmental instability and ineffectiveness). France between 1951 and 1955 did seem to have moved into calmer waters after the turbulence of the late 1940s. Even defeat in Indochina in 1954 had only a limited impact on the French as a whole. Only a tiny part of the French armed forces were touched, for the war in Indochina was waged by a small professional expeditionary corps (swelled by contingents from French imperial territories such as Madagascar, Senegal and North Africa). At home the Fourth Republic was presiding over a genuine economic boom and industrial modernization in the early and middle 1950s, one much admired by contemporary Anglo-American observers.

190

This period of tranquillity and rising material prosperity enabled French people to take stock of their experiences in the Second World War. The phenomenon to agitate them most in the 1950s was not what had happened during the campaign of 1940, why, and who was responsible. Rather, the French were excited and polarised by a struggle to establish orthodoxies or dominant myths about the Resistance after the defeat, between 1940 and 1944. Quickly the portrayal of Resistance assumed a Manichean character. On the one hand, Resistance was depicted as something entirely the work of the French Communists, the party of the 75,000 martyrs executed by the Germans for courageous acts of Resistance. On the other stood the charge by liberal-Catholic-nationalist Resisters that the Communists had excelled only at propaganda for their own cause to gain post-war electoral advantage and in the war had done little, and nothing at all till instructed by their puppet-masters in Moscow in June 1941, to resist the Germans.

This may seem peripheral to our concerns with the historiography of the 1940 campaign. In fact it is crucial. For it was the military operations that proved utterly marginal to French national debates. The 1950s and 1960s were dominated by memoirs, polemics and an increasing volume of serious academic scholarship about the Resistance. The French constructed a comforting version of their nation's Second World War history and conduct in these years. This was largely the work of a small band of distinguished French historians, notably Henri Michel and Claude Lévy. Around them a team edited the *Revue d'Histoire de la Deuxième Guerre Mondiale* and directed from the rue de Leningrad in Paris by the French Centre for the History of the Second World War. They assembled hundreds of tape-recorded testimonies and a wealth of leaflets, tracts, pamphlets and underground newspapers printed by Resistance groups between 1940 and 1945 across the length and breadth of France. The work of the French Committee has left a treasure trove for later historians of Second World War Resistance.

Much of the activity and motivations of wartime French resisters was never confided to paper. Written minutes of resistance meetings would have been tantamount to suicide notes under the wartime German occupation. Michel and Lévy realized that the first-hand evidence to account for Resistance motivations, actions and plans for post-war France was embodied in the veterans themselves. The sources for the future resistance histories were the oral testimonies to be garnered from the men and women who had taken part. Teams travelled to the small towns and countryside of France during the later 1950s and 1960s. There they painstakingly tape-recorded former Resistance activists and retrieved the fragile pamphlets, fly-sheets and tracts often printed on flimsy wartime paper that constituted such a paper trail as survived from wartime clandestinity. Many of the resisters have now died. Without the dedicated work of the French Committee vast swathes of Resistance activity and ideas would now be lost permanently from the historical record. In the main, then, the French were concerned in the 1950s and 1960s with what Resisters did, where they did it and when they did it. Few had much concern for the war of 1939–1940.[21]

Notwithstanding the domination of the historical agenda by Resistance histories written and argued over *fortissimo*, there was some debate in the 1950s and 1960s (albeit distinctly *diminuendo*) about the military nature of the defeat. For this Basil Liddell Hart was partly responsible. He helped ensure that Colonel Adolphe Goutard's book, *1940, La Guerre des occasions perdues* (French edition, Hachette, 1956) appeared in English translation and wrote a foreword to the English edition published in 1958. The book had rarity value, especially coming from a French military historian. For it put up a spirited challenge to the view that France had been a demoralized nation in 1940, riddled with pacifism, her army's morale rotted by enforced idleness in the Maginot Line during the so-called Phoney War. Goutard rejected assumptions about inevitable defeat at the hands of an overwhelmingly superior Germany. Instead he suggested that the French need not have lost and that, in losing, they had only themselves and their deficient military institutions, generals and fighting methods to blame.[22]

Defeat on the Meuse, in Flanders and on the Somme and Seine was a result of blunders by the high command, poor use of troops and equipment, contingencies and missed opportunities during a confusing and highly fluid campaign. The Germans had made mistakes, too, noted Goutard. He concluded that the Germans prevailed because they made fewer, and the Allies let them get away with those they did make. For Goutard, it was not foreordained that France would lose. Indeed, he argued, a stalemate ought to have been achieved by the Allies. This was an outcome that many German commanders and staff officers greatly feared in early 1940 and one that Hitler himself would have viewed as a grave strategic defeat.[23]

Besides prefacing Goutard's book, Liddell Hart befriended General André Beaufre. Beaufre was a rising star of a rejuvenated French officer corps after the Suez débâcle of 1956 and the Algerian quagmire. Like General Pierre Gallois, regarded by some as the father of the French nuclear force, and General Charles Ailleret, Beaufre was a technocrat. These officers had largely avoided tarnishing their names in the failed wars to retain French Indochina and Algeria. De Gaulle, returning as President of France in 1958, promoted them rapidly, especially when the attempted military putsch of 1961 convinced him he should thoroughly purge the army's senior officer corps. He used Beaufre, Gallois and Ailleret to remodel the French military and prioritize French nuclear weapons.

Beaufre won a high reputation in the 1960s as a serious strategic thinker. He wrote numerous works on military power and geo-strategy in the nuclear age and was the closest France had to a Bernard Brodie or a John Slessor. Of greater concern to us is that in 1965 he wrote a book, *Le Drame de 1940*. Impressed by this, Liddell Hart helped set up an English translation published in London in 1967 and in New York in 1968 under the title, *1940. The Fall of France*.[24] Beaufre's volume was part memoir – he had served as a captain at the French general headquarters in 1940 – and part history. It, too, presented a trenchant critique of the French 'military system' of the later 1930s and did not spare the French army or commanders such as Gamelin by pandering to comforting military alibis about defeat stemming from Fifth Columnists or civilian pacifists. Also in 1965 the writer Claude Gounelle first published his book about the battle for the Meuse crossings, *Sedan, 1940*.[25] These works reflected the fact that in the middle 1960s France was again comparatively secure and politically tranquil. French people could look back and debate the events of twenty-five years before, without much fear of stirring controversies or polemics likely to destabilize a fragile contemporary political situation.

After the 1960s, however, there was a long hiatus. The riots of May 1968 switched public concern onto the stagnation of the Gaullist Fifth Republic, the unfulfilled modernization of society, the claims of women for inclusion and full political rights and the emergence of a vibrant youth culture. The political left was ascendant. Intellectual debates, led by Jean-Paul Sartre, Simone de Beauvoir, Regis Debray, Raymond Aron and others looked forward, not back. In November 1970 even de Gaulle died. A page seemed definitively turned on the sepia-tinted and largely forgotten war of 1939–1940 and its actors.

By the mid-1970s there was scarcely a scholar in France with any interest in 1940. This was not just a matter of the mood of the time. It was also a result of the inaccessibility of the archives and a consequence of the wholesale 'turn' of French academic historians to a very different type of history. For the 1960s and 1970s were the heyday of the *Annales* school of historians in France, who traced their roots to the foundation of the journal *Annales d'histoire économique et sociale* in 1929 by Lucien Febvre and Marc Bloch. This school was led with massive prestige in the 1960s by the most celebrated French historians of the age, Fernand Braudel and Emmanuel Le Roy Ladurie. Trade, plague and bread prices in early-modern Europe were in fashion; the alternative was to be led to the methodological barricades by Albert Soboul, Michel Vovelle and François Furet, Marxist standard-bearers for a new explanation of the 1789 Revolution. These were the fields on which an ambitious French historian could make a name. Locked into a Marxist paradigm, French university history in the 1960s and 1970s was concerned to explain the course of the past not as the outcome of human actions but as the product of immense and irresistible socio-economic currents.

With historians also 'discovering' computers, this approach was buttressed by the penchant for quasi-scientific data analysis. French historians became seduced by the chimerical promises of computers, quantitative approaches and social-scientific number crunching. The *forces profondes* and the *longue durée* – the deep socio-economic and demographic undercurrents of the past – gripped imaginations. The knock-on effects for French academe included the distribution of the vast bulk of the research grants to projects in social, economic, demographic and cultural history. Up-and-coming scholars saw that they could only flourish if they latched onto the coat-tails of the grandees, and undertook the long doctoral studies essential to a university career.

Only one significant grouping swam against the tide. This was the school of historians of contemporary international relations at the Sorbonne (Paris I), founded by Pierre Renouvin and Maurice Baumont. This spawned disciples such as Jean-Baptiste Duroselle and, from the second half of the 1970s, René Girault, Georges-Henri Soutou, Denise Artaud, Jacques Bariéty, Maurice Vaïsse, Elisabeth du Réau and others. But even they had, in the 1970s and 1980s, little concern for the history of strategy, let alone with the operational conduct of war (though, by the late-1970s, they did begin to explore the emerging history of intelligence and secret services.

The French army's and air force's operational performance in 1940 contains elements of great potential interest to military historians. Unfortunately, however, to declare any interest in military history was profoundly unfashionable, even a kiss of death, in French universities from the 1960s to the mid-1980s. Indeed this remains disappointingly true even in the year 2001. Some modest recovery did occur. Military history could be 'respectable' in the 1990s, especially if it engaged with 'society' and culture, better still on relations between soldiers and the 'home front' or on attitudes, outlooks, *mentalités*. The view continues to prevail that operational military history – studies of what armed forces actually do in war rather than how they are recruited and organized in peace – should be left to the professional military officers who have received formal academic training as historians.

This is why most of the serious works in French on the campaign of France and Flanders in 1939–1940 have been written by the staff of the historical services of the French army, navy and air force. These are, ironically enough, located at the former headquarters of General Gamelin himself at the Château de Vincennes. It may come as a surprise to note the lasting quality of works from the French Army Historical Service (SHAT) produced as early as the late 1940s, such as Major Pierre Lyet's book *La Bataille de France* (1947) and articles by the head of the Service in the late 1940s, Colonel Charles de Cossé-Brissac, that should have left stillborn the legend of German victory achieved by overwhelming numbers of armoured and air forces.[26] Overdue for acknowledgement, too, are the important publications of General Jean Delmas, head of the SHAT for much of the 1980s, and successive heads of the SHAT Research and Studies Section, Colonels Henry Dutailly, Michel Turlotte and Frédéric Guelton.[27]

Similarly, the staff of the French air force historical service (SHAA) have produced major works on air operations over France and Flanders in 1939–1940. Worth underlining are books such as that by Patrick Fridenson and Jean Lecuir on Anglo-French air force relations, 1935–39, published as long ago as 1975, and studies on French air intelligence about the Luftwaffe by Patrice Buffotot and on the French aviation industry's problems in rearming swiftly enough by General Charles Christienne.[28] The SHAA, under Christienne's leadership from the mid-1970s to the early 1980s, hosted several important colloquia. This practice happily continued under Christienne's successor, General Lucien Robineau, in the later 1980s and early 1990s.[29] These colloquia spawned multi-author works and volumes of conference proceedings. By the later 1990s SHAA staff were publishing substantial single-authored books such as Patrick Facon's on the French air force in the 1940 campaign and that of Claude d'Abzac Epézy on aviation under Vichy.[30]

On the French navy important work was produced for many years by Philippe Masson of the *Service Historique de la Marine* (SHM).[31] This has been reinforced, latterly, by other SHM staff historians. One, Philippe Lasterle, has begun publishing the fruits of his doctoral thesis on Admiral Gensoul and the drama of Mers-el-Kébir.[32] Numerous works have come from the prolific naval historian Hervé Coutau-Bégarie and his co-author Claude Huan. The most significant are their quasi-definitive biography of Admiral François Darlan (chief of French naval staff, 1937–1941), an edited collection of Darlan's diaries and personal correspondence, and Coutau-Bégarie's study of the maritime strategic theorist, Admiral Raoul Castex, who was commander of the Channel zone of operations and '*Amiral Nord*' in 1939, based at Dunkirk.[33]

A key development for those lacking the privileged access open to the military's official historical branches was the softening of French archival laws in May 1975. This resulted from a decree promulgated for the thirtieth anniversary of VE day by Valéry Giscard d'Estaing, then President of France. From that date consultation of the primary sources for French defence and diplomatic policies, rearmament and military doctrine for the period 1919–July 1940 became easier, even if the lack of detailed inventories, catalogues and finding-aids still made work in French government papers highly laborious until the late 1980s. 'Outsider' historians had to rely greatly on the generous help of *Service Historique* archivists with detailed knowledge of the holdings by carton-series, such as Jean Nicot, Jean Devos, Patrick Wakjsman and Patrick Facon. Thanks to these 'insiders', the 1975 archive law relaxation was used to advantage, albeit mainly by historians from North America, including John C. Cairns, Robert J. Young, Robert A. Doughty, Jeffery A. Gunsburg, Nicole Jordan and Eugenia C. Kiesling, and by a small number of Britons including the present writer. In spite of easier access, however, 1940 and the reputation of the major French protagonists remained a sensitive matter. As late as 1975 a senior staff historian in the SHAT, Colonel Pierre Le Goyet, had his career terminated for publishing a book on Gamelin without first obtaining full ministerial and family authorization.[34]

Only from the early 1980s have mid-career French officers been encouraged to undertake military and naval history as part of their professional development. They have done so under the supervision of French academics such as Professor Guy Pédroncini, the leading historian of Pétain's command of the French armies in 1916–1918, and Professor Maurice Vaïsse, the first Director of the Centre for the Study of Defence History (CEHD).[35] These officers have gained the French *maîtrise* by thesis or, in more recent years, the reformed and now shorter university doctorate. Among those officer-scholars whose dissertations concerned the 1930s and 1940 were Claude Carré (who wrote a seminal study on the interwar French military attachés), Dominique de Corta (whose work tackled the role of the French military attaché in Madrid during the Spanish Civil War) and André Bach, whose *maîtrise* examined the re-establishment of Franco-Soviet military and diplomatic relations in the years 1932–1936. In an encouraging development (and a rare case of a military placement of a 'round peg in a round hole'), Bach returned to military history at the end of his army career by finishing as Director of the SHAT between 1997 and 2000.

During the 1990s, furthermore, growing numbers of civilian French students, particularly from the history of international relations programme at the Sorbonne (Paris I) under Professor Robert Frank, were pushed to undertake research into military topics. Recent subjects have included the operational functioning of the Franco-British task forces in the Suez crisis, Franco-American naval relations in the Mediterranean in the 1950s and Franco-German defence relations in the late 1950s and early 1960s.

These represent exciting and uplifting indications of greater openness, of minds as well as archives. Unfortunately, despite the generally more favourable climate, the story is not entirely encouraging for the historiography of 1940. During the 1990s French interest in their recent past has lain predominantly with the history of 'The Dark Years'.[36] Vichy and collaboration has been an 'ever-present Past', in the haunting formula of Eric Conan and Henry Rousso.[37] The intensity of the spotlight on the Occupation has not dimmed, the glare being kept bright by the highly public trials of Klaus Barbie, Gestapo chief in Lyons in 1943–1944, and of the Vichy milice leader Paul Touvier and the collaborationist sub-prefect of the Gironde in 1942–1944, Maurice Papon.

In 1997 the CEHD, at the instigation of its Director, Maurice Vaïsse. convened a colloquium on the events of May–June 1940 through the eyes of 'foreign' (non-French) historians.[38] This was a welcome antidote to the cold-shouldering of non-French students of the defeat a generation earlier. Yet the sixtieth anniversary of 1940 was dominated in the French media not by Hitler's triumph in the West and its terrible consequences, nor was it even taken over by more on Vichy and collaboration. Rather, the media and historians have been caught up with dramatic controversies and confessions from a more recent dark era, the French war in Algeria of 1954–1962. It seems symptomatic that the year saw at least two major colloquia on the Algerian War, the first in May in Montpellier and the second in Paris in November (despite the year 2000 offering no special anniversary peg on which to hang them). Welcome though it is to see French attention to the Algerian War, one hopes this will not be totally to the exclusion of research and debate on 1940.

Yet just one conference in Paris marked the campaign in France and Flanders. This, held from 16–18 November 2000 in the refurbished Musée de l'Armée at Les Invalides, was as notable for what it did not tackle as for what it did. There was only one British academic on the programme (the present author), and one other in the audience. Only one German historian presented a paper, and one Belgian.[39] The role of intelligence was tackled by a single speaker (in a paper by Olivier Forcade, a professor at the French military academy of St. Cyr-Coëtquidan, that focused on the French secret services rather than the organization, functioning, coordination and shortcomings of Allied intelligence as a whole). Wholly absent were the approaches that have during the 1990s, in the hands of British, Canadian and Australian historians, transformed our understanding of armies' operational problems and how they were overcome in the First World War. Thus questions of supply and logistics were entirely invisible. Military technology got very short shrift, being tackled specifically in just one paper about the manufacture of signals communications equipment, even though signals and radio communications gear were identified as a truly crucial area of Allied weakness in the campaign as long ago as 1985 by the American historian and West Point history professor, Robert Doughty.[40]

It is a telling commentary on French academic historians' priorities that not until 1998 was a serious account of the French air force in the 1940 campaign written, and then it was written by Patrick Facon, head of the Studies Section at the Air Historical Service, the SHAA, not by anyone holding a university post. This is symptomatic of a continuing, if nowadays less blatant, French academic disdain for military history. The French university regard for historical research into military subjects is weak at best. This disdain, or at least neglect, is compounded by the fact that, unlike the British, Canadians, Australians, South Africans and Americans, the French do not write official histories of their wars. There is nothing comparable on 1940 to the volume by Major L.F. Ellis, *The War in France and Flanders*, nor to the volumes produced by the German historians Wilhelm Deist, Manfred Messerschmidt *et al.* at the Military History Research Office, Potsdam, on *Germany in the Second World War*.[41] It is only a slight exaggeration to say that the military history of the late 1930s and the 1940 campaign is 'ghetto-ized' in the official armed services historical branches.

Many writers on the French defeat have taken their cue from the book of reflections written shortly after the defeat by the celebrated French medieval historian, Marc Bloch, to which we referred earlier, *Strange Defeat: A Statement of Evidence written in 1940*. Bloch, a co-founder of the Annales school of history, had fought bravely on the Western Front in 1914–1918. He served during the war of 1939–1940 as a reservist captain in charge of an army fuel depot in Northern France. His highly personal account of what he heard and saw has hugely influenced two generations of French and non-French writers about the defeat. It gained poignancy from the fact of Bloch's execution as a Jew and a resister in 1944. Even Bloch, however, was more concerned with puzzling out why French people so readily acquiesced in – many even enthused about – the overthrow of the Third Republic and its values. In other words, Bloch picked away at why military defeat led so swiftly to a decisive change in French political orientation, causing such emotional grief to a Republican like himself.

For the sixtieth anniversary Andrew Shennan has re-examined the historiography of 1940 in an excellent new work of synthesis, *The Fall of France, 1940*. This concludes that the campaign and military defeat in France and Flanders is a matter of limited interest primarily concerning specialists in strategic/military history. It does not, at bottom, interest the French. There has been no '1940 syndrome'.[42] This was also the line adopted recently by Stanley Hoffmann, for over forty years one of American academe's most respected and prolific commentators on French politics and mentalities. In a chapter to conclude Joel Blatt's edited collection, *The French Defeat of 1940: Reassessments*, Hoffmann noted the absence of a '1940 syndrome'.[43]

199

This apathy over 1940 contrasts with the notorious 'Vichy syndrome' identified by Henry Rousso in the late 1980s, and with what Martin Evans, writing of the trauma being caused to the French by revelations about use of torture in Algeria, has termed a 'colonial syndrome'.[44]

Admittedly the French historian Jean-Pierre Azéma described 1940 as 'The Terrible Year'.[45] Yet he did so not primarily because the military defeat was terrible but because of the terrible political, ideological and fratricidal consequences that flowed *from* the defeat. The military events of April, May and June 1940 are far from being the dominant problem of the Second World War for the French and for French historians. The defeat has not been what mattered for them, but rather the results of the defeat. It is the consequences that stemmed from defeat, and even more from the change of régime at Vichy in July 1940, that continue to matter to the French. Sadly, oversights extend to the experiences of rank-and-file French combatants in 1940. Some graphic diaries and first-hand accounts exist. There are well-known journals and memoirs by subsequently famous men – Georges Sadoul, later France's most celebrated cinema critic, and Pierre Dunoyer de Segonzac of the semi-monastic leadership college at Uriage, founded to forge a new generation of leaders to make France great again in a post-war world.[46]

But there are also fascinating narratives from long-forgotten combatants. These include the journal of Robert Felsenhardt of the 18th Corps, Lucien Carron's account of his battalion's heroic but hopeless battle to defend the Aisne, and Claude Armand-Masson's diary of service in the Maginot Line.[47] All repay attention. Together they can help us recover a picture of the brave, often bewildered, French soldiers who fought (100,000 of whom died) in the 1940 campaign. Except for a chapter by the present author in the book *Time To Kill* (1997), however, the often deadly war experienced by French troops, NCOs and junior officers remains to be researched and written.[48] Historians have not, to date, done justice to the bravery of the French soldiers of 1940.[49]

One should conclude by recalling how weakly Britain and France were linked as allies in 1939–1940. They were, in too many key respects, neighbouring nations conducting a war in parallel rather than as one unified endeavour. The linkages between the two national historiographies of the opening round of the Second World War are at least as weak: these are close neighbours that underwent the same events but experienced radically divergent outcomes from them. These are neigbours with two parallel national myths about 1940 as a result, and two literatures set to continue to run alongside one another rather than converge. In 1940, in France and Flanders, there were French and British, not Franco-British, war efforts and military operations; sixty years later there are French and British historiographies of 1940, not a Franco-British one.

Notes

1   See, indicatively, Christine Lévisse-Touzé, 'Le Général de Gaulle et les débuts de la France Libre', in *Revue Historique des Armées. Numéro spécial: L'année 1940* no. 219 (June 2000), pp. 63–70.

2   J.A. Gunsburg, *Divided and Conquered. The French high command and the defeat of the West, 1940* (Westport, CT: Greenwood Press, 1979).

3   On Norway, see François Kersaudy, *Stratèges et Norvège, 1940. Les jeux de la guerre et du hasard* (Paris: Hachette, 1977); and Wesley K. Wark, 'Sir Edmund Ironside: The Fate of Churchill's First General, 1939–40', in Brian Bond (ed.), *Fallen Stars. Eleven Studies of Twentieth Century Military Disasters* (Oxford: Brassey's, 1991), pp. 141–63; Major-Gen. Sir John Kennedy, *The Business of War* (London: Collins, 1957); T.K. Derry, *The Campaign in Norway* (London: HMSO, 1952).

4   See the interesting re-evaluation of the campaign by Ernest R. May, *Strange Victory: Germany and the defeat of France, 1940* (Cambridge, Mass: The Belknap Press, 2000).

5   Exempted from this stricture is the magisterial two-volume work by Jean-Louis Crémieux-Brilhac, *Les Français de l'An 40* (Paris: Gallimard, 1990).

6   For fascinating reflections on this theme, see P.M.H. Bell, *France and Britain, 1904–1940: Entente and Estrangement* (London: Longman, 1996).

7   See the memoir by one of French premier Paul Reynaud's close advisors at the time, Dominique Leca, *La Rupture de 1940* (Paris: Fayard, 1978).

8   Quoted in C. Christienne, 'La RAF dans la bataille de France à travers les rapports Vuillemin de juillet 1940', in *Recueil d'Articles et Etudes (1981–1983)* (Vincennes: Publications du SHAA, 1987), p. 328; cf. P.M.H. Bell, 'Shooting the rapids: British reactions to the Fall of France, 1940', in *Modern and Contemporary France. Review of the Association for the Study of Modern and Contemporary France* 42 (July 1990), pp. 16–28.

9   A. Horne, *To Lose a Battle: France 1940* (London: Macmillan, 1969; re-issued 1980). The earlier works referred to are: J.-B. Duroselle, *Politique*

étrangère de la France: La Décadence, 1932–1939 (Paris: Imprimerie Nationale, 1979), which was followed by the same author's *L'Abîme, 1939–45* (Paris: Imprimerie Nationale, 1983); and E.M. Gates, *End of the Affair. The Collapse of the Anglo-French Alliance, 1939–40* (London: George Allen & Unwin, 1981).

10 See, for example, Paul Huard, *Le colonel de Gaulle et ses blindés. Laon, 15–20 mai 1940* (Paris: Plon, 1980); and Henri de Wailly, *De Gaulle sous la casque: Abbeville 1940* (Paris: Albin Michel, 1990).

11 General Albert Lelong (French military attaché, London, 1936–40), 'Etude sur la participation de l'Angleterre dans l'éventualité d'une action commune franco-britannique en cas de guerre', 8 Nov. 1938, in Papiers Edouard Daladier: 4 DA 8, dr. 3, sdr. b, Archives Privées 496 AP, Archives Nationales, Paris; Conseil Supérieur de la Défense Nationale, study for Daladier (minister of national defence and war), no. CU/1, 'La puissance des forces armées franco-britanniques', 22 Nov. 1938, Carton 5N579, dr. 2, Archives du SHAT, Vincennes; Patrick Fridenson and Jean Lecuir, *La France et la Grande-Bretagne face aux problèmes aériens (1935–mai 1940)* (Vincennes: Publications du SHAA, 1976); Robert J. Young, *In Command of France. French foreign policy and military planning, 1933–1939* (Cambridge, MA: Harvard University Press, 1978), pp. 218–19.

12 For an excellent analysis of this supposed tradition, see David W. French, *The British Way in Warfare, 1688–2000* (London: Unwin-Hyman, 1991).

13 See Arthur J. Marder, *From the Dardanelles to Oran. Studies of the Royal Navy in peace and war* (Oxford: Clarendon Press, 1974).

14 Gustave Folcher, *Marching to Captivity. The War Diaries of a French Peasant, 1939–45* (London and Washington: Brassey's, 1996); Jacques Benoist-Méchin, *La moisson de quarante. Journal d'un prisonnier de guerre* (Paris: Albin Michel, 1941); Robert Guerlain, *Prisonnier de guerre* (London: Hachette, 1944); Roger Ikor, *O soldats de quarante!* (Paris: Albin Michel, 1986); Yves Durand, *Captivité, histoire des prisonniers de guerre français 1939–1945* (Paris: Editions FNCPG-CATM, 1980); idem, 'Prisonniers du Grand Reich', in *Le Monde Aujourd'hui* (14–15 Apr. 1985).

15 M. Bloch, *L'Etrange Défaite. Témoignage écrit en 1940* (Paris: Editions Franc-Tireur, 1946); translated as *Strange Defeat. A Statement of Evidence Written in 1940* (trans. by Gerald Hopkins, New York: W.W. Norton, 1968). See also Carole Fink, *Marc Bloch. A Life in History* (Cambridge: Cambridge University Press, 1989).

16 General M.-G. Gamelin, *Servir* (Paris: Plon, 3 vols. 1946–47).

17 J. Minart, *P.C. Vincennes. Secteur 4* (Paris: Berger-Levrault, 2 vols. 1945).

18 C. Grandsard, *Le 10e Corps d'Armée dans la bataille, 1939–1940* (Paris: Berger-Levrault, 1949); Gen. Arlabosse, *La Division de Fer dans la Bataille de France. 10 mai–25 juin 1940* (Paris: Charles Lavauzelle, 1943); J. Prioux, *Souvenirs de guerre, 1939–43* (Paris: Flammarion, 1947); Edmond Ruby, *Sedan. Terre d'épreuve: avec la IIe Armée, mai–juin 1940* (Paris: Flammarion, 1948); E. Requin, *Combats pour l'honneur, 1939–1940* (Paris: Charles Lavauzelle, 1946); V. Bourret, *La Tragédie de l'Armée française* (Paris: La Table Ronde, 1947); G. Prételat, *Le Destin tragique de la Ligne Maginot* (Paris: Berger-Levrault, 1950).

19 Gen. M. Gauché, *Le Deuxième Bureau au travail, 1935–1939* (Paris: Amoit-Dumont, 1953); Gen. L. Koeltz, *1940, ou comment s'est joué notre destin* (Paris: Hachette, 1957).

20 M. Weygand, *Memoirs. Recalled to Service* (London: Heinemann, 1954).

21 It is right to record, however, that although most of Henri Michel's books were histories of the French underground, the 'shadow war', the Resistance work of Jean Moulin and Free France, he did write three books concerning the defeat of 1940: *La Drôle de Guerre. De guerre lasse . . .* (Paris: Hachette, 1971); *Le Procès de Riom* (Paris: Albin Michel, 1979); and *La Défaite de la France. Septembre 1939–juin 1940* (Paris: Presses Universitaires de France, 1980).

22 Colonel A. Goutard, *The Battle of France, 1940*. Translated by Captain A.R.P. Burgess. Foreword by Captain B.H. Liddell Hart (London: Frederick Muller, 1958).

23 See also A. Goutard, 'La surprise du 10 mai 1940', in *Revue de Paris* (10 May 1966).

24 A. Beaufre, *Le Drame de 1940* (Paris: Plon, 1965); English translation by Desmond Flower, *1940. The Fall of France* (London: Cassell, 1967; New York: Alfred A. Knopf, 1968).

25 C. Gounelle, *Sedan, mai 1940* (Paris: Presses de la Cité, 1965; reprinted 1980). Cf. Robert A. Doughty, *The Breaking Point. Sedan and the Fall of France, 1940* (Hamden, CT: Archon Books, 1990); Florian K. Rothbrust, *Guderian's XIXth Panzer Corps and the Battle of France. Breakthrough in the Ardennes, May 1940* (New York: Praeger, 1990); Karl-Heinz Frieser, *Blitzkrieg-Legende, der Westfeldzug, 1940* (Munich: Oldenbourg Verlag, 1995).

26 Commandant P. Lyet, *La Bataille de France (Mai–Juin 1940)* (Paris: Payot, 1947); C. de Cossé-Brissac, 'Combien de chars français contre combien de chars allemands le 10 mai 1940?', *Revue de Défense Nationale (RDN)* 5 (July 1947), pp. 75–91; idem, 'Combien d'avions allemands contre combien d'avions français le 10 mai 1940?', *RDN* 4 (June 1948), pp. 741–59.

27 Dutailly wrote an excellent book, *Les Problèmes de l'Armée de terre*

française, 1935–1939 (Paris, 1980). Turlotte completed a mémoire de mâtrise for the Sorbonne on inter-war Franco-Polish military relations; Guelton is editor of *Le 'Journal' du général Weygand, 1929–1935. Edition commentée* (Montpellier: CNRS-ESID, 1998).

28 Fridenson and Lecuir, *La France et la Grande-Bretagne face aux problèmes aériens (1935–mai 1940)*, op. cit.; P. Buffotot, 'Le réarmement aérien allemand et l'approche de la guerre vus par le 2e Bureau Air français (1936–39)', unpub. paper read at the Franco-German historians' colloquium, Bonn, Sept. 1978; C. Christienne, 'L'Industrie aéronautique française de septembre 1939 à juin 1940', in *Français et Britanniques dans la Drôle de Guerre. Actes du Colloque franco-britannique tenu à Paris du 8 au 12 décembre 1975* (Paris, 1979), pp. 389–410.

29 For example, L. Robineau, 'L'Armée de l'Air dans la Bataille de France', in *Les Armées françaises pendant la Seconde Guerre Mondiale, 1939–1945: colloque international tenu à Paris du 7 au 10 mai 1985.*

30 P. Facon, *L'Armée de l'Air dans la tourmente. La bataille de France 1939–1940* (Paris: Economica, 1997); C. d'Abzac-Epézy, *L'Armée de L'Air de Vichy, 1940–1944* (Vincennes: Publications du SHAA, 1997).

31 P. Masson, *La Marine française et la guerre, 1939–1945* (Paris: Tallandier, 1991 and revised edn. 2000). Also important on the French navy are William Gregory Perrett 'French Naval Policy and Foreign Affairs, 1930–1939', Stanford University Ph.D (Ann Arbor: University Microforms International, 1978); and Ronald Chalmers Hood, *Royal Republicans. The French Naval Dynasties between the World Wars* (Baton Rouge, LA: Louisiana State University Press, 1985).

32 P. Lasterle, 'Marcel Gensoul (1880–1973), un amiral dans la tourmente', in *Revue Historique des Armées. Numéro spécial: L'année 1940* no. 219 (June 2000), pp. 71–91. M. Lasterle, to whom I extend warm thanks for supplying a copy of this special issue of the *RHA* at short notice, is writing a thesis on the French navy, 1938–46, at the Université de Paris I Panthéon-Sorbonne, supervised by Robert Frank. See also H. Coutau-Bégarie and C. Huan, *Mers-el-Kébir (1940), la rupture franco-britannique* (Paris: Economica, 1994).

33. H. Coutau-Bégarie and C. Huan, *Darlan* (Paris: Fayard, 1989); H. Coutau-Bégarie, *Castex: le Stratège inconnu* (Paris: Economica, 1985).

34 P. Le Goyet, *Le Mystère Gamelin* (Paris: Plon, 1976).

35 *Centre d'Etudes d'Histoire de la Défense* (Centre for the Study of Defence History), also located at the Château de Vincennes.

36 F. Bédarida, *Les années noires. La France et le guerre, 1939–45* (Paris: Seuil, 1995).

37 E. Conan and H. Rousso, *Vichy: An Ever-Present Past* (Hanover, NH: University of New England Press, 1998).

38 M. Vaïsse (ed.), *Mai–Juin 1940. Défaite française, victoire allemande,*

sous l'oeil des historiens étrangers (Paris: Editions Autrement, 2000), esp. the chapter by Klaus-Jürgen Müller, 'La nouvelle historiographie de la campagne de 1940', pp. 23–8.

39 In the audience was Douglas Johnson, Emeritus Professor of French History at University College, London. The German paper was by Stefan Martens of the German Historical Institute, Paris; the Belgian by Jean Vanwelkenhuyzen, the retired director of the Centre de Recherches et Etudes Historiques sur la Seconde Guerre Mondiale, Brussels.

40 R.A. Doughty, 'The French armed Forces, 1918–1940', in Allan R. Millett and Williamson Murray (eds.), *Military Effectiveness*. Vol II: *The Interwar years* (Boston: Unwin-Hyman, 1986), pp. 49–54.

41 M. Messerschmidt, W. Deist, H.-E. Volkmann, W. Wette et al., *Germany and the Second World War* (Oxford: Oxford University Press, 4 vols. to date, 1990, 1991, 1995, 1998).

42 A. Shennan, *The Fall of France, 1940* (Harlow: Pearson Education, 2000), esp. Part Two: 'The Defeat in History', pp. 113–66.

43 S. Hoffmann, 'The Trauma of 1940. A Disaster and its Traces', in J. Blatt (ed.), *The French Defeat of 1940: Reassessments* (New York: Berghahn, 1998), pp. 354–70.

44 M. Evans, 'From colonialism to post-colonialism. The French Empire since Napoleon', in Martin S. Alexander (ed.), *French History since Napoleon* (London: Arnold, 1999), pp. 391–415.

45 J.-P. Azéma, *1940: L'Année terrible* (Paris: Seuil, 1990).

46 G. Sadoul, *Journal de Guerre (2 septembre 1939–20 juillet 1940* (Paris: les Editeurs Français Réunis, 1977); P. Dunoyer de Segonzac, *Le Vieux Chef: mémoirs et pages choisies* (Paris: France-Empire, 1971).

47 R. Felsenhardt, *1939–40 avec le 18e corps d'armée* (Paris: La Tête de Feuilles, 1973); L. Carron, *Fantassins sur l'Aisne. Mai–Juin 1940* (Paris: Arthaud, 1943); C. Armand-Masson, *Ligne Maginot, bastion inutile* (Paris: Fasquelle Editeurs, 1941).

48 Martin S. Alexander, '"No Taste for the Fight?": French combat performance in 1940 and the politics of the Fall of France', in Paul Addison and Angus Calder (eds.), *Time to Kill. The Soldier's Experience of War in the West, 1939–1945* (London: Pimlico, 1997), pp. 161–76. Cf. Gen. Léon Menu, *Lumières sur les ruines: les combattants de 1940 réhabilités* (Paris: Grasset, 1953).

49 See, however, Thibault Richard, 'La 43e Division d'Infanterie en Basse-Normandie, l'impossible renaissance, 4–26 juin 1940', in *Revue Historique des Armées. Numéro spécial: L'année 1940* no. 219 (June 2000), pp. 43–52.

THE GERMAN VIEW

MUNGO MELVIN

The Campaign in History

When teaching at the Army Staff College at Camberley and more recently at the new Joint Services Command and Staff College, the present author always stressed, to borrow Liddell Hart's famous title, the need to consider *The Other Side of the Hill*.[1] The military maxim of assessing the opponent's standpoint as well as one's own should be matched in any balanced historical analysis. Thus the aim of this chapter is to offer an insight into the German historiography of the 1940 campaign in the west, presenting a bibliographic survey rather than giving a narrative of events. With a few important exceptions, only translated German sources have been quoted in order to keep this chapter as accessible as possible to the majority of readers.

In terms of approach, a particular area of professional interest for many years has been 'the operational art', and the associated study of the dynamics of the three principal levels of war: tactical, operational and strategic. Perhaps the former Tsarist officer A.A. Svechin provides the most enduring and succinct definition: 'Tactics form the steps from which operational leaps are assembled, strategy points out the path.'[2] Yet during the Second World only the Germans, and more particularly the Soviets, had any real understanding of the operational level of war, a term absent from the Anglo-American military lexicon of that time. In looking at 1940 'sixty years on', and in considering the German interpretation of the campaign in the intervening period, it is necessary to differentiate between tactical success, operational impact and strategic outcome.

Specifically, this contribution addresses three principal thematic issues: first, the authorship and development of the campaign plan; secondly, German higher-level decision-making during the first phase of the battle for France; thirdly, the reasons for the startling German tactical and operational success. In this way, a German perspective of the 'Blitzkrieg' victory, and its overall strategic effect, is explored in relation to some key events. In common with the rest of the book, this chapter focuses on the planning and conduct of *Fall Gelb* (Operation Order Yellow), the first operational phase of the German campaign in the west which opened on 10 May 1940 and concluded with the Anglo-French evacuation at Dunkirk between 27 May – 4 June 1940. The second phase *Fall Rot* (Operation Order Red), which saw the defeat of the remaining French forces in June 1940, is not considered.

In reviewing the German historiography, four main strands of work have appeared since 1940. The first, and not considered here in any detail, is the contemporary propaganda of both book and film[3] which extolled the extent of the German victory and Hitler's pre-eminent part in it. After the War, the next set of writing was the series of highly readable senior commanders' personal reminiscences that started to appear in the 1950s. Most prominent among these are the memoirs of Manstein and Guderian, foreign language editions of which continue to sell well abroad.[4] This 'post-mortem' school was followed in the 1960s and 1970s with greater numbers of more scholarly academic works, sets of edited documents and the first official histories by staff of the German Armed Forces Research Institute for Military History.[5] These works are of more value to the researcher as they draw on primary sources such as war diaries and other records, both official and personal. Unfortunately, the vast majority of this material, including oral histories, is available only in German. This period of work merged into the 1980s and 1990s which saw a number of significant revisionist studies by 'official' researchers and others, only some of which have been translated.[6] Of these four sets of writing, the most recent is probably of most interest and enduring value for two main reasons. First, such work paralleled a reawakening of operational thought in the Germany Army and therefore has become a focus for professional military education and training in schools, formation headquarters and units.[7] Secondly, and perhaps of more academic interest, the Germans have revisted not only earlier German interpretations of events but have also reviewed British and French studies of the campaign. Not surprisingly, a key source for this chapter stems from the latest German research work.

Of the primary sources available, the war diaries of Chief of the Army General Staff, Colonel General Franz Halder, are particularly valuable and continue to be quoted frequently.[8] As Hans-Adolf

Jacobsen observed in his preface to the German edition, Halder gives an immediate impression of how events unfolded at the interface of politics and war. Reading Halder, much of the atmosphere, culture and methodology of the Army General Staff at the time is revealed, thus affording an insight into how the German Army High Command planned and conducted the campaign in the west on behalf of Hitler.[9] Yet Halder's contemporary account, written under intense time pressure in uncorrected note form, could not include any detailed analysis of decisions and events. Halder's war diaries (sometimes inaccurately referred to as his private war journal) would more properly be described as semi-official notebooks and warrant careful interpretation accordingly.[10]

Manstein's memoirs, on the other hand, were written with the advantage of reflection and hindsight, and helped to secure the author's place in history. Nonetheless, *Lost Victories* represents a rich seam of information about the development of the campaign plan. The one main caution about using the English edition is that it is abridged. For example, Chapter 5, 'The Operation Plan Controversy', runs to 31 pages. The German reader gets somewhat more: 33 pages of main text and no less than 6 appendices (a further 45 pages) that include various directives and estimates of the situation. In some respects it is a pity that these documents have never been translated and incorporated in the English edition. Without them, it it is difficult to follow Manstein's own advice: "The war historian or officer reading military history might well find it worth his while to study this intellectual tussle over an operation plan in its entirety."[11] Yet, as Helmuth Schmidt sagely observed, historiography is not only the art of understanding past events. It is also the "art of omitting and distilling facts – particularly for those periods for which a great number of documents and testimonies are available".[12] In the face of a wealth of primary and secondary material available for researching the German view of the campaign, only a very compressed and highly selective analysis can be given in this short chapter.

Development of the Campaign Plan

Today many military commentators would identify the success of what later became termed the German *Sichelschnitt* (Sickle Cut) plan in 1940 with one man in particular, Erich von Manstein.[13] He must thank Liddell Hart for much of his pre-eminent position in Anglo-American military history. Liddell Hart's public relations campaign for the German field marshal started in *The Other Side of the Hill*, was sustained during Manstein's war crimes trial at Hamburg in 1950 and continued with the writing of the foreword to the English edition of his memoirs in 1958.[14] Highly respected, if not hugely liked by his fellow officers, Manstein is perhaps the one individual, if any, who can put in a serious claim to be the 'Father of the Campaign Plan'.[15] German officers during and after the Second World War regarded him as a master of strategic and operational planning. For many Manstein was the true originator of the stunning German victory in the West and saviour of many a dark day later on in the war in the East, most notably his brilliant counter-stroke at Kharkov in the spring of 1943.

Success, of course, has many fathers, whilst failure is typically an orphan child. Detailed post-war German research, whilst remaining generally supportive of Manstein, has indicated that some of the credit normally attributed to him should be shared with others. Principal decision-makers in the chain of command above Manstein included his immediate superior, Colonel General (as he then was) Gerd von Rundstedt, commander of Army Group A. Above Rundstedt stood the Chief of the Army General Staff, Colonel General Franz Halder, the Commander in Chief of the Army, Colonel General Walther von Brauchitsch, and ultimately the Führer, Adolf Hitler. Closely aligned to the latter was Colonel General Wilhelm Keitel, who as 'Chief of OKW' fulfilled the function of a high level chief of staff to the Supreme Commander.[16]

The first version of the German campaign plan in the West was very much a re-run of the Schlieffen plan with the main weight of the attack lying in northern Belgium. Manstein presented six memoranda up the chain of command between the end of October 1939 and January 1940, pressing for the main effort to be switched to the south from Bock's Army Group B to von Rundstedt's Army Group A. Only in this way could the '*partial* victory', the likely outcome of the original operation plan, be converted into a 'final victory' in France. So it comes as little surprise that this irritating element to the High Command (and particularly to Halder) was removed and posted to command the 38th Infantry Corps at Stettin in far-off Pomerania.[17] Manstein, the erstwhile creative director, was thus condemned to a walk-on part in the coming drama. He appeared late in the first act to perform a minor tactical role on the Lower Somme, before making a dazzling operational entrée in the second act (*Fall Rot*) with his 'storm march' to the Loire.

In his memoirs Guderian supports Manstein's account of the development of the campaign plan. He includes a fascinating description of how Manstein consulted him over the 'going' for armoured forces in the Ardennes. Guderian recalls:

> One day in November [1939] Manstein asked me to come to see him and outlined his ideas on the subject to me; these involved a strong tank thrust through southern Belgium and Luxembourg towards Sedan, a break-through of the prolongation of the Maginot Line in that area and a consequent splitting in two of the whole French front. He asked me to examine this plan of his from the point of view of a tank man. After a lengthy study of maps and making use of my own memories of the terrain from the First World War, I was able to assure Manstein that the operation he had planned could in fact be carried out. The only condition I attached was that a sufficient number of armoured and motorised divisions must be employed, if possible all of them.[18]

So here we have key technical and terrain analysis supporting an operational idea which was to have enormous strategic consequences. Yet the challenges of 'selling' the idea to a sceptical and traditionally minded high command were many. These included overcoming institutional opposition to deploying armour so far forward of the infantry, and in forming a mobile group of armoured and motorized forces or what the Soviets later termed an operational manoeuvre group. Within Army Group A, von Kleist's Panzer Group formed an experimental ad hoc grouping. The next challenge to conventional German military thinking was to consider crossing the Meuse between Sedan and Dinant on the fifth day of the offensive without pausing for the infantry to join up and awaiting full artillery support.[19] The final risk (and potentially the biggest) was the need to press home the attack towards the Channel coast with scant regard to open flanks in order to preserve operational momentum. But only by such calculated risk-taking, and by avoiding half-measures, argued Manstein, could the German offensive in the West "force an issue by land".[20]

So does Manstein indeed deserve the main credit for the success of *Sichelschnitt* in balancing this delicate military cost/risk assessment?

According to Günther Roth, Manstein's operational analysis can be summed up in two theses. First, "Driving the enemy back in a frontal offensive toward the Somme does not bring about an operational result. This can only be achieved by an enveloping manoeuvre from the flanks." Secondly, "The German offensive thrust will be threatened by an operational counterattack against its southern flank." Thus, the "ingenious aspect of Manstein's proposed solution was that it would solve both operational problems at the same time."[21] Yet an enduring and fundamental question remains: do *operational* solutions, however elegant, necessarily guarantee *strategic* success and hence lasting political settlements?

In determining the final nature of the campaign plan, post-war historical analysis indicates that other factors apart from Manstein's personal views were involved in causing the German Army High Command to shift its view on the positioning of the main effort. The 'Mechelen Affair', when a copy of the German operation plan was lost on 10 January 1940 and its partially burnt remains came into the hands of the Allies, was no doubt a concern to Hitler who remained obsessed throughout the war with the need for secrecy and surprise. Delays in finalising the date of the attack, and hence providing more time for consideration of other ideas, were also caused by the continuing bad weather and concerns about Allied and neutral countries' (Belgium and the Netherlands) military preparations and intentions. More significant perhaps was the impact of two wargames (*Kriegsspiele*) held in February 1940 by Headquarters Army Group A in Koblenz.[22]

Wargaming, a routine part of German general staff work, gets no particular emphasis in the German accounts, and being unfamiliar to many foreign authors its significance in the operational planning process is often overlooked. Significantly there were no equivalent planning events on the Allied side in 1939–1940. Whilst the German official history suggests that Halder began to come round to Manstein's and Guderian's thinking whilst attending the wargame of 7 February 1940, Halder's own diary entry is rather ambiguous on this point.[23] We do know for certain, however, that prior to taking up command of his corps in Stettin, Manstein briefed a willing Hitler in Berlin on 17 February 1940. In a written report to his former Army Group Headquarters, Manstein summarized his presentation to Hitler and described the overall strategic intention in the following terms:

The aim of the offensive must be to achieve decisive results on land. The political and military stakes are too high for the limited objectives defined in the present Operation Order, i.e. defeat of the largest possible elements of the enemy in Belgium and occupation of parts of the Channel coast. Final victory on land must be the goal. The operations must therefore be directed towards winning a final decision in France and destroying France's resistance.[24]

Significantly, neither Britain nor her armed forces gains a detailed mention here in Manstein's analysis. Yet, notwithstanding the authorship of the campaign plan, Guderian is perhaps over-stating his case when he declares that only Hitler, Manstein and himself actually believed in a successful outcome to the campaign.[25] Keitel and Halder differ here in their interpretations of events. Keitel has little concrete to tell us save giving exclusive credit in hindsight to Hitler:

I will only go as far as to make it quite plain that it was Hitler himself who saw the armoured break-through at Sedan, striking up to the Atlantic coast at Abbeville, as the solution; we would then swing round [northwards] into the rear of the motorised Anglo-French army, which would most probably be advancing across the Franco-Belgian frontier into Belgium and cut them off.

I had some misgivings, as this stroke of genius [Hitler's] could go awry if the French tank army [not specified] did not do us the favour of automatically driving through Belgium towards our northern flank, but held back instead until they recognised Hitler's planned break-through operation.[26]

Hitler did indeed fall victim to his fears about the threat from the southern flank. But one fact stands out in most German accounts. Manstein, who provided the original germ of a brilliant operational *idea*, was not wholly responsible for that idea's full development in an operational *plan*. Halder, who had originally opposed the switch of main effort, belatedly and enthusiastically endorsed the revised operational scheme of manoeuvre. By subordinating the mass of the German mobile forces (eventually seven panzer and three motorized infantry divisions) to Army Group A, he in fact gave the main effort greater substance than Manstein.

Postioned between the field commanders' early accounts and the later official history, Hans-Adolf Jacobsen presents a dispassionate German commentary. His analysis bears out a view of *shared* authorship of the plan. He notes that the ultimate decision on the campaign plan was taken on 18 February 1940 (one day after Manstein's briefing) at a meeting between Hitler, Brauchitsch and Halder. Jacobsen considers that "OKH has at least the credit of casting the German deployment in a form that was of decisive importance for the success of the campaign". He concludes that the plan had two masters: "The new deployment plan of February 24th, 1940, was thus based on the brilliant operational methods of Manstein and Hitler's own ideas."[27] What is also clear is that until 17 February 1940 Manstein and Hitler were thinking independently. Yet there was a curious link nonetheless between them: Hitler's Chief Adjutant (Personal Staff Officer) Colonel Schmundt had visited Manstein and his staff in Koblenz.

The German official history gives due credit to Halder, Hitler and Manstein. Noting that time was "working for Manstein's operational concept" and drawing on Jacobsen's detailed study of the evolution of the campaign plan, the history concludes that there was a fortunate "convergence of Manstein's inspired concept and Hitler's ideas".[28] Thus the official history implies that once Halder had understood the commonality of Hitler's and Manstein's ideas, he then applied the final, professional polish to the fourth and final version (24 February 1940) of the German campaign plan. In the German records and postwar research work there is little corroboration of the view presented in the British Official History that von Rundstedt contributed much, if any, original thought to the campaign plan.[29] This perhaps can be put down to a typically British misunderstanding of the pivotal role of a senior German general staff officer and operational level chief of staff such as Manstein. Another cause might have been a false assumption, on inspecting the captured documentation under Rundstedt's signature, in attributing this to Rundstedt personally.

The most recent, and very comprehensive, German military analysis of the campaign offers a different perspective. In his exhaustively researched study *Blitzkrieg Legends – The Campaign in the West 1940*, Karl-Heinz Frieser suggests that Manstein's *Sichelschnitt* plan is forever being misinterpreted.[30] Roughly translated, he believes that Manstein's brilliant contribution was in finding an operational escape route out of a strategic blind alley. Time was working for the Allies with their economic and maritime power. Once Hitler had manoeu-

214

vred Germany into such a "catastrophic strategic situation", the only option for the German military was to provide a solution by gambling at the operational level. So Manstein's revolutionary operation plan can be regarded as taking a desperate 'flight forwards'. Frieser also exposes Halder's attempts after the war to influence historical analysis by exaggerating his creative contribution to the campaign plan at the expense of Manstein.[31]

Significantly, however, there remained concerns about the campaign plan within the subordinate army groups after its publication. Headquarters Army Group A, for example, now divested of Manstein's brainpower and creativity, did not want to commit its armoured forces until the infantry had forced a breakthrough at the Meuse. Had this 'conventional' thinking prevailed, notes Frieser, then the whole operational object and desired effect of von Kleist's Panzer Group of 1222 tanks, 41,140 vehicles and 134,370 men would have been nullified.[32] After all, its mission was to thrust through Luxembourg and southern Belgium and to gain the western bank of the Meuse in a surprise attack. Thus speed and surprise were essential ingredients of the German plan. Once the campaign clock started on 10 May 1940, time would work against the German armed forces at the tactical, operational and strategic levels as the Allies began to act in response. Despite its inherent risks, the plan worked *because* it was so risky and thus so unexpected. Such is the basis of absolute surprise. Yet the plan also worked in the inevitable chaos of war because, when mistakes were made on both sides, the Germans generally recovered from these and the Allies did not. Initiative once lost is very difficult to regain. Despite the spectacular success of the German offensive, it was not without internal frictions, and there was plenty of hard fighting for those in the vanguard of attack.[33]

Conduct of the Campaign

Space does not permit a detailed description of the German offensive in the West, the key elements of which are covered in other chapters. Most of the main points, however, can be made with reference primarily to the progress of Kleist's Panzer Group and Guderian's 19th Panzer Corps. Under the cloak of Army Group B's operations, these mobile forces of Army Group A represented the sharp, hardened armoured tip of the extended German lance that stabbed out of the

Ardennes and cut deep into the Anglo-French under-belly. Yet the 'infantry' shaft of that lance was brittle and thus very fragile.[34] From an Allied perspective, the challenge was to find and fix the tip and to strike decisively at its shaft before receiving a mortal blow. Contemporary German views, meanwhile, on the conduct of the campaign not surprisingly differ according to their position relative to the lance. If Guderian and Rommel are at the tip, Kluge and Rundstedt are somewhere down the shaft, and Halder, Brauchitsch, Keitel and Hitler are at its base.

German accounts describe the tense disagreements within the German leadership that occurred following the unexpectedly swift forcing of the Meuse between 13–15 May 1940. The fluid, confused and uncertain situation began to rattle the traditionalists in the miltiary hierarchy. Whilst no modern web of phase lines cluttered the battlefield, synchronisation among the German forces often broke down. There was also growing disharmony within the German chain of command. There were two battles being fought: one at the front with the opponent and another within the German high command between the progressive and more traditional thinkers. To take one well-documented example, Hitler, Rundstedt and Busch, commander-in-chief of the Sixteenth Army, were concerned about the continuing threat of a French counter-attack into the lengthening open southern flank. On the morning of 17 May 1940 Guderian was ordered to halt and to report personally to von Kluge. After an argument, Guderian asked to be relieved of his command. Although von Kluge accepted, sense prevailed later in the day when von Rundstedt re-instated Guderian to corps command. Reconnaissance in force was permitted and the advance continued, quickly picking up momentum by 18 May. Guderian's memoirs suggest that the order to halt had originated from the Army High Command.[35] Halder's diary indicates the contrary:

> Continuance of our drive in south-western direction is based on the condition that Army Group A does not tie up any of its strength on the southern flank, but keeps pushing westward in echelon formation. This involves no risk, as the enemy here is too weak to attack at this time.[36]

The truth would appear that Rundstedt had ordered the temporary halt and that Hitler had a part to play in this decision. Halder and

216

the OKH staff were less nervous than either the subordinate army group or the political leadership. Hitler continued to mistrust his own luck and remained nervous about the state of the armoured forces. In the absence of detailed forward planning, German orders for a rapid exploitation of the situation were developed on a rushed ad hoc basis, and tensions within the chain of command were fuelled accordingly. It is also easy to forget that success brings its own pressures; commanders at all levels were becoming tired and fractious.[37] Halder recorded further on 17 May: "Rather unpleasant day. The Führer is terribly nervous. Frightened by his own success, he is afraid to take any chance and so would rather pull the reins on us. Puts forward the excuse that it is all about his concern for the left flank."[38]

Yet the northern (right) flank also posed a danger to Army Group A. The British tank action at Arras on 21 May 1940 threatened the integrity of Rommel's panzer division for a few hours. The small tactical action by an incomplete brigade, rather than the intended Anglo-French multidivisional operational level counter-stroke, caused a ripple rather than a tremor up the German chain of command. Whilst Rommel does not appear to have been unnerved unduly, and Halder took the incident in his stride, Army Group A was less sanguine. After the war Rundstedt talked about the event to his (gullible) British captors:

A critical moment in the drive came just as my forces reached the Channel. It was caused by a British counter-stroke southward from Arras on 21 May. For a short time it was feared that our armoured divisions would be cut off before the infantry divisions could come up to support them. None of the French counter-attacks carried any serious threat as this one did.[39]

The most controversial halt order, however, was Hitler's sudden pulling of the emergency brake which stopped the panzer forces reaching Dunkirk, barely ten miles' march for the leading elements of Guderian's corps. This brake on the unfolding of the campaign plan, a fatal decision from the German perspective, prevented the complete defeat of the British Expeditionary Force and downgraded, in German eyes, a strategic victory into an operational one. All accounts of the complicated series of orders and counter-orders over the period 23–26 May 1940 indicate a marked divergence of views and lack of

217

mutual understanding about aims and objectives between the various levels of command. The main issue was the decision by the Army High Command to give Army Group B the responsibility for concluding the defeat of the Anglo-French forces north of the Somme, so turning Army Group B into the 'hammer' and Army Group A into the 'anvil', the reversal of Halder's idea. Yet the only mobile striking force available was in Rundstedt's Army Group.

German analysis of the infamous Halt Order indicates that a number of closely interrelated factors played on the minds of the key decision-makers at the time. Comparing a considerable number of sources, no very clear picture emerges; a number of factors influenced Hitler and his principal subordinates. At the operational level these included worries about the wet terrain and the poor going for the armoured forces; a need to conserve these in any case for the rest of the campaign; an associated switch of planning focus to operations south of the Somme; continuing concerns about the threat from the southern flank; and an over-reliance on the Luftwaffe to compete the destruction of the enemy. All these matters were compounded by a lack of reliable intelligence. Frieser dismisses, however, the reasoning reflected by a number of earlier authors that Hitler deliberately offered a 'golden bridge' allowing the British to escape at Dunkirk.[40] Frieser considers that a more likely answer lies in the continental thinking of the Germans who under-estimated their opponents' ability to stage a large-scale evacuation. The potential synergy of the Royal Air Force and the Royal Navy was overlooked.

German research into the Halt Order has also indicated that the human factor was very much at play and has focused on the states of mind of and personal relationships between the principal actors involved. Hitler was flexing his muscles over the German High Command in an effort to exert his tight personal rein (for good and bad) over events. Paradoxically, Hitler's need to demonstrate his soldierly decision-making prowess led to indecision and delay in the execution of the campaign. Rundstedt was thus an unwitting ally to Hitler, both fed on each other's concerns, prejudices and fears.

Analysis of the Campaign

In the heady days of such a spectacular victory, contemporary German authors and propagandists extolled the nature of *Hitler*'s success:

Neither by adherence to the 'Schlieffen Plan' nor to the Cannae-doctrine nor to any other rigid theory, but by way of free artistic creation, resulting from the inspiration of his martial genius, has the Führer led the German Wehrmacht to the most glorious victory in its laudable history.[41]

Serious post-war writers later investigated the campaign objectively, highlighting the chances taken and the opportunities missed. From a modern German military historical point of view, Frieser has championed Manstein's role and investigated the campaign in un-paralleled detail in a number of studies. In 1988 he offered three principal conclusions about the nature of the campaign. First, he considered one of the fundamental causes of the Allied defeat was the fact that their commanders could react to the "operational challenge of the German tanks only at a tactical level". The Allies were there-fore unable to concentrate their tank force, superior in quantity and quality, for an operational counter-attack. Secondly, the campaign which saw the "first instance of an employment of tanks on an oper-ational level" was a "leap in the dark". Exercises, which could have served to test the new operational concept, were out of the question simply for security reasons. But Frieser also noted that "all deficien-cies were more than compensated by the effect of surprise". Thirdly, in his view the German advance to the Channel coast led both to a "climax of operational freedom of action and to its reversal when Hitler began to interfere increasingly with the control of military oper-ations".[42] In this manner Frieser echoes the earlier remarks by Halder and by battlefield commanders in their memoirs about increasing meddling by the Supreme Commander.

By 1995, however, Frieser had developed nine closely interrelated reasons for the startling German success in the 'Blitzkrieg' campaign in the West. Of these nine factors, four main issues can be distilled in the present author's opinion: operational art, the application of tech-nology, manoeuvre and method of command.

Historically, Germany, constrained by the realities of geostrategic position and facing the trauma of a war on two or more fronts, sought to exploit her internal lines and to fight short wars, seeking quick victory in these through decisive battle. German operational art emphasized the need to overcome strategic inferiority by achieving operational superiority in concentrating the right forces in time and space. In this manner Blitzkrieg reflected a fundamental German way of war by overcoming inherent strategic weakness through creative operational virtuosity.

Considering the power of modern weapons, Schlieffen had regarded breakthrough operations as unfeasible and so favoured encirclement. Frieser is of the view that neither side in the First World War achieved an *operational* breakthrough on the Western Front. Thus Manstein's plan to break through the French line at the Meuse by launching an immediate attack from the line of march might appear "abstruse", yet the nature of war had changed. The balance of advantage between fire and manoeuvre had swung back towards manoeuvre. Guderian believed, for example, that armour and air power (rather than depending on mass artillery that would take precious time to bring up and support logistically) now provided sufficient punch to achieve any necessary breakthrough operations. The Germans exploited modern mobile radio communications, combined arms tactics and the employment of the air force as flying battlefield artillery. In stark contrast to the French, the Germans concentrated their air power and armour in the right place to achieve operational success. In this respect, Frieser quotes the French armoured general Charles Delestraint: "We possessed 3000 tanks, a similar number to the Germans. But whereas we employed a thousand groups of three tanks, the Germans employed three groups of a thousand tanks each."[43] The principle of concentration of force, in the best German tradition, was employed to turn an absolute enemy strategic superiority into one's own operational superiority in forces, time and space.

According to Frieser, Manstein also struck against another of Schlieffen's taboos: the open flank. In effect, Guderian and Manstein adapted the German *Stosstrupp* or Hutier tactics of the First World War through the use of an armoured 'wedge' to attack the enemy without regard to threats from the flanks. Instead of concentrating reserves against the enemy's strongest point (the Allied method), the Germans employed their reserves against the enemy's weakest point at Sedan. Thus Manstein's *Sichelschnitt* plan combined breakthrough and encirclement operations in two complementary phases: a frontal attack to break through the Meuse line at Sedan and an attack in the enemy's rear to achieve encirclement. Moltke the Elder had encircled the French at Sedan on 1 September 1870. Subsequently Schlieffen had praised this Cannae-like battle which had achieved the complete defeat of the enemy, a classic battle of annihilation. During the First World War, however, the only true battle of encirclement was achieved at

220

Tannenberg in 1914 against the Russians on the Eastern Front. By 1940 vertical envelopment and the interdiction of the enemy was now possible due to the application of airpower.

In Frieser's view, however, the most important factor behind the German success was their system of command that differed from Allied methods in two important respects: command style and the position of the commander. German *Auftragstaktik* (also known as directive control or mission orders) sets particular emphasis on ordering only *what* was to be achieved, not *how* it was to be achieved. This decentralized command doctrine gives subordinate commanders a maximum freedom of action and sets the conditions for the exercise of individual initiative at the lowest practical level. This method of command is based on the German principle of providing a sound conceptual framework of thought, mutual understanding and trust brought about by a common military education and doctrine. Determined tactical level commanders such as Guderian, Rommel and Balck did not hesitate to make their own decisions in order to maintain momentum, to seize and to retain the initiative. In this way – while leading from the front – leaders could act instantly and exploit the tactical situation to best operational effect.

To summarize, German historiography of the campaign seeks answers to a number of fundamental questions. How brilliant was the Manstein-Hitler operational idea, strategically? Was it realistic in its objectives to "force a decision on land", to crush the enemy and end the war in Germany's favour? Was the French defeat a forgone conclusion to German eyes? Would the defeat of the BEF on the sands of Dunkirk have decided the war in Germany's favour? From a German perspective, however, there is no easy set of answer to these questions. In 1940 it was difficult to predict the outcome of the campaign with any certainty, the stakes were high, the risks considerable. Personal accounts and war diaries often indicate apprehension and tension rather than confidence and euphoria.

Professional Wehrmacht commanders were amazed by the speed of the German success, by the collapse in French morale and by the pluck of the British escape. The modern historian, however, works with one particularly supportive ally at his side: General Hindsight. Thus from a British perspective, sixty years on, we might make much of the German failure to consummate their victory at Dunkirk. Modern German analysis is more forgiving. A recent study declares:

Even if the experts agree that the omission at Dunkirk was a major operational, even strategic blunder, such a blunder cannot be attributed to the lack of an overall concept of the war on the German side. Whereas it is probably incorrect to call the 'miracle of Dunkirk' the fundamentally decisive turn of the war, it still proved to be a fatal blow for German strategy.[44]

Denied an enduring strategic victory, the Germans achieved nonetheless a stunning operational success, profiting from their opponents' mistakes and overcoming most of their own in a climate of considerable discord in the chain of command. As German writing since 1940 has demonstrated, the campaign offers much material for academic and military enquiry on all sides. Neither the debate nor the history is closed.

Notes

1   B.H. Liddell Hart, *The Other Side of the Hill* (London: Cassell, 1948). Under this title, later published in America as *The German Generals Talk*, Liddell Hart gave a mouthpiece to imprisoned German military commanders' views of the Second World War. The reliability of this evidence, however, may be questioned in view of Liddell Hart's overriding need to rebuild his reputaton that had suffered during the Second World War and the German generals' attempts to exonerate themselves from 'Mitschuld' [collective blame] in Hitler's war. See Alex Danchev, *Alchemist of War: The Life of Basil Liddell Hart* (London: Weidenfeld & Nicolson, 1998), pp. 223–5 for an account of how this book came to be written.

2   A.A. Svechin, *Strategiia* [Strategy] (Moscow: Voenizdat, 1927). Quoted by David M. Glantz and Jonathan House, *When Titans Clash* (Kansas: University Press, 1995), pp. 7–8 and 322, fn. 7.

3   Of particular note is the German film 'Triumph in the West', itself a triumph of propaganda that implied that the mass of the all-conquering German forces was mechanized. In fact the German army remained predominantly horse-drawn for the entirety of the Second World War.

4   Field-Marshal Erich von Manstein, *Lost Victories*, ed. and trans. by Anthony G. Powell (London: Methuen, 1958), originally published as *Verlorene Siege* (Bonn: Athenäum-Verlag, 1955). References in this chapter are to the 1982 Arms and Armour Press London edition. General Heinz Guderian, *Panzer Leader*, trans. by Constantine Fitzgibbon

(London: Michael Joseph, 1952), originally published as *Erinnerungen eines Soldaten*. References here are to the 1979 Zenger Publishing New York edition. There are also useful commentaries of the campaign in a number of other translated memoirs. See, for example, General Siegfried Westphal, *The German Army in the West* (London: Cassell, 1951), originally published as *Heer in Fesseln*, 1950; Major-General F.W. von Mellenthin, *Panzer Battles* (London: Cassell, 1955); General Frido von Senger und Etterlin, *Neither Fear nor Hope*, (London: Macdonald, 1963), published as *Krieg in Europa* (Cologne and Belin: Kiepenheuer & Witsch, 1960). For further details of German sources available up to 1982, see Albert Seaton, *The German Army 1933–45* (London: Weidenfeld and Nicolson, 1982), pp. xiii–xv.

5   The most important work is the as yet uncompleted ten-volume history of the German armed forces in the Second World War being compiled by the Militärgeschichtliches Forschungsamt der Bundeswehr (MGFA) [Research Institute for Military History of the Federal Armed Forces] under the title *Das Deutsche Reich und der Zweite Weltkriege* [German and the Second World War], (Stuttgart: Deutsche Verlags-Anstalt, 1979–). Publication of this series, which can be regarded as the German official history, is underway in English. Therefore an indispensable source for this chapter is Hans Umbreit, 'The Battle for Hegemony in Western Europe' in Klaus A. Maier et al, ed. by MGFA and trans. by Dean S. McMurry and Ewald Osers, *Germany and the Second World War*, ii, *Germany's Initial Conquests in Europe* (Oxford: Clarendon, 1991), pp. 227–326. Although originally published in 1979, of particular significance to researchers is the comprehensive bibliography in which works published between 1979 and 1987 have been added to the Oxford (1991) edition.

6   The most recent and controversial work is Heinz Magenheimer, *Hitler's War: Germany's Key Strategic Decisions 1940–1945* (London: Cassell, 1999), first published as *Die Militärstrategie Deutschlands 1940–1945* by F.A. Herbig Verlag, 1997. Magenheimer rejects, for example, the commonly-held view that the German war effort was "hopeless from the very beginning".

7   Facing a growing conventional Warsaw Pact threat, a renaissance of operational level thinking in the German Army occurred in the 1980s. At the same time, the operational level of war was introduced into the British and United States armies. Within the German Army, the pressing requirement for an understanding of operational art and the need to think in campaign terms was first expressed officially in *Operative Richtlinie* [Operational Guidelines] published by the Chief of the German General Staff in 1987. In the same year the subject was reflected in the curriculum of the German Armed Forces Staff College. Supporting

military historical research studies such as *Operational Thinking in Clausewitz, Moltke, Schlieffen and Manstein* had appeared in 1988.

8   Generaloberst Halder, *Kriegstagebuch*, i, *Vom Polenfeldzug bis zum Ende der Westoffensive* (14.8.1939 – 30.6.1940) (Stuttgart: Kohlhammer, 1962). References in this chapter are to the English translation published by T.N. Dupuy Associates (Boulder, Colorado: Westview Press, 1976). The Dupuy edition is a reprint of the 1948 translation prepared by the Office of the Chief of Counsel for War Crimes, Office of the Military Government, United States, originally edited by Arnold Lissance. Whilst a detailed comparison of the German and English editions is beyond the scope of this chapter, there would appear to be a number of inconsistencies in translation.

9   See also Walter Görlitz, *History of the German General Staff 1657–1945* (New York: Praeger, 1953), originally published as *Der Deutsche Generalstab*, who devotes a detailed chapter to the campaign and associated controversies.

10   The most detailed analytical work on Halder is the as yet untranslated monograph by Christian Hartmann, *Halder Generalstabschef Hitlers 1938–1942* [Halder: Hitler's Chief of the [Army] General Staff 1938–1942]. (Paderborn: Schöningh, 1991).

11   Manstein, *Lost Victories*, p. 95.

12   In his preface to Johannes Steinhoff, Peter Pechel and Dennis Showalter, *Voices from the Third Reich – An Oral History* (New York: De Capo, 1994), p. ix.

13   'Sichelschnitt' was not a term used by Manstein or by other Germans at the time. However, it has since become an accepted term in the history of the campaign, including the German official and specialist military histories. For a detailed account of Sichelschnitt and Blitzkrieg, see [Lieutenant Colonel Dr] Karl-Heinz Frieser, *Blitzkrieg-Legende: Der Westfeldzug 1940* [Blitzkrieg Legends: The Campaign in the West] (München: Oldenbourg, 1995), pp. 95–116.

14   Liddell Hart also wrote supportive forewords to the English editions of Guderian's and von Senger und Etterlin's memoirs. He also edited *The Rommel Papers* (London: Collins, 1953) the first chapter of which contains Rommel's account of the German breakthrough on the Meuse.

15   Von Mellenthin, *Panzer Battles*, p. 11, gives a typically supportive view of Manstein: "Manstein had the best brain in the German General Staff, but his manner was blunt; he said what he thought and did not disguise his opinions even when they were not flattering to his superiors. In consequence he had been 'put in cold storage' and was allotted a relatively minor rôle in the campaign which he had so brilliantly conceived."

16   One of the best internal perspectives of the German Armed Forces High Command (OKW) and its relations with the Army High Command

(OKH) is given by Walter Warlimont, trans. by R.H. Barry, *Inside Hitler's Headquarters* (London: Weidenfeld and Nicolson, 1964). [First published in Germany under the title *Im Hauptquartier der deutschen Wehrmacht 1939–1945* by Bernard & Graefe, Frankfurt am Main, 1962.]

17 Halder, *Diaries*, p. 192, includes a note dated 22 January 1940 about personnel changes including requiring to get Rundstedt's opinion of Manstein, and a note of 26 January 1940 (p. 196) about "Manstein, Commanding General" which indicates a new appointment was being considered. Halder's entry note of 31 January 1940 indicates that the decision on selecting Manstein's relief (Sodenstern) was made on 1 February 1940, apparently in consultation with Keitel. Doubts were to creep in later on – see Halder, *Diaries*, p. 260).

18 Guderian, *Panzer Leader*, p. 89.

19 Guderian's preference for this forcing the Meuse on 'A plus 4' Day with his (19th) and von Wietersheim's (14th) Corps is corroborated by Halder. See Halder, *Diaries*, p. 214.

20 Manstein, *Lost Victories*, p. 103.

21 MGFA, ed., *Operational Thinking in Clausewitz, Moltke, Schlieffen and Manstein*, (Freiburg in Breisgau, 1989), p. 48.

22 Umbreit, 'The Battle for Hegemony in Western Europe', pp. 242–7.

23 Halder, *Diaries*, p. 213–14. Halder would now appear to have accepted the merits of concentrating 19th and 14th Corps together. However, he specifically noted that a "concerted attack across the Meuse would be impossible before the ninth or tenth day of the offensive".

24 Manstein, *Lost Victories*, p. 121.

25 Guderian, *Panzer Leader*, p. 91.

26 Walter Görlitz (ed.), trans. by David Irving, *The Memoirs of Field-Marshal Keitel* (London: William Kimber, 1965), p. 115.

27 Hans-Adolf Jacobsen and Jürgen Rohwer (ed.), trans. by Edward Fitzgerald, *Decisive Battles of World War II: The German View* (London: André Deutsch, 1965), pp. 33–8. [Originally published in German under the title *Entscheidungsschlachten des Zweiten Weltkrieges* by Bernard & Graefe, Frankfurt am Main, 1960.]

28 Umbreit, p. 247. Hans-Adolf Jacobsen, *Fall Gelb: Der Kampf um den deutschen Operationsplan zur Westoffensive 1940* (Wiesbaden: Publications of the Institute for European History Mainz, 16, Department of General History, 1957).

29 L.F. Ellis, *The War in France and Flanders 1939–1940* (London: HMSO, 1953), pp. 337–44. Von Mellenthin, *Panzer Battles* (p. 11) was the first German to challenge Ellis publicly: "I am aware that the British official history . . . minimizes Manstein's influence, but in my view the evidence of Guderian and other officers is decisive."

30 Recent communication (January 2001) with Dr Frieser indicates that an English language translation of his work is being undertaken by a publisher in the United States, due for completion in 'a couple of years'.

31 Frieser, *Blitzkrieg-Legende*, pp. 82–91. Hartmann, *Halder* (pp. 17–23) provides the evidence. Between 1946 and 1961 Halder was employed by the United States Army Europe Historical Division. As leader of an ambitious military research project employing up to 150 staff, Halder was involved in over 2500 'studies'. Later German military research has questioned the objectivity and value of this work.

32 Frieser, *Blitzkrieg-Legende*, pp. 119–24.

33 Personal account given to the author at Sedan in July 1996 by Obersleutnant Wackernagel, commander of the first (7th) company of Infantry Regiment Grossdeutschland to cross the Meuse at Sedan at 1600 hours on 13 May 1940 and involved subsequently in the bitter bridgehead battle at Stonne.

34 The lance analogy is advanced by Frieser, *Blitzkrieg-Legende*, p. 39.

35 Guderian, *Panzer Leader*, p. 110.

36 Halder, *Diaries*, p. 405. [Entry for 17 May 1940]

37 The present author observed this phenomenon after only 100 hours of operations during the Gulf War in which the Coalition forces, including the British, were more stressed by their own rapid manoeuvre than by the half-hearted actions of the Iraqis.

38 Halder, *Diaries*, p. 406. [Entry for 17 May 1940]

39 Quoted by Liddell Hart, *The Other Side of the Hill*, p. 184.

40 See, for example, Westphal, *The German Army in the West*, p. 87, and Görlitz, *History of The German General Staff*, p. 376.

41 Konstantin Hierl, 'Die deutsche Oberste Führung im Westfeldzug und der Schlieffen-Plan', in Wilhelm Weiss, ed., *Triumph der Kriegskunst*, 2d ed., (München: 1942), pp. 67–74. Quoted by Jehuda L. Wallach, *The Dogma of the Battle of Annihilation* (Westport, Connecticut and London: Greenwood, 1986), p. 262.

42 Karl-Heinz Frieser, 'The Execution of "Case Yellow" ("Sickle Cut") Exemplified by Panzer Group Kleist (10–21 May 1940)' in (ed. MGFA) *Operational Thinking in Clausewitz, Moltke, Schlieffen and Manstein*, pp. 79–80.

43 Frieser, *Blitzkrieg-Legende*, p. 416.

44 Magenheimer, *Hitler's War: Germany's Key Strategic Decisions 1940–1945*, p. 25.

THE BRITISH VIEW

BRIAN BOND

The experience of the British Field Force in France in 1939–1940, once the subject of frequent personal memoirs, critical analyses and *post mortems*, has now suffered the fate of many 'opening rounds' in past wars, namely to be eclipsed by the more dramatic events that followed. Thus, in the British case, in recent anniversary years, such as 1990 and 2000, publishers and the media have focused almost exclusively on Dunkirk (and in particular the heroic exploits of 'the little ships') and the Battle of Britain (the 'finest hour' and the somewhat exaggerated triumph of 'the few' over the many). Professional soldiers' interest is mainly confined to the remarkable German achievement in their speedy crossing of the Meuse and subsequent break-out which virtually settled the outcome in the first week. British officers find some consolation in the small-scale but briefly successful 'counter-attack' at Arras on 21 May which may have influenced the enemy's 'halt order' three days later and so made possible the Allied escape from Dunkirk. Television has shown some interest in these events in terms of the now popular 'counter-factuals': what if the 'halt order' had not been given? Would the British Army then have been trapped and captured and, if so, would Churchill have been toppled from power by a minister bent on seeking a negotiated peace, such as Lord Halifax? Fiction writers and film producers have long been fascinated by an alternative counter-factual of a successful German invasion of Britain: how gallant and prolonged would the resistance have been, and what would then have happened to the individuals listed in the Nazis' *Black Book*?

This volume has been commissioned and edited on the assumption that the operations in France and Belgium in 1939 and 1940 still have many interesting aspects for serious students of history. To provide just one example here: newspapers have recently called attention to the need for funds to preserve the site near Wormhoudt where British

227

prisoners were massacred in particularly horrific circumstances on 28 May 1940. No German officer has ever been successfully prosecuted for this atrocity (*Daily Telegraph*, 11 November, 2000).

A brief survey of some outstanding landmarks in the historiography of the campaign will show how our knowledge of, and perspectives on, these operations have been formed, while also enabling us to spot the gaps or problems which still deserve serious scholarly attention.

Major L.F. Ellis' official history *The War in France and Flanders, 1939–1940* was published as early as 1953. Though not a trained historian, he produced a clear and generally reliable day-by-day narrative which, with truly excellent maps, still provides a good starting point. But Ellis was too close to the events and confined by his official position to evaluate the role of individuals or criticize high-level decisions. The publication of much more inside information, some examples to be discussed here, and a longer perspective on this campaign in a historical context, suggest that a revised or completely new official history would be worthwhile.

In the following year Sir Edward Spears' brilliantly written recollections *Assignment to Catastrophe* captured the drama of the last days of Reynaud's premiership and the break-up of the Anglo-French alliance in almost epic mode. Spears was Churchill's personal representative with the disintegrating French government. His pro-French stance had been so marked that in the House of Commons he had been known as 'the member for Paris', but in these memoirs we see bitter disillusionment setting in as the French leaders failed to inspire the heroic resistance he had witnessed in the First World War and increasingly sought to blame the British for their impending defeat and humiliation. We should not be surprised that, as the tragedy reached its climax, Spears played the role of impassioned patriot rather than objective diplomat or scholar. We cannot accept his judgements on individuals and decisions at face value. As John Cairns' deeply-informed account of the climax of Anglo-French friction over Dunkirk reveals, mistakes, deceptions and duplicity were not a monopoly of one party in the alliance.

In 1960, only three years after its subject's death, R.J. Minney published his curiously titled study *The Private Papers of Hore-Belisha*, which was indeed heavily dependent on the former War Minister's personal documents, and which made the strongest possible defence of its subject. Here was a case of an early attempt at a biography, written under the watchful eye of the late minister's former secretary and guardian of his reputation, Hilde Sloane, which clearly needed a more scholarly replacement that would encompass new sources, such as the Ironside and Pownall diaries, and would explore more fully his controversial 'partnership' with Liddell Hart. Several would-be biographers have shown an interest in this colourful personality but have apparently been deterred by the paucity of the surviving private papers. Hore-Belisha, as War Minister between May 1937 and December 1939, undoubtedly played a crucial role in preparing and equipping the Field Force. Furthermore, as will be discussed later, his sudden and puzzling fall from office constitutes a dramatic episode in British civil–military relations.

The Chief of the Imperial General Staff from September 1939, whose frigid relations with Hore-Belisha rendered the War Office an unhappy and inefficient institution, was General Sir Edmund Ironside. His remarkably outspoken and revealing diaries (covering the years 1937–1940) were edited, and published in 1962, by his loyal assistant Colonel Roderick Macleod. Macleod's editorial intentions were pious rather than scholarly: believing his former chief had been right on all important issues he reorganized the diaries to show that this was so. By his own admission, Ironside was a field commander rather than a staff officer, and he proved to be inherently unsuited to the most stressful and responsible desk job in Whitehall. Though Gort and his staff were excessively critical of 'Tiny' Ironside ('like a bull in a china shop' was one description), he evidently did not give the Field Force the consistent and informed backing it needed; for example in allowing troops destined for France to be sent to Norway in April 1940. The War Cabinet realized his limitations and on 22 April 1940 Sir John Dill was sent home from France to act as his Vice-Chief and successor a month later.

In the late 1960s I accepted the difficult, but ultimately rewarding, task of editing the longhand diaries of Lt General Sir Henry Pownall, eventually published as *Chief of Staff* (2 volumes, 1972–1973). Pownall was an intelligent, acerbic gunner with orthodox and somewhat conservative professional views, evident, for example, in his admiration for Gort and detestation of Hore-Belisha and Liddell Hart, whom he held jointly responsible for the unpreparedness of the Army in September 1939. As a member of the C.I.D. secretariat (1933–1936), Director of Military Operations and Intelligence (1938–1939) and Chief of Staff to the Field Force (1939–1940), Pownall seems to have controlled his vehement opinions and powerful emotions in public on all but a few occasions. As with many people in high-tension, stressful occupations, Pownall used his diary to 'let off steam'; otherwise it is hard to credit how such a choleric, opinionated individual could have performed efficiently alongside high-ranking politicians, officers of the other Services and, above all, foreign allies. In this trait he could be compared with Alan Brooke, an even more acerbic and irascible character.

For me, personally, Pownall's well-informed insider's stance was a useful corrective to the more radical outsider's view of my then mentor Basil Liddell Hart. On the much-disputed Continental role of the Field Force particularly, Pownall's diaries made a powerful case that the Army's small size and deficiencies in material, manpower and training in 1939 were mainly due to political vacillation and refusal to face unpleasant facts throughout the previous decade. As for the politics and strategy of the Field Force in France, Pownall's diaries are truly an invaluable source; indeed it is hard to imagine how little was known about the view from G.H.Q. and its activities before 1972. Space permits reference here to only a few of the most important revelations – and limitations – of the diaries in relation to the topics covered in this volume.

First, the lengthy and vitriolic diary entries towards the end of 1939 reveal Pownall as Gort's hatchet-man who played the leading role in bringing down Hore-Belisha. One would like to believe that Pownall's hostility was due entirely to professional irritation with the War Minister, but nasty references to his Jewishness (also present in Ironside's diaries) cannot be overlooked. Pownall 'bent the ears' of the Prime Minister and even of the King in his determination to oust Hore-Belisha from the War Office, noting at one point that he was a greater menace than the enemy across the Rhine!

Second, during the operations in May 1940 Pownall's protective loyalty towards Gort as a 'gallant gentleman' cannot conceal the Commander-in-Chief's professional limitations and lack of mental robustness in frustrating conditions where his aggressive warrior qualities were redundant. Pownall unwittingly reveals the near-paralysis at G.H.Q. caused by Gort's insistence on flitting from one advance post to another: most notably at fault when he failed to arrive in time at the one attempt to co-ordinate Allied strategy at Ypres on 21 May.

Third, and by contrast, Pownall makes a strong case in favour of Gort's refusal to heed Churchill's and the War Cabinet orders, backed

230

up by a visit from Ironside, to march south to try to link up with the French forces supposedly massing for a counter-attack northward across the Somme. Gort's bold, unilateral decision, in the evening of 25 May, to retreat to the Channel coast with a view of embarking the Field Force, was bitterly criticized at the time (as John Cairns' contribution shows), but proved to be justified by subsequent events, at least from a British viewpoint.

Finally, readers have to be wary and discriminating in assessing Pownall's frequently sarcastic and even contemptuous references to Belgian and French politicians and generals. His superior, insular attitudes were probably commonplace among officers of his seniority and background (Rugby School and Royal Horse Artillery), and were most likely rooted in his experience as a young officer in the First World War. He was unfavourably impressed by French soldiers' slackness and their staff officers' obsession with ill-thought-out *projets* during the 'Phoney War'; and by their nominal commanders' (especially Billotte's) failure to give clear orders during the critical days after 10 May. The Belgians had exasperated him by clinging stubbornly to their neutrality until actually invaded, and then obliging the Field Force to advance into unknown and chaotic conditions in an attempt to support them. Pownall's anti-Belgian outbursts culminated on 27 May with their sudden announcement of an imminent ceasefire. Like many critics, he found a scapegoat in King Leopold, but, as would soon be revealed, the faults were not all on one side, and G.H.Q. had had ample warning that Belgian resistance was coming to an end. Thus we may conclude that, although there were many genuine and legitimate reasons for Pownall's irritation with particular French and Belgian officers with whom he came into direct contact, his deep-seated prejudices and need to relieve stress through his diary caused him to generalize to an extent that was unfair and misleading.

In the same year (1972) that the first volume of *Chief of Staff* appeared, John Colville published his remarkably fair and beautifully written biography of Gort entitled *Man of Valour*. Colville achieved the difficult feat of establishing a positive impression of Gort, both as a man and a soldier, while frankly exposing his intellectual limitations and his guardsman's obsession with petty details. While Gort deserved better than the dismissive French description of him as "a jovial battalion commander", it does seem clear that he had been promoted above his ceiling, first as C.I.G.S. and then as Commander-in-Chief. His lonely and painful last days soon after the war must incline us to

231

temper criticism with sympathy: his reputation certainly could not have been given fairer treatment than in Colville's biography.

Among a batch of books published to mark the fortieth anniversary of the Battle of France in 1980 was Nicholas Harman's *Dunkirk: the Necessary Myth*, of which it might be said that the contents did not fulfil the promise of a perceptive sub-title. The book was marred by factual errors and provoked outrage in the regiments concerned by suggesting, without supporting references, that German atrocities at Wormhoudt and Le Paradis had been provoked by some specific British units killing their prisoners after the fighting around Arras on 21 May. More significant was Harman's comparatively moderate puncturing of the excessive nostalgia and propaganda built up around the evacuation from Dunkirk and the beaches, particularly in exaggerating the role of the 'little ships', and the depiction of all their skippers and crews as heroes. Harman was surely right to suggest that 'the myth' of Dunkirk, though absolutely necessary at the time to muffle the extent of the Allied defeat, should not be allowed to dominate historical understanding forty years on, as, alas, it largely still does a further twenty years later.

In 1982 David Fraser published an excellent biography of *Alanbrooke* which did its subject proud, as had Colville for Gort, though in Alanbrooke's case his career culminated in a towering success, as chairman of the Chiefs of Staff Committee and principal strategic adviser to Churchill, while his limitations, if such they were, were of temperament rather than intellect. Fraser's careful analysis went far to supercede the exaggerated claims for Brooke and the eccentric editing of Sir Arthur Bryant's *The Turn of the Tide* (1957).

As Michael Piercy's contribution demonstrates, Brooke had done very well as a Corps Commander, particularly during the crisis caused by the Belgian ceasefire, but his performance as commander of the second expeditionary force, dispatched to Normandy in June in a vain political gesture to encourage the French, was necessarily less heroic. With the ruthless pragmatism he would later display as C.I.G.S. in opposing some of Churchill's wilder projects, Brooke showed from the outset that he had no confidence in the scheme: the French will to continue fighting was ebbing and his improvised force would be operating beyond the range of air cover from England. Brooke displayed no great urgency in returning to France and, having arrived, almost immediately decided that his troops must be evacuated forthwith. This resulted in a telephone confrontation with Churchill in which Brooke prevailed. A second, little-known evacuation took place from Normandy and the Biscay ports in which most of the troops were rescued but a vast amount of stores and weapons was abandoned. Brooke's career survived this inglorious episode, which understandably received little publicity at the time, and has attracted few historians since. An exception was Basil Karslake whose father, Lt. General Sir Henry Karslake, had been given a belated and ill-defined command of British forces south and west of the Somme in June 1940. Basil Karslake's spirited defence of his father in *1940: the Last Act* (1979) also showed that these scattered and ill-coordinated operations had many interesting features but, apart from the enforced surrender of the 51st Highland Division at St Valery-en-Caux, these have so far failed to attract modern scholars.

The final choice of a landmark in the historiography of the campaign may seem an odd one, namely Ronald Atkin's *Pillar of Fire: Dunkirk 1940* (1990), which portrays the chaotic character of the British retreat to the coast through a compilation of eye witness accounts – in diaries, letters and post-war recollections. The method is not new, but the author, better known as a sports journalist, has cast his net very wide and has assembled his evidence – much of it drawn from manuscripts and recorded interviews held at the Imperial War Museum – in a compelling way. Very little motor transport was available; lack of water was an acute problem and some units were abandoned by, or lost contact with, their officers. Atkin's foray into this campaign in terms of the soldiers' experience, as distinct from tactics and strategy, draws attention to a rich and varied array of sources which have been surprisingly little used. Needless to say, there are several vivid published memoirs relevant to this campaign, including Anthony Rhodes' *Sword of Bone* (1942, paperback edition, 1986), Christopher Seton-Watson's *Dunkirk-Alamein-Bologna* (1993) and Bruce Shand's *Previous Engagements* (1990), but most are by junior officers and cover their Second World War experience as a whole, with 1940 often only a prelude to longer spells in North Africa and Italy.

It is received wisdom among military historians that it is usually a matter of extreme ill-fortune to hold a senior command in a British army at the start of a great war. Generals Sir John French, Smith-Dorrien and Ian Hamilton were among the commanders unstuck or *dégommé* in 1914–1915, and Lord Gort in effect suffered a fatal eclipse as commander-in-chief of an Army driven off the Continent after less than a month of active fighting. To be rendered an ineffectual spectator as his troops were forced into a disorganized retreat was a cruel fate for this aggressive and much-decorated officer. Whether or not he had lost Churchill's confidence is unclear, but he was not given another field command during the war. After a frustrating period in England he was made Governor of Gibraltar in May 1941, and, exactly a year later, assigned to an extremely active role as Governor of Malta from May 1942 until July 1944 where his successful defiance of fierce German air and sea attacks was perhaps his greatest achievement, earning him his Field Marshal's baton. In October 1944 he was appointed High Commissioner and Commander-in-Chief in Palestine, but after a year was forced to resign by what proved to be a terminal illness.

However, apart from Gort and a few other senior officers such as M.G.H. Barker of I Corps, the leading officers in the Field Force did not fare badly. Rather surprisingly, Pownall's reputation was not adversely affected by the débâcle in France. Quite the contrary, Churchill gave him a succession of commands in actual or potential trouble spots before he eventually ended his career in another senior staff appointment, namely as Chief of Staff to Mountbatten in South-East Asia Command in 1943–1944. Before that he had been given the Herculean task of organizing the Local Defence Volunteers (better known as the Home Guard), and this was followed by the command in Northern Ireland when a German invasion seemed quite possible. When that threat diminished, Churchill sent him to take over the Far East command at Singapore, but his arrival coincided with that of the Japanese invading army, so instead he became Chief of Staff to Wavell in the short-lived American, British, Dutch and Australian (ABDA) command. His final commands (in 1942–1943) were in Ceylon and then, briefly, in what proved to be the comparatively uneventful Persia-Iraq theatre. After the war Pownall joined the select group of senior officers and scholars who assisted and advised Churchill in producing his six-volume *History of the Second World War*.

Ironside's military career after the Battle of France was necessarily short. He was already 60 years old in 1940 and had reached the apex of the Army career structure as C.I.G.S. On his own admission he was temperamentally unsuited to be C.I.G.S., and it was his own misfortune (and perhaps the nation's also) that he had not been given command of the Field Force, which he had reasonably expected, in September 1939. His bizarre strategic ideas and poor handling of

234

ground operations in Norway probably caused his stock to plummet more than anything concerned with the Battle of France, during which he was little more than a helpless and out of touch spectator. On 27 May 1940 he was replaced by Sir John Dill as C.I.G.S., moved sideways to become Commander-in-Chief Home Forces, and was promoted Field Marshal. Fortunately, this did not provide an opportunity for a culminating act of death or glory in resisting a German invasion, and he retired on 19 July 1940.

Alan Brooke, another gunner like Pownall, Dill and Ironside, was reckoned to have enhanced his reputation as commander of II Corps in the Field Force particularly, as Michael Piercy's contribution demonstrates, in his handling of the complicated manoeuvre which plugged the gap suddenly created by the Belgian ceasefire. As already mentioned, his brief return to France in mid-June as commander of the reconstituted Field Force was, to say the least, inglorious, but his physical vigour and razor-sharp mind (accompanied by a rapid machine-gun style of speech) attracted Churchill, who quickly put him in command of Home Forces in place of Ironside. When Dill was sent to Washington in December 1941 as British representative to the Joint Chiefs of Staff, Brooke (though not the Prime Minister's favoured candidate) replaced him and remained C.I.G.S. until January 1946. His unique achievement in that post, particularly as the tough, pragmatic foil to Churchill's exuberance and waywardness in strategic matters, is well-established. Indeed Brooke has strong claims to be considered Britain's most important serving officer in the Second World War.

Two successful division commanders in the Battle of France whose subsequent careers are too well known to require elaboration were Montgomery (3rd Division) and Alexander (1st). Montgomery's excellence as a trainer and commander was well established before the battle and, as we have seen, he was outstanding in the retreat to the coast. Alexander was promoted to the command of I Corps and of the remaining British troops inside the Dunkirk perimeter on 31 May. Alexander, a *beau sabreur* with a guardsman's acute sense of honour, was put in an impossible position *vis-à-vis* Admiral Abrial and other French leaders by receiving contradictory orders from Churchill and the War Office – the former ordering him to stay and provide the rearguard while ensuring that an equal number of French troops were evacuated, whereas the latter gave priority to the evacuation of British troops and the speedy termination of the rescue operation. John

235

Cairns' admirably detailed reconstruction of Anglo-French disagreements in the final phase at Dunkirk shows that, while inclining to the War Office's instructions to put British interests first, Alexander also tried, without much success, to convince the French that Britain remained a loyal and steadfast ally.

Lastly, mention should be made of one of the unsung, or at any rate less famous, heroes of the Dunkirk evacuation, General Sir Ronald Adam. As Gort's deputy (Vice C.I.G.S.) before the war Adam had displayed diplomatic tact and first class administrative ability in his relationship with the difficult War Minister. Then, having relinquished command of III Corps, as Jeremy Crang's contribution shows in detail, he was ordered to organize the British sector of the perimeter around Dunkirk, and did so with impressive calm and efficiency. He was subsequently appointed Adjutant-General and remained in that important office throughout the war, implementing enlightened policies in military education and welfare, and preparing the Army for demobilization and the transition to post-war soldiering.

The contributors to this volume have attempted either to throw new light on well-known controversies, such as Anglo-French friction at Dunkirk and the Royal Navy's role in the evacuation, or to explore less familiar aspects such as 'the manoeuvre that saved the Field Force', the reporting of the campaign by the British media and the long-term influence of the operations on British doctrine. But it is also important that collective enterprises like this volume should reveal gaps in our knowledge and suggest topics where further research would be rewarding. Thus, for example, there is no single publication which does full justice to the RAF's role in the campaign; despite the many interesting books on Dunkirk, there is still no outstanding overview of the whole operation; and the second phase in western France after 5 June has been badly neglected. Finally, as suggested earlier, there are very large and under-used sources on the campaign in terms of military, but also social and cultural experience, including relations with French citizens, entertainments, disciplinary problems and atrocities, both established and alleged. In sum, historians must convince a wider readership that there is much more of interest in the campaign of 1939–1940 than the exploits of Guderian, the dithering of Hitler and the immortal exploits of 'the little ships'.

INDEX

238

240